PREDICATES and TEMPORAL ARGUMENTS

PREDICATES and TEMPORAL ARGUMENTS

Theodore B. Fernald

New York · Oxford

Oxford University Press

2000

Oxford University Press

Oxford New York
Athens Auckland Bangkok Bogotá Buenos Aires Calcutta
Cape Town Chennai Dar es Salaam Delhi Florence Hong Kong Istanbul
Karachi Kuala Lumpur Madrid Melbourne Mexico City Mumbai
Nairobi Paris São Paulo Singapore Taipei Tokyo Toronto Warsaw

and associated companies in
Berlin Ibadan

Copyright © 2000 by Theodore B. Fernald

Published by Oxford University Press, Inc.
198 Madison Avenue, New York, New York 10016

Oxford is a registered trademark of Oxford University Press

All rights reserved. No part of this publication may be reproduced,
stored in a retrieval system, or transmitted, in any form or by any means,
electronic, mechanical, photocopying, recording or otherwise,
without the prior permission of Oxford University Press.

Library of Congress Cataloging-in-Publication Data
Fernald, Theodore B.
Predicates and temporal arguments / Theodore B. Fernald.
p. cm.
Includes bibliographical references and index.
ISBN 0-19-511435-3
1. Grammar, Comparative and general—Verb phrase. 2. Grammar,
Comparative and general—Syntax. 3. Grammar, Comparative and
general—Temporal constructions. 4. Semantics. I. Title.
P281.F47 2000
415—dc21   98-45488

1 3 5 7 9 8 6 4 2

Printed in the United States of America
on acid-free paper

For B. H. H.

Preface

This book is about the distinction between individual- and stage-level predicates, a semantic distinction that interacts with syntax and pragmatics in complex ways. Because of these interactions, the distinction has been significant for theories of the interfaces between these fields. In this volume, I survey the most prominent views of the distinction, taking new data and perspectives into consideration, and then I adopt and explore an underexamined portion of Kratzer's (1988) proposal that there is a type-theoretic distinction between the two sorts of predicate.

This book began as my doctoral dissertation (1994) at the University of California, Santa Cruz, supervised by William A. Ladusaw. Roughly two-thirds of it is substantially different in the current volume. I have benefited from the input of scholars I did not know as a graduate student, and I have had the chance to learn more and to reflect on the issues involved. My opinions on smaller points have undergone many adjustments. My fundamental views have not changed substantially, although I think I have better reasons for holding them, and they are expressed with greater clarity than in the dissertation.

Many people have contributed to this book through written comments, correspondence, and consultations. Bill Ladusaw invested a large amount of time in me and my work while I was at Santa Cruz. I am also grateful for insightful contributions from dissertation committee members Geoffrey Pullum and Donka Farkas, who is always generous with her time and ideas. I have benefited from conversations with Michael Johnson, Chris Kennedy, Louise McNally, and Peter Svenonius. When I needed a boost during the most recent evolution of this book I got one from Greg Carlson, Donka Farkas, Sheila Glasbey, Gerhard Jäger, Eloise Jelinek, Manfred Krifka, Donna Jo Napoli, Hana Philip, Carlota Smith, and two anonymous reviewers for Oxford. Many of them contributed key ideas that developed into major points in the analysis.

I would like to thank former Swarthmore College students Dan Heider, Tom Kornack, and Heather Mateyak for lively discussion, ongoing interest, and original ideas. And thanks go to Hanan Hussein for word-processing labor and discussion.

I am grateful for the support and encouragement of Willard and Elizabeth Fernald.

Huge thanks go to Betsy Horner, Marena Fernald, and Eleda Fernald.

Contents

ONE
Predicates and Predicaments   3

TWO
Patterns of Interpretation and Grammaticality   12

THREE
Traditional Explanations   36

FOUR
The Distinction and Its Slipperiness   63

FIVE
Taking Stock   74

SIX
Nonuniformity   87

SEVEN
Of Time and Predicates   117

Notes   143

References   147

Index   153

PREDICATES and
TEMPORAL ARGUMENTS

1

Predicates and Predicaments

The distinction between individual-level and stage-level predicates has interested grammarians for a number of reasons. In English, this distinction interacts with a variety of apparently unrelated syntactic constructions. In some constructions the different sorts of predicates show a contrast in interpretation, and in others they show a contrast in grammaticality. This is particularly interesting because the distinction is not a matter of traditional syntactic category like noun or verb phrase. It seems to be a semantic classification, although delineating it precisely in terms of meaning has proven difficult, at least outside a particular theoretical viewpoint. Complicating things further, a number of contextual and pragmatic factors can affect the tests taken to be diagnostic of the distinction. Many languages display grammatical effects due to the two kinds of predicates, suggesting that this distinction is fundamental to the way humans think about the universe.

This study is confined, for the most part, to data from English, and so it overlooks a growing body of work on the ILP/SLP distinction in other languages: for example, Diesing (1992) on German, Doherty (1996) on Irish, Kratzer (1988) on German, Kuroda (1992) on Japanese, Willie (1999) on Navajo, and Sasse (1987) on a wide variety of languages.

1. Characterizations of the Distinction

Since the work of Milsark (1974) and Carlson (1977), the distinction between individual-level predicates (ILPs) and stage-level predicates (SLPs) has been at the forefront of the development of theories about the syntax-semantics interface (e.g., Kratzer 1988, Diesing 1992, Krifka et al. 1995). Milsark's (1974, 1977) original proposal of the distinction between "state-descriptive" (SLP) and "property" (ILP) predicates is introduced as follows:

4 Predicates and Temporal Arguments

> It would be of great value at this point to be able to point out some independent criteria for telling the difference between state-descriptive and property predicates. The best I can do is to suggest some tendencies and rules of thumb, plus an imprecise definition or two. Properties are those facts about entities which are assumed to be, even if they are not in fact, permanent, unalterable, and in some sense possessed by the entity, while states are conditions which are, at least in principle, transitory, not possessed by the entity of which they are predicated, and the removal of which causes no change in the essential qualities of the entity. (1974:212)

This discussion presents the distinction as one that distinguishes essential, permanent properties of an entity from accidental states that the entity might be found in. In Milsark (1977), this is repeated:

> States [are] conditions in which an entity finds itself and which are subject to change without there being an essential alteration of the entity... [Properties] are descriptions which name some trait possessed by the entity and which is assumed to be more or less permanent or at least to be such that some significant change in the character of the entity will result if the description is altered. (1977:12f.)

Milsark (1974) offers the following lists of representative predicates:

(1) SLPs   ILPs
     sick   all NP PREDs
     hungry   shapes
     tired   colors
     alert   intelligent
     clothed   beautiful
     naked   boring
     drunk   crazy
     stoned   etc.
     closed
     open
     etc.

This classification applies to verbal predicates as well, as Milsark (1977) notes. Most are stage-level (e.g., *kick over a trash can, eat supper, think lovely thoughts*), but some are individual-level (e.g. *own a bank, have long arms, know how to fly an airplane*). And Hana Philip pointed out to me that nominals are not ILPs in all languages: in the Slavic family, case markers seem to make a difference in the sort of predicate one has.

In introducing this distinction, connections are made on one hand between being a property predicate and tending to remain true of an entity over time, and on the other between being a state-description and freely changing applicability over time. While the latter connection does not seem to be problematic, the former is: even though predicates like *be blond(e)*, and *be French* are individual-level, they are not literally permanent properties because we can imagine an individual changing status, even repeatedly, with respect to the property. On the other hand, as Carlson (1977:72) notes, some SLPs—like *be dead*—are permanent. Whatever sense of permanence is crucial to this distinction, it must be a very weak notion. For example, Chierchia proposes that ILPs are *tendentially* stable while SLPs are not:

> The main characteristic of i[ndividual]-level predicates is that they ascribe tendentially permanent properties to their arguments. It seems that one can say of an argument with an i[ndividual]-level property P, "Once a P, tendentially always a P." (1995b:198)

Chierchia proposes that the non-necessary tendency toward permanence that ILPs have is a result of inherent genericity. However, the tendential stability characterization is problematic as well. Predicates like *be an infant*, and *be a child* are classified as individual-level, but by no means do we expect infants to remain infants or children to remain children. On the contrary, in a world in which everything follows its normal course, these states will occupy a relatively small portion of an entity's existence. We must admit, then, that the permanence of ILPs is intuitive but elusive. In our discussion of the diagnostic tests, and in particular in our later discussion of "coercion," the temporally persistent nature of ILPs will be an important theme.

Carlson's (1977) discussion of this distinction views the difference as essentially one of domain for the predicates: ILPs are predicates of individuals, while SLPs are predicates of "stages." He writes, "A stage is conceived of as being, roughly, a spatially and temporally bounded manifestation of something. . . . An individual, then, is (at least) that whatever-it-is that ties a series of stages together to make them stages of the same thing" (68). Carlson later wrote:

> [The ILP/SLP distinction] is correlated with the sort of entity the predicate meaningfully applies to. If the predicate speaks of general characteristics, or dispositions, we represent it as applying to a set of objects. If something more fleeting is intended, somehow more temporary, and in some sense less intrinsic to the nature of a given individual, the predicate is represented as denoting a set of stages. This distinction is intended to correspond to the basically atemporal nature of individuals as opposed to their time-bound stages. (1979:57)

The difference between ILPs and SLPs, on this view, is that the former characterize individuals, while the latter present eventualities that take place and involve the stage of an individual. Carlson's characterization commits stage-level predications to an essential spatiotemporal location. This theme is continued in Kratzer (1988), where SLPs are distinguished as having an inherent spatiotemporal argument that ILPs lack.

The ILP/SLP distinction has been assumed to give rise to a number of grammatical effects. These effects involve the grammaticality requirements and interpretational possibilities of a number of constructions. These will be examined in detail in chapter 2, but I will summarize them here. The existential construction permits only SLPs in its coda (Milsark 1974, 1977). Bare plural and indefinite subjects also show ILP/SLP effects: as we will see, subjects of ILPs must be construed strongly (Milsark 1974, 1977). This phenomenon forces bare plural subjects of ILPs to have a generic interpretation rather than an existential one (Carlson 1977), and indefinites that cannot be construed strongly (e.g., *sm* and, ordinarily, *a*) sound quite odd in this environment. Another diagnostic is the position of the predicate in the small clause complement to perception verbs; only SLPs are grammatical in this environment (Carlson 1977). *When* adjuncts (Carlson 1979, Kratzer 1988) and absolute adjuncts (Stump 1985) show a contrast in possible interpretations depending on whether they contain a SLP or an ILP. Finally, Carlson (1982) and Kratzer (1988) have argued that temporal and locative modifiers are grammatical only when the main predicate of a sentence is stage-level. Other researchers have proposed additional constructions in which the ILP/SLP distinction has a role, but the ones that will be central to our investigation are mentioned above.

The terms used in this classification of predicates are due to Carlson, who distinguishes SLPs and ILPs from a third level that he calls "kind-level predicates" (KLPs). KLPs denote properties that logically cannot have individual objects as their arguments. Rather, they are predicates of kinds, species, or classes of objects. The examples below contain KLPs:

(2) a. Wolves were widespread in North America.
    b. Dinosaurs are extinct.
    c. This kind of tree is indigenous to California.

These examples cannot be interpreted as generalizations about members of a group. For example, (2a) does not mean that in general, if you find a wolf it will be widespread in North America, and (2c) does not mean that a particular individual tree is indigenous. Instead, these are claims about the class of wolves and the kind of tree being indicated. Carlson (1977) is the classical work on kinds and their predicates; see also Krifka et al. (1995) for a recent overview of relevant issues and previous work. Issues involving KLPs are not of central concern in this investigation, but they will occasionally enter into the discussion. ILPs and SLPs interact with each other in subtle ways, but KLPs do not interact with the other levels in the same way, and this is the reason that they will generally be ignored.

2. Stativity

In the course of this investigation, issues involving Aktionsart will keep popping up. Aktionsart deals with the aspectual characteristics inherent in sentences and determined largely by the head of the sentence's main predicate. Vendler (1967) distinguishes four verbal classes: *states*, *activities*, *accomplishments*, and *achievements*. Dowty (1979), in his discussion of "the Aristotle-Ryle-Kenny-Vendler Verb Classification," provides a summary of earlier work on Aktionsart. Verkuyl (1972) shows that the distinction must really take the whole verb phrase into account and not simply the verb. Dowty (1979) has examples, discussed below, which appear to show that even the subject of the sentence can contribute to the classification. Work on Aktionsart is ongoing: Smith (1991) adds *semelfactive* as a distinct class; and see Verkuyl (1993) and ter Meulen (1995) for recent accounts of these phenomena.

The ILP/SLP distinction overlaps significantly with the stative/non-stative aspectual distinction, but the two distinctions do not quite make the same division among the non-KLP predicates. Lakoff (1965) provides a number of tests for the stative/non-stative distinction, some of which involve the orthogonal issue of agentivity. Those that do not test for agentivity involve the ability to appear in the progressive and the ability to appear in the pseudo-cleft construction; Lakoff claims that only non-statives have both of these abilities. These claims are supported by the data below:

(3) a. *Robin is knowing the answer.
   b. *What Robin did was know the answer.

(4) a. Robin is reaching a decision.
   b. What Robin did was reach a decision.

Carlson (1977) claimed that individual-level verbs cannot appear in the progressive, and this raises the question of whether the progressive is properly seen as excluding states or as excluding ILPs.

As it turns out, all ILPs are stative, and all non-statives are SLPs. The only reason we have for positing the existence of the ILP/SLP distinction at all is that there exist some stative SLPs. Some of these are PPs and APs that are overtly locative (e.g., *on the lawn, airborne*), but others are not (e.g., *out of their minds with worry, drunk, naked*). For simple verbal predicates, the ILP/SLP distinction coincides nearly exactly with the stative/non-stative distinction, although things will get more complicated when we consider predicates with clausal complements in chapter 6. There is one group of verbs, discussed by Dowty (1979), which displays complex behavior in this respect. These are verbs like *sit, stand,* and *flow,* which are sometimes used statively and sometimes not. In particular, they can appear in the progressive with certain subjects, but not with others. Dowty notes the following contrasts, from his examples (62) & (67):

(5) a. The socks are lying under the bed.
   a'. ??New Orleans is lying at the mouth of the Mississippi River.
   b. Your glass is sitting near the edge of the table.
   b'. ??John's house is sitting at the top of a hill.
   c. The long box is standing on end.
   c'. ??The new building is standing at the corner of First Avenue and Main Street.
   d. One corner of the piano is resting on the bottom step.
   d'. ??That argument is resting on an invalid assumption.

Dowty proposes that in the cases in which the progressive is permissible, the VP is being used as a SLP, and when it is not, the VP is used as an ILP. These predicates, which Dowty calls "interval statives," are taken to be individual-level just in case the subject denotes the sort of thing that cannot ordinarily change its physical position from the one described by the predicate: New Orleans always lies at the mouth of the Mississippi River, but the socks do not always lie under the bed. It seems, then, that there are stative verbs that can serve as the heads of SLPs, and that these statives can appear in the progressive. These are the only stative verbs that appear able to head a stage-level predicate.

The progressive does not make a clearcut distinction between all ILPs and SLPs, however, and this makes it difficult to use as a diagnostic for the ILP/SLP distinction, at least until we consider its coercive effect:

(6) a. *Sam is being on the ship.
   b. Sam is being a hero.

(7) a. Sam is being careful.
    b. Sam is being an idiot.

The locative in (6a) is a SLP, and the nominal predicate in (6b) is an ILP, and yet the progressive is acceptable with the latter and not with the former. In chapter 4 we will see reasons to believe that the progressive can "coerce" a stative predicate into becoming a non-stative predicate (all of the latter are SLPs), with a predictable change in interpretation resulting. Dowty (1979:114, 115) argues that in (7), *careful* and *an idiot* are ambiguous between stative and agentive readings, and that copular predicates in the progressive, therefore, adhere to the stative/non-stative distinction (see 130, fn. 6). However, his analysis of the examples in (5) suggests that for verbal predicates, the progressive is sensitive to the ILP/SLP distinction, supporting Carlson's claim to this effect.

Kenny (1963:175) notes an additional means of distinguishing stative and non-stative verbs. English non-stative verbs tend strongly to have a habitual or generic interpretation when they appear in the simple present:

(8) a. Sam sits by the fire after supper.
    b. Surgeons cook for themselves.

Such sentences can also have a "reportive present," typified by a sportscaster's play-by-play or newspaper headline usage; however, they do not have the ordinary existential reading found with other tenses. Although we will see that the unavailability of existential readings for bare plural subjects and the ungrammaticality of weak nominal subjects can be indications that the predicate is individual-level, the judgments in (8) arise independently of the ILP/SLP contrast. Note that a generic interpretation is required even when the subject is independently referential, as in (8a). This is not what we see when the predicate is individual-level (cf. *Sam is intelligent*). Further, the predicates in (8) pass the tests for stage-level status when they appear in the past tense. We clearly do not want to say, however, that it is a characteristic of SLPs that they have generic readings in the simple present; stative SLPs (e.g., *be excited, be available*) do not have the generic reading, and they allow weak subjects:

(9) a. Sam is excited.
    b. Surgeons are prepared for the operation.
    c. Sm surgeons are prepared for the operation.

Thus, we must conclude that the generic reading for the simple present and the ungrammaticality of weak subjects is a property of non-stative predicates, and that this issue is independent of the ILP/SLP distinction. This discussion shows that the bare-plural and weak-subject tests for SLP status (discussed in chapter 2) cannot be applied blindly in the simple present for non-stative predicates. The tests are reliable, however, in the present progressive, present perfect, and past tenses (with any aspect). The English simple present is idiosyncratic in requiring generic interpretations for non-stative predicates. Other languages (e.g., German) do not have this restriction, and the simple present can mean what English speakers use the present progressive for. Because there are other languages that do not have this restriction, it is clear that the English facts are due to a quirk of grammar and not to some deep principle of logic.

We conclude that the ILP/SLP distinction cannot be reduced to previously known aspectual distinctions. The fact that stative SLPs exist makes reduction to the stative/non-stative distinction impossible. Because the stative/non-stative distinction is so close to the ILP/SLP distinction, we must exercise caution in our work; otherwise, we may accidentally identify a stativity distinction as one of predicate levels. By including stative SLPs in our diagnostics, we can avoid this problem.

3. The Theses

If the ILP/SLP effects are really indicative of a binary, lexical classification of predicates, then the constructions that show the effects should always yield consistent results when taken as diagnostics for the binary classification. Carlson (1977) and Stump (1985) showed that there is a class of copular predicates which behave like typical SLPs from the point of view of the existential construction and the indefinite subject effect, but which are ungrammatical in the small clause complement to perception verbs. Later, Kratzer (1988) pointed out that there is another class of predicates (the "unaccusative" ILPs, in her terminology) which behave like SLPs for the existential construction and the indefinite subject diagnostics, but not for temporal and locative modification. Previous work has focused primarily on data involving very simple predicates; when predicates of greater syntactic complexity are considered, the uniformity of the effects will be seen to break down still further. I will investigate such cases in chapter 6. Carlson (1977) briefly discusses what happens when predicates of different levels are embedded in the complements of raising verbs; in the present work, they will be subjected to a wider range of diagnostics. The effects of embedding ILPs and SLPs in the complements of control verbs and propositional attitudes will also be examined, along with cases in which SLPs appear as modifiers of heads that are independently classified as ILPs.

Some of the differences between ILPs and SLPs result from the ability or inability of a clause to delimit cases for the purpose of quantification; these effects are seen with *when* and with absolute adjuncts when they restrict certain modals. Other effects are due to the ability or inability of clauses to delimit *multiple* cases for the purposes of quantification; this is evident when absolute and *when* adjuncts appear with adverbs of quantification. I will use the term "subject effects" to include the existential construction and the diagnostics that concern bare plurals and the possibility of indefinite subjects to be construed weakly. The grammaticality of perceptual reports constitutes a fourth set of effects.

There are, I think, a number of widely held assumptions about individual- and stage-level predicates that have not been sufficiently scrutinized. Certain previous analyses have suffered because of their assumption that the ILP/SLP distinction depends entirely on a classification of the predicate's head (along with, perhaps, some ill-understood pragmatic factors). In this book I will argue that, in many cases, it is necessary to consider the entire predicate before its proper classification can be attempted with success.

It has been widely assumed that predicates that are not KLPs fit into either the SLP or the ILP group, or else they are ambiguous, but it is constantly acknowledged that there are ways in which a predicate from one level can be taken to be a predicate from the other level. But making such a claim should have empirical consequences. In general, language users are quite adept at concocting interpretations for strings of words that are thrown at them and are purported to be sentences. When a predicate of one level is used in an environment that favors predicates of the other level, the interpretation of the predicate is *coerced* according to a small number of predictable patterns. Once we identify the patterns, we can test whether coercion has actually occurred in any given instance.

The analysis developed in this book draws heavily on existing work, particularly that of Kratzer (1988) and Carlson (1977). The cases of nonuniformity that we find among the diagnostics will naturally be explained by trying to be clearer about what each of the tests diagnoses. I will claim that ILPs and SLPs have a conglomerate of properties that different diagnostics pick out. The heart of my analysis is built on a fairly implicit assumption in Kratzer (1988): that there is a type-theoretic distinction between ILPs and SLPs because only the latter can have a spatiotemporal argument. Of course, Carlson (1977) was the first to propose that the predicates be distinguished type-theoretically. We will see evidence from perceptual reports and from free and absolute adjuncts that the ILP/SLP distinction can be maintained after the predicate composes with its subject. An assumption compatible with Kratzer's distinction will fare better in allowing a formal treatment of this observation. In addition to the type-theoretic distinction, we will find reason to believe that SLPs are potentially anaphoric and that ILPs are not, suggesting that a dynamic analysis is called for. We will also identify what sorts of pragmatic factors are involved with certain diagnostics, and we will develop precise ways of telling when they are exerting their influence.

In chapter 2, the traditional diagnostics will be examined with respect to simple predicates. Chapter 3 presents traditional analyses for each of these groups of effects; the discussion will focus on the work of Carlson, Stump, Kratzer, Diesing, and de Hoop and de Swart. In chapter 4, we pause to consider again the basis of the ILP/SLP distinction, and then we investigate coercion, the precise means by which the classification of a predicate can be changed. We will explore what possibilities Kratzer's and Carlson's theories allow for the change in meaning that accompanies coercion. Chapters 5 and 6 lay the groundwork for the theory developed in chapter 7. The first of these considers the consequences of previous work, arguing for three large points: first, that the ILP/SLP distinction is visible at syntactic nodes dominating tenseless clauses; second, that adverbial quantification is subject both to a prohibition against vacuous quantification (Kratzer 1988) and to a plurality condition (de Hoop and de Swart 1989); and finally, that SLPs are anaphoric but ILPs are not. Chapter 6 follows this with a presentation of data that have received little discussion in previous work. The effects of definite nominals, clausal complements, and clausal modifiers will be considered. This is followed by consideration of ways of extending the analyses of Kratzer, Diesing, and Carlson to account for more complex predicates. This discussion poses serious problems for the Mapping Hypothesis of Diesing (1992) and Kratzer (1988), and it calls for a theory that allows SLPs and ILPs to be derived compositionally.

Finally, chapter 7 develops the analysis based on the type-theoretic distinction implicit in Kratzer (1988). I focus only on the temporal portion of the extra argument found in SLPs and consider the predictions that the analysis makes for how time is used in propositions described by SLPs as opposed to ILPs. Because time is an argument of SLPs but not of ILPs, time will be a constituent in a SLP-based proposition.

As for the basis of the distinction, rather than claiming that ILPs are tendentially stable, or that we assume they are, I will conclude what the formal account forces me to conclude: that SLPs describe characteristics of individuals that hold in space and time—we might even say that they describe spatiotemporal slices of the world; and that ILPs are independent of space and time.

2

Patterns of Interpretation and Grammaticality

In this chapter I will survey the range of grammatical phenomena that have been proposed as sensitive to the ILP/SLP distinction. These phenomena have been used as diagnostic tests by which predicates can be sorted into two classes. Consideration of these diagnostics in some detail is important because, as noted in the introduction, an independent definition of the contrast has thus far eluded investigators. The constructions discussed in the following sections have traditionally been assumed to divide the (non-kind-level) predicates into two classes. Past investigations have focused on syntactically simple predicates, and this initial discussion will be confined to that domain.

1. The Diagnostics

1.1 The Existential Construction

The existential construction consists of the expletive *there* followed by a form of *be*,[1] followed by a nominal expression called the "pivot," and ending with a predicate called the "coda." The pivot functions as the logical subject of the coda. This construction has been discussed extensively by Milsark (1974), Lumsden (1988), McNally (1992), and others, and recently in McNally (1998). Milsark showed that the coda cannot contain just any sort of predicate, and that the pivot is also restricted. Much of the work on this construction has focused on the correct way to state the necessary restrictions.

Milsark (1974) noticed that existential sentences are grammatical only when the coda contains a SLP (which he called "state-descriptive"); ILPs ("properties," in his terminology) are ungrammatical in this position. Data like the following motivated this observation (the coda is italicized):

(1) a. There were people *sick*.
    b. There were people *drunk*.
    c. There were doors *open*.

(2) a. *There were people *intelligent*.
    b. *There were people *tall*.
    c. *There were doors *wooden*.

The existential construction is acceptable only in (1), in which the predicates in the codas are stage-level. The examples above show that stage-level adjective phrases are grammatical in the coda position but individual-level ones are not.

Milsark also noticed that there appear to be no nominal predicates that are grammatical in the coda position of the existential. The following are examples:

(3) a. *There were people *doctors*.
    b. *There was a surgeon *a happy woman*.
    c. *There were clouds *a welcome sight*.

Because ILPs and NPs were both identified as being ungrammatical in the coda, this led to the generally accepted (but not necessary) conclusion that all nominal predicates are individual-level. Most PPs and participial VPs are grammatical in this position:

(4) a. There were insects that I couldn't identify *on the windowsill*.
    b. There was a student who had never ridden a rollercoaster before *at the boardwalk*.
    c. There were three cars that had been designed in Sweden *rolling down the hill*.
    d. There was a woman that I knew in college *running along the beach*.

Some VPs are not, however:

(5) a. *There are three people that know you *thinking about overthrowing the government*.
    b. *There was a tycoon that Lynne met on an expedition *owning this company*.
    c. *There was a student who ordinarily sits in the front row *knowing the answer*.

The ungrammaticality of the examples in (5) has been taken to show that the VPs in the coda are individual-level. Carlson (1977) pointed out that KLPs are also excluded from the coda position:

(6) a. *There were bears that my brother told me about *widespread*.
    b. *There are tires *in short supply*. (Carlson's ex. V (27b))

ILPs and KLPs are ungrammatical as the coda of the existential construction. In general, it is claimed that SLPs are always acceptable there; but, of course, if the predicate is a VP, it must be in present participial form. These participial cases are open to the alternative analysis of being reduced relatives, however. We will consider this further in section 2.2.

In addition to observing that ILPs are ungrammatical as the coda of the existential construction, Milsark (1977) noticed that certain determiners are ungrammatical in the pivot:

(7) a. *There was every horse available.
    b. *There were most horses running wild.

c. *There were some horses in the stable.
d. *There was the horse available.[2]

(8) a. There was a horse available.
b. There were six horses running wild.
c. There were *sm* horses in the stable.
d. There were rabbits all over the yard.

Milsark proposed that nominals can be given a "weak" (or "cardinal") construal, or a "strong" (or "quantificational") construal. Some determiners are necessarily construed weakly, some are necessarily construed strongly, and some can be construed either way. Milsark showed that strong construals are ungrammatical in the pivot of the existential construction, and that weak ones are grammatical. Weak determiners include *a*, *some*, number determiners, and what Milsark argued was a null determiner appearing with bare plurals and mass nouns when they have a non-universal (or non-generic) reading. "Strong" NPs contain determiners that are definite or quantificational. Bare plurals and mass terms with a generic reading are strong. Numerals and the quantifier *many* are examples of determiners that can be construed either way. The phonetically reduced determiner *sm*, seen in (8c) is also weak. *Sm* is discussed by Postal (1969). Its orthographic representation is *some*, but it is usually pronounced with a reduced vowel. It cannot be used in the partitive (*sm of the people . . .*), and it differs from *some* in that *sm* can appear only with plural nouns. We should recognize that sentential stress patterns can have the effect of reducing *some* to something that sounds like *sm* independently of the ILP/SLP distinction. In applying the diagnostic, we need to control for this by making sure that the subject has a weak interpretation.

Barwise and Cooper (1981) reconstruct the Milsark distinction in their theory of generalized quantifiers by distinguishing weak from strong determiners. Their definitions are as follows:

(9) A determiner D is *positive strong* (or *negative strong*, resp.) if for every model M = <E,|| ||> and every A ⊆ E, if the quantifier ||D||(A) is defined then A ∈ ||D||(A). (Or A ∉ ||D||(A), resp.). If D is not (positive or negative) strong then D is *weak*.

Barwise and Cooper then give the following sentence form as a test for this classification:

(10) *D* N is a N/are Ns

The N chosen for the test is not significant as long as it is a count noun. Barwise and Cooper write that a sentence of this form will be either a tautology, a contradiction, or contingent. If it is a tautology, the determiner used in it is positive strong; if the sentence is a contradiction, the determiner is negative strong; if the sentence is contingent, the determiner is weak. Thus, *Most dogs are dogs* and *Neither dog is a dog* show that *most* and *neither* are positive and negative strong, respectively. But *Some dogs are dogs* is taken to be contingent on the model with respect to which the sentence is interpreted: if there are no dogs in the model, the sentence will be false, but if there are any dogs, the sentence will be true. Weak nominals thus entail the existence of some member of the set denoted by the common noun; strong nominals do not.

Barwise and Cooper offer an additional diagnostic for the weak/strong distinction. They describe a quantifier as a "sieve." if it "separat[es] ... the VP denotations into those that do and those that do not combine with it to make a true sentence" (1981:179). The sifting process has degenerated, however, if the quantifier lets through every set or lets through no set. Barwise and Cooper define a sieve as a quantifier that does not permit either of these degenerate cases to occur. Because strongly construed nominals are generalized quantifiers, they are degenerate when not construed as sieves. Weakly construed nominals, however, need not be interpreted as sieves because they are not quantificational. This contrast is shown in the examples below (Barwise and Cooper's exx. 21–23). From the utterance of (11a), we might be justified in inferring (11b); when we do, we are interpreting *no boy* as a sieve. But since (11c) is not contradictory, (11b) is at best an implicature of (11a):

(11)   a. No boy at the party kissed Mary.
       b. There were boys at the party.
       c. No boy at the party kissed Mary since there weren't any boys at the party.

In (11c), *no boy* is interpreted as a non-sieve, and this indicates that *no* is a weak determiner.

With *every*, the inference of (12b) from (12a) is unavoidable, and (12c) sounds quite odd (Barwise and Cooper's ex. 24):

(12)   a. Every man at the party kissed Mary.
       b. There were men at the party.
       c. ?Every man at the party kissed Mary, but only because there weren't any men at the party.

Thus, a sieve interpretation is possible for NPs containing *every*, but a non-sieve reading is almost contradictory.

Milsark concluded that the existential construction requires its pivot to be a weakly construed nominal. He also noticed that the weak/strong distinction interacts in another important way with the ILP/SLP distinction, as we shall see in the following section.

1.2 Indefinites and Bare Plurals

In addition to this contrast in the existential construction, Milsark noticed that the weak/strong distinction among nominals interacts in a crucial way with the ILP/SLP distinction.

The examples in (13) pair ILPs with weak subjects (adapted from Milsark 1977, exx. 29 and 30):

(13)   a. *Sm people were tall. (Cf. Some of the people were tall.)
       b. *A man was intelligent. (Cf. All men were intelligent.)
       c. People were clever in those days. (generic only)

It has become customary to use the ungrammaticality asterisk with examples like these, although they probably are not quite as unacceptable as this suggests. However, when the predicate is stage-level, weak indefinites in subject position are fully grammatical with an existential interpretation:

(14) a. *Sm* people were sick.
b. A man was drunk outside.
c. People were hungry. (existential possible)

As examples (13c) and (14c) suggest, an existential reading is possible for a bare plural subject of a SLP, but not for that of an ILP. Carlson (1977) discusses the interpretation of bare plurals at great length, arguing that they are names of kinds and thus are distinct from indefinite nominals. Below are some additional examples:

(15) a. Potato chip manufacturers are upset. (existential possible)
b. Sales representatives are annoyed.
c. Surfers are lying on the beach.

(16) a. Potato chip manufacturers are intense. (generic only)
b. Sales representatives are annoying.
c. Surfers are laid-back.

Existential interpretations of the bare plural subject are possible for the examples in (15), which contain SLPs, but not for the examples in (16) which contain ILPs.

The crucial observation made by Milsark is that ILPs do not allow their subjects to be given weak interpretations. The weak subjects in the examples above exhibit two patterns of behavior. Some nominals have only weak interpretations (e.g., those with *sm*, and some cases with *a*, to be discussed below) and therefore are ungrammatical as subjects of ILPs. Bare plurals, however, can be interpreted weakly (existentially) or strongly (generically); when they appear as subjects to ILPs, they admit only a generic construal. Finally, certain nominals (e.g., those with *many*, *several*, *three*, etc.) are like bare plurals in their ability to be construed either weakly or strongly. However, I have found it difficult to obtain consistent judgments for these, and so I will omit them from consideration in this study.

In the examples above, indefinites with the determiners *a* or *sm* sound quite odd when the predicate is individual-level. Krifka et al. (1995) point out that when the predicate is an essential property of the subject, as opposed to an accidental one, an *a* indefinite is grammatical with a generic interpretation:

(17) a. ??A madrigal is popular.
b. A madrigal is polyphonic.

(18) a. A hero is popular.
b. ??A hero is polyphonic.

Since popularity is an essential property of heroes but not of madrigals, a generic reading is available for (18a), but not for (17a). Krifka et al. (1995) acknowledge that the underlying reason for this is not clear. We conclude that *a* indefinites may have a generic interpretation in these environments, and so care must be exercised when employing this diagnostic.

To summarize this section, indefinite subjects provide the following diagnostics for the ILP/SLP distinction. There is a fairly clear difference in grammaticality when *sm* is used as the determiner: *sm* is ungrammatical with an ILP and grammatical (with an existential interpretation only) with a SLP. A bare plural subject has the possibility of an existential reading only when the predicate is stage-level (generic readings are often possible in these cases as well). When the predicate is individual-level, a bare plural subject must be interpreted generically. The determiner *a* cannot have an existential reading when the predicate is individual-level; either the subject will be interpreted generically (this is the case when the predicate denotes an essential property), or the sentence will be ungrammatical.

1.3 Perceptual Reports

One of Carlson's (1977) diagnostics for stage-level predicates is the predicate position following the postverbal NP complement of *see*:

(19) a. Martha saw the policemen walk home.
 b. *Martha saw the policemen intelligent.

(20) a. I saw Sam tower over his friends.
 b. *I saw Sam taller than his friends.

Jack Hoeksema called my attention to the second minimal pair. In each case an ILP in the perceptual report leads to ungrammaticality.

Syntactic work in the Government & Binding framework (see, e.g., Chomsky 1981, 1986) and its descendants, and in Head-Driven Phrase Structure Grammar (Pollard and Sag 1994), has commonly argued that the predicational complements to *see* and other verbs of perception are syntactically small clauses (Stowell 1981, 1989; cf. Williams 1983 in dissent). A small clause is a syntactic constituent consisting of a subject and a predicate, but with no tense inflection. The syntactic category to which small clauses belong is a matter of ongoing dispute and is not relevant to the present discussion.

When a verb of perception has a full clause complement, the contrast in acceptability is not maintained, and both ILPs and SLPs are fully acceptable as the embedded predicate:

(21) a. Martha saw that the policemen walked home.
 b. Martha saw that the policemen were intelligent.

(22) a. I saw that Sam towered over his friends.
 b. I saw that Sam was taller than his friends.

Thus, the ILP/SLP distinction makes a difference only when *see* has a small clause complement and not when its complement is a full clause.

As Barwise (1981) and others have pointed out, when *see* has a complement that is a full clause, the sentence can be interpreted as expressing that the root subject has indirect evidence for believing that the denotation of the complement is true. Thus, (23) does not entail that Cathal saw Peter washing the dishes (in fact, saying it would ordinarily implicate that he did not), but it entails that Cathal observed something unspecified that led him to believe that Peter had done the dishes:

(23) Cathal saw that Peter had washed the dishes.

If Cathal has gone out for the evening, leaving behind a pile of dirty dishes, and returns home to find that they are all clean, then, if he believes that Peter was the only person in the house, he may draw the conclusion that Peter did the dishes.

This is the kind of situation in which (23) can be used. However, the following sentence is false under these circumstances:

(24) Cathal saw Peter wash the dishes.

When perception verbs have a small clause complement, direct perception is entailed and ILPs are ungrammatical as the predicate in the complement.

Because all ILPs are stative, in order to be confident that the contrast we have seen is due to a prohibition against ILPs and not one against states, we must show that stative SLPs are acceptable in descriptions of perceived eventualities. The following sentences show that this is true:

(25) a. Martha saw the policemen agitated.
      b. Jason saw the snake asleep.
      c. Chris saw the provost drunk.

Since these grammatical sentences contain stative SLPs in the small clause complement to *see*, we conclude that the contrast is due to a prohibition against ILPs, and not to a prohibition against states in this environment.

1.4 When *Adjuncts with Generic Quantification*

Work in the tradition of Lewis (1975), Kamp (1981), and Heim (1982) has argued that indefinite nominals are best interpreted as restricted free variables. *When* adjuncts can be used to form the restriction of a null generic operator, and the clause to which they are adjoined can be used as its nuclear scope. In such cases, *when* has an atemporal reading, as noted by Carlson (1979) and by Farkas and Sugioka (1983), for example. Kratzer (1988) points out that this quantificational reading is possible only when a variable is present for the quantifier to bind (Kratzer's exx. 15a and 15b):

(26) a. *When Mary knows French, she knows it well.
      b. When a Moroccan knows French, she knows it well.

The only difference between these examples is that (26b) contains the indefinite *a Moroccan* in place of the definite *Mary* in (26a), and there is a contrast in the acceptability of the sentences. These sentences are taken to express generic quantifications. The adjunct expresses the restriction, and the main clause expresses the nuclear scope. If a *when* adjunct is not used to restrict a quantifier, the same adjunct appearing in (26a) is grammatical:

(27) When Mary knows French, she will be able to advance to candidacy.

The adjunct can be paraphrased as *when Mary learns French*. A generic interpretation is not possible, except in a bizarre world in which Mary alternates between states of knowing and not knowing French and in which advancing to candidacy can happen repeatedly.

Kratzer (1988) notes that the examples in (26) have the logical representations shown below, on the assumptions that the adjunct restricts the null generic quantifier and that the main clause contributes the nuclear scope:

(28) a. *When Mary knows French, she knows it well.
 *G [knows (Mary, French)] [knows well (Mary, French)]
 b. When a Moroccan knows French, she knows it well.
 G_x [Moroccan(x) & knows (x, French)] [knows well (x, French)]

The difference between the two logical representations is that, in (a), the quantifier has no variable to bind. Thus, Kratzer proposes the following well-formedness constraint on logical representations (1995:131):

(29) *Prohibition against vacuous quantification*
For every quantifier Q, there must be a variable x such that Q binds an occurrence of x in both its restrictive clause and its nuclear scope.

Violations of this constraint are taken to result in ungrammaticality.

The examples in (26) contain ILPs in the adjunct and in the main clause. Interestingly, if SLPs take the place of the ILPs in (26a), the sentence becomes fully grammatical (Kratzer's ex. 15d):

(30) When Mary speaks French, she speaks it well.

Since this is grammatical, it must not violate the prohibition against vacuous quantification. But this sentence does not have any more indefinite nominals in it than (26a) had: neither one has any. Kratzer proposes that SLPs themselves contribute a variable to the logical representation of the sentence, and this variable prevents (30) from being a case of vacuous quantification:

(31) When Mary speaks French, she speaks it well.
 G_l[speaks (Mary, French, l)] [speaks well (Mary, French, l)]

We will discuss what this variable is in the next chapter when we examine Kratzer's proposal in detail.

The constraint in (29) requires a variable to appear in the main clause as well as in the adjunct. Example (32a) is acceptable because the adjunct contains an indefinite and the main clause contains a pronoun with the indefinite as its antecedent. Example (32b) has a variable in the adjunct clause, but not in the main clause:

(32) a. When Mary knows a foreign language, she knows it well.
 G_x[foreign language(x) & knows (Mary, x)] [knows well (Mary, x)]
 b. *When Mary speaks French, she knows it well.
 *G_l[speaks (Mary, French, l)] [knows well (Mary, French)]

De Hoop and de Swart (1989, 1990) point out that there is more to be said on this topic. In particular, (33) contains the same SLP in both the adjunct and the main clause (as well as an indefinite in the adjunct and a pronoun with an indefinite antecedent in the main clause), but the sentence is ungrammatical:

(33) *When a Moroccan kills Fido, she kills him quickly.

The key observational insight of de Hoop and de Swart was that *when* adjuncts, interpreted as restrictions of an adverb of quantification, presuppose that the eventuality denoted by the adjunct clause has happened at least twice. Example (33) is ungrammatical because, no matter who kills Fido, Fido can be killed at most one time. Any predicate that can hold only once (a "once-only" predicate) will violate the presupposition, and the sentence in which it appears will have a bizarre interpretation.

The analyses of Kratzer (1988) and of de Hoop and de Swart (1989) will be discussed in greater detail in chapter 3. The crucial question that arises is whether the phenomena discussed here are the result of one factor or two. Kratzer proposed that ILPs fail to delimit cases (without the aid of an indefinite) because they do not contribute a variable to the logical representation of a sentence. De Hoop and de Swart showed that clauses must delimit multiple cases in order to restrict an adverbial quantifier. If the latter requirement is sufficient for the interpretations of *when* adjuncts, it may not be necessary to assume that SLPs contribute a variable after all. We will resolve these issues in chapter 5.

Finally, we should note that the starred sentences above do not seem all that ungrammatical; they just have to be interpreted in a way that makes them a bit odd. With all the *when* adjuncts, the material in the adjunct must be interpreted as forming multiple cases to be quantified over. For (26a), the speaker must believe that Mary sometimes knows French and sometimes she doesn't; only under very unusual circumstances could this be possible. Sentence (30) can be true under much more normal circumstances: sometimes Mary speaks French, and sometimes she doesn't, but when she does, she does it well. Thus, this diagnostic ultimately depends on intuitions about what kinds of eventualities can be quantified over in the required way. The reliance on this kind of intuition is unfortunate for us because it makes the results of the diagnostics unclear at times. Consider *own*, an ILP, as an example:

(34)   a. When Sam owns that house, he has parties every weekend (but when Mary owns it, she never invites anybody over).
        b. When Lex Luthor owns the world, Clark Kent wants to throw him off a skyscraper (but when he doesn't, Clark isn't annoyed by him as much).

Both these sentences require the interpretation that the ownership of the house and the world must change hands from time to time, and that, at least more than once, Sam and Lex Luthor hold title to them, respectively. Neither sentence seems ungrammatical, although (34b) presupposes a less likely set of circumstances. Should we conclude from this that *own* is stage-level? I will argue that the answer is *no*, contrary to what the *when*-adjunct diagnostic seems to indicate.

In sum, atemporal *when* adjuncts provide another diagnostic for the ILP/SLP distinction. To use this diagnostic, it is necessary to fill in all the arguments in the adjunct with definite expressions; ILP adjuncts are grammatical when they contain an indefinite because the indefinite provides a variable that allows cases to be defined. The main clause must contain either the same SLP as the adjunct, or an indefinite nominal that is coreferential with an indefinite in the adjunct. When no indefinites appear in the adjunct, and when either a SLP or an indefinite appears in the main clause, the sentence will be grammatical without a bizarre interpretation, as long as the adjunct contains a SLP that is not once-only. *When* adjuncts containing ILPs and no indefinite nominals will always be bizarre on a quantificational interpretation.

1.5 Free and Absolute Adjuncts

Stump (1985) pointed out that certain kinds of adjuncts display variations in interpretation that depend on the status of the predicate they contain. Stump distinguishes three varieties of adjuncts which he calls "absolute constructions." (Stump's ex. 1):

(35) a. The free adjunct construction:
   Walking home, he found a dollar.
   b. The nominative absolute construction:
   His father being a sailor, John knows all about boats.
   c. The augmented absolute construction:
   With the children asleep, Mary watched TV.

Stump usually reserves the term "absolute" for adjuncts of the variety shown in (b) and (c), and I will follow him in this. The difference between the free adjuncts and the absolutes is that the latter have an explicit subject and thus are necessarily saturated, but the former are analyzed as either unsaturated or having obligatorily controlled subjects. Stump notes that object control is also possible for free adjuncts (hence the name "free"), but these cases are not relevant to our investigation.

Stump noticed that free adjuncts and augmented absolute adjuncts have differing interpretations depending on whether they contain a SLP or an ILP.[3] When these adjuncts contain SLPs, they can have a "weak" interpretation, as he calls it. That is, they can serve as the restriction of a modal, frequency adverb, or generic operator. When an adjunct does not serve as a restriction of such an operator, it is said to have a "strong" interpretation.

The following examples contain free adjuncts with modals in the main clause. When the adjunct contains a SLP, the sentence may be paraphrased as a conditional, as in (36a,b) and (37a,b), but this is not the case when the adjunct contains an ILP, as in (36c,d) and (37c,d). (These examples are taken from Stump, chapter 2, examples 1-8):

(36) a. Standing on a chair, John can touch the ceiling.
   b. If he stands on a chair, John can touch the ceiling.
   c. Having unusually long arms, John can touch the ceiling.
   d. If he has unusually long arms, John can touch the ceiling.

(37) a. In first gear, the truck might reach the top of that hill.
   b. If it were in first gear, the truck might reach the top of that hill.
   c. Weighing only a few tons, the truck might reach the top of that hill.
   d. If it weighs only a few tons, the truck might reach the top of that hill.

Stump notes that the examples containing SLPs do not entail that the condition denoted by the adjunct holds for the denotation of the subject: thus, in (36a) and (37a), there is no entailment that John is standing on a chair or that the truck is in first gear. However, when the adjunct contains an ILP, the condition is entailed to hold for the denotation of the subject: in (36c) and (37c), John is entailed to have long arms and the truck is entailed to weigh only a few tons.

Stump is careful to point out that SLPs need not be interpreted as restrictions of the main clause modal. The following example (Stump's ex. 50) does have an interpretation entailing that John is standing on the chair and able to see over the fence at the time of the utterance:

(38) Standing on the chair, John can see over the fence.

The augmented absolutes show the same contrast in interpretation shown by the free adjuncts: only when they contain a SLP can the adjunct restrict the interpretation of a modal (examples from Stump, chapter 5, 7–9):

(39) a. With the truck in first gear, we would coast gently downhill.
 b. With her hair braided, Jane must resemble Mary.
 c. With the children asleep, Mary might watch TV.

The following augmented absolutes contain ILPs and the conditional interpretation is not available (examples from Stump, chapter 5, 10–12):

(40) a. With his mother being a doctor, John would know the way to the Med Center.
 b. With the water being a little cold, the children must stay on the beach.
 c. With his arm being in a cast, Bill might not be asked to participate.

Thus, augmented absolutes reveal a contrast in the interpretations of ILPs and SLPs. SLPs allow two interpretations for augmented absolutes: in one, the adjunct is interpreted as the restriction of a modal; in the other, it is not, and the eventuality denoted by the adjunct is presupposed to hold in the world of discourse.

Stump argues that the unaugmented nominative absolutes cannot have this conditional interpretation[4] (examples from his chapter 5, 4–6):

(41) a. The truck in first gear, we would coast gently downhill.
 b. Her hair braided, Jane must resemble Mary.
 c. The children asleep, Mary might watch TV.

ILP nominative absolutes receive the same interpretation:

(42) a. His mother being a doctor, John would know the way to the Med Center.
 b. The water being a little cold, the children must stay on the beach.
 c. His arm being in a cast, Bill might not be asked to participate.

In all these examples, there is an entailment that the eventuality denoted by the adjunct holds. This, of course, is not the case with the augmented examples in (39).

Most of the examples surveyed above contain modals in the main clause, and when the adjunct contains a SLP, it can be interpreted as restricting that modal. Stump also notes that augmented absolutes can appear with no overt operator in the main clause, and in such cases, a generic reading may be available. This is the case with the following augmented absolutes which contain SLPs (from Stump, chapter 5, 44–46):

(43) a. With her hair braided, Jane reminds us of Mary.
 b. With her children asleep, Mary watches TV.
 c. With his work done, John goes straight to bed.

Sentence (43a), for example, can be taken to be a generalization over cases in which Jane's hair is braided; it asserts that when such cases hold, she reminds us of Mary. If we assume the existence of a null generic operator, we see that the adjunct can be interpreted as its restriction. This is not the case when the absolute contains an ILP—then, the adjunct cannot restrict the generic operator:

(44) a. His left arm being in a cast, John doesn't like to play volleyball.
b. His father having been a wheat farmer, John works at the Board of Trade.
c. The water being a little cold, Bill stays on the beach.

When the adjunct does not restrict an operator, it is entailed to hold in the world of discourse. This is the only possible reading for the examples in (44).

The examples in (43) and (44) show a contrast in the ability of predicates to restrict a generic operator: SLPs are suitable for this and ILPs are not. This is exactly what was seen with the diagnostic involving *when* adjuncts, discussed in the previous section. We have also seen in this section that SLPs in free and augmented absolute adjuncts can restrict a modal, and, again, ILPs cannot. Clearly, something about SLPs makes them better suited than ILPs to restricting these operators.

1.6 Temporal and Locative Modifiers

Carlson (1982) and Kratzer (1988) point out contrasts like the following:

(45) a. Manon is dancing on the lawn.
b. ?Manon is a dancer on the lawn.

(46) a. Manon is dancing this morning.
b. ?Manon is a dancer this morning.

SLPs can be modified by temporal and locative expressions without resulting in an unusual interpretation for the predicate. ILPs, on the other hand, can be interpreted only with rather odd meanings when modified in this way. We should add a caveat here that different temporal modifiers have different effects. The ones that show a SLP/ILP contrast are of fairly short duration. Those with longer duration are fully acceptable with ILPs:

(47) a. I was a dancer in 1978.
b. I was a dancer when I was younger.

However, as Donka Farkas has pointed out to me, even modifiers of short duration can be fully acceptable:

(47) c. John is a goalie this morning (although he usually plays forward).

In the context of sporting events, it is not unusual for individual-level properties to hold only for the duration of a particular game. In fact, (46b) strikes me as fully acceptable if Manon is a performer who assumes different roles on different occasions. The same may be true any time individuals assume roles of short duration. Should we conclude that *be a goalie* and *be a dancer* are "being used" as stage-level predicates in these contexts? This is an important question, and the answer depends on what one takes to be the definitive properties for the two sorts of predicate. We will return to this question in the discussion of coercion in chapter 4.

Related to the idea that only SLPs are grammatical with temporal and locative modifiers is the idea that ILPs express properties that are independent of at least a spatial location. For example, if someone named Mary knows Latin, she can change her location without losing her knowledge of Latin. On the other hand, if Mary is swimming and her location changes, say to her dining room, she may well no longer be swimming. We might try to use this idea as the basis of a diagnostic for the ILP/SLP distinction. SLPs would denote properties that can or must change when an individual changes physical location. But "can" is too weak in this statement and "must" is too strong: many ILPs express properties that *can* change when the subject moves, and many SLPs express properties that need not change with a change in location. In fact, some SLPs seem crucially to have physical locations and others do not. Obviously, locatives do, and I agree with Chierchia (1995b) that episodic verbal predicates usually seem to. Non-locative SLPs that are aspectually stative, however, seem not to depend on location at all. These include *drunk* (as noted by Chierchia), *naked, tired, bored, unhappy,* and perhaps *available,* although the last probably depends on exactly what it is that one is available for and whether that purpose is somehow crucially located. Thus, it seems that our proposed diagnostic runs the risk of bifurcating the class of SLPs and of grouping some of them with ILPs. And this grouping is different still from the stative/non-stative aspectual distinction.

It is clear that SLPs differ from ILPs in the ability to be located in space and time. This discussion also suggests that the SLPs do not constitute a uniform class in this respect; although all SLPs can be modified by a spatial locative, some seem to be intrinsically located in space and others seem not to be. Louise McNally suggested to me that it might be profitable to attempt an analysis that makes a distinction between space and time. Things get complicated quickly, however, so we will not pursue this idea here.

1.7 Additional Complement Selection Cases

Bolinger (1973) presents evidence that three verbs, when they appear with clausal complements of certain syntactic categories, require their complements to contain ILPs, which he calls "essence" predicates. *Think,* when it appears with a small clause or infinitival complement, seems to require this, as do *hold,* with an infinitival complement, and *feel,* with a *that*-clause complement. When the same verbs appear with other categories of clausal complement, no such restrictions appear. The examples below, taken from Bolinger (1973:62–63), show a contrast among predicates embedded in small-clause and infinitival complements to *think*:

(48) a. I thought him (to be) clever.
 b. I thought him (to be) sickly.
 c. I thought him (to be) tiresome.
 d. I thought him (to be) weak in character.

(49) a. *I thought him (to be) ready.
 b. *I thought him (to be) ill.
 c. *I thought him (to be) tired.
 d. *I thought him (to be) weak from loss of blood.

The embedded predicates in all these examples are adjective phrases. Bolinger adds some examples with nominal complements. All of the latter are acceptable, a significant fact in view of the common assumption that all English nominal predicates are ILPs. The following examples, then, support the conjecture that the ILP/SLP contrast is involved:

(50) a. I thought him (to be) a man of honor.
b. I thought it (to be) a good example.
c. Do you think that animal (to be) a gorilla?

Bolinger gives one example of a PP predicate and notes that it is not acceptable because it does not describe its subject in terms of its essence:

(51) *I thought the concert (to be) in the park.

PPs that denote essential characteristics are hard to find. *Out of x's mind* is one that I think is ambiguous between ILP and SLP interpretations. If so, Bolinger would expect the following to be acceptable, and I think that it is:

(52) Robin thought Pat (to be) out of her mind.

In the cases examined thus far, the non-finite complements of *think* seem to accept the class of ILPs but not of SLPs, making this construction a useful diagnostic for the distinction. Although Bolinger does not discuss them, VPs can grammatically appear in non-finite complements to *think*, but they have to appear without *be*:

(53) a. I thought her to know French.
b. Robin thought Pat to have a Ph.D.
c. Leslie thought this problem to require additional attention.

(54) a. *I thought her to reach a decision.
b. *Robin thought Pat to kick the trash can.
c. *Leslie thought Sam to solve the problem.

These examples show a fairly clear ILP/SLP contrast. However, this construction is not used very frequently, and it strikes me as mannered. In addition, many of the sentences that are starred do not seem fully ungrammatical, although there is usually a clear contrast in naturalness between predicates of the two classes. These features detract from the usefulness of these cases as a diagnostic with more complicated predicates. However, these are important data that a theory of the ILP/SLP distinction should be able to handle.

Bolinger (1973:64) also claimed that infinitival complements of *hold* also show a contrast of grammaticality owing to the class of the embedded predicate. He used examples like the following:

(55) a. I hold him to be clever.
b. Robin held Pat to be out of her mind.
c. I hold him to be a man of honor.

(56) a. *I hold him to be ready.
b. *I held the concert (to be) in the park.

VPs other than those headed by *be* are ungrammatical in this complement position, making this diagnostic less versatile than the complement of *think*:

(57) a. *I held her to know French.
b. *I held her to have known French.

Next, Bolinger offers examples of *that* complements of *feel*, which also accept only essence predicates:

(58) a. I feel that he is insane.
b. I feel that he is pretty impertinent.
c. I feel that he is a man of honor.

(59) a. *I feel that he is queasy.
b. *I feel that he is here.
c. *I feel that he is chopping the wood.

To these examples of Bolinger's we can add contrasting prepositional phrases:

(60) a. Robin feels that Pat is out of her mind.
b. *Robin feels that Pat is on the porch.

Below are cases with VP predicates:

(61) a. Leslie feels that Sam understands the situation.
b. *Leslie feels that Sam kicked the chair.

However, I find the following with SLPs much better than sentences like (61b):

(62) a. Leslie feels that Sam may have kicked the chair.
b. Lyle feels that Bo never helps with the dishes.

In these examples, the SLP appears within the scope of a modal or adverbial quantifier. This kind of environment also makes non-verbal SLPs acceptable:

(63) a. Robin feels that Pat is always on the porch when there is work to be done.
b. Marion feels that Robin always gets sleepy early.

We have a strong generalization; however, (64a) below contains a SLP that does not appear to be in the scope of any operator:

(64) a. Leslie feels that the group lost momentum.
b. Leslie feels that the group has lost momentum.

I believe that (64a) has a past perfect interpretation just like that of (64b). The interpretation of the past perfect will have a scope. If the SLP is caught in it (at least on a particular interpretation), the clause will be grammatical as a complement of *feel*.

The examples with *feel* are particularly important. Bolinger's data appeared to show that *feel* somehow has a selectional restriction for an ILP in an embedded full clause. Then we noticed that SLPs are acceptable in complement clauses only if they are in the scope of an operator. We will discuss this further in chapter 7. Anticipating that analysis, I will say that SLPs can be used deictically unless they are bound by some operator. I will take the position that it is Kratzer's extra spatiotemporal argument that gives SLPs these characteristics.

Bolinger (1973:65) also claims that *feel* appears grammatically with infinitival complements only when the complement is individual-level:

(65) a. I feel him to be insane.
b. I feel him to be pretty impertinent.
c. I feel him to be a man of honor.
d. Robin feels Pat to be out of her mind.

(66) a. *I feel him to be queasy.
b. *I feel him to be here.
c. *I feel him to be chopping the wood.
d. *Robin feels Pat to be on the porch.

Full VPs are not acceptable, however:

(67) a. *Leslie feels Sam to know French adequately.
b. *Leslie feels Sam to have kicked the chair.

Other verbs with meanings similar to those presented here allow predicates of both classes. The following examples are given by Bolinger (1973:64) to illustrate this:

(68) a. I consider him (to be) ready.
b. I consider her (to be) intelligent.
c. I supposed him to have been weak from loss of blood.
d. I supposed him to have been weak in character.
e. I knew them to be alarmed about it.
f. I knew them to be clever.
g. I found them to be ready.
h. I found the text to be indecipherable.
i. I judged them to be ready.
j. I judged them to be well qualified.

These examples show that there is no direct pairing of complement category with predicate restriction. Small clause complements may be required to contain SLPs, as with the familiar case of perceptual reports; or they may be required to contain ILPs, as with *think*; or they may allow either class of predicate, as is the case with *consider*. I am not aware of any infinitival complements that are acceptable only with SLPs, but Bolinger points out that *think* and *hold* require their infinitival complements to contain ILPs, and that many verbs, like those in (68), impose no such restrictions on their complements. Finally, *that* complements of *feel* are required to contain ILPs or else SLPs within the scope of an operator; many other verbs that take full-clause complements are unrestricted (e.g., *believe, think, know, imagine*). These observations are very significant, because they eliminate the possibility of an account based solely on category selection and/or semantic selection.

Finally, we should note that sentences of the types discussed in this section are not used all that frequently, and the judgments are fairly subtle. Consequently, this investigation will not rely too heavily on these contrasts. Nevertheless, they constitute important data that we will need to account for.

1.8 Other cases

There are several other cases that seem to show a contrast between ILPs and SLPs and thus deserve brief mention.

First, Bolinger notes that "we do not ordinarily conjoin complements that in Spanish would call for different verbs" (1973:58). In other words, we do not ordinarily conjoin an ILP with a SLP. He offers the following examples (Bolinger 1973:58):

(69) a. *He's wicked and afflicted.
 b. *He's home wise.
 c. *What and where is the theater?

These contrast with the following:

(70) a. He's sick and afflicted.
 b. He's home free.
 c. Who and what are these people?

Another construction that shows a similar contrast involves predicate complements of *get*:

(71) a. Mary got sick.
 b. He got free by stratagem, and came to America.
 c. Water gets hard as it freezes.

These SLPs are acceptable, but the ILPs below are less natural:

(72) a. *Mary got intelligent.
 b. *He got American by stratagem, pretending to know the Constitution and fooling the judge into naturalizing him.
 c. *Water gets ice as it freezes.

Second, Bolinger (1973:66–67) points out a contrast in what he calls "specifying *in*" phrases, like the following:

(73) a. He is like his brother in irritability.
 b. He is like his brother in cowardice.
 c. She resembles you in appreciativeness.

The individual-level predicates above are acceptable. They contrast with the SLPs shown below:

(74) a. *He is like his brother in anger.
 b. *He is like his brother in fear.
 c. *She resembles you in gratitude.

Bolinger (1973:60–62) also argues that the use of *all* as a predicate intensifier is acceptable only with stage-level predicates:

(75) a. He's all ready.
 b. He's all wrong about that.
 c. I'm all afraid.
 d. Poor thing, she's all toothless.

(76) a. *He's all intelligent.
 b. *He's all clever.
 c. *I'm all cowardly.
 d. *The snake is all toothless by nature.[5]

This also appears to reflect the ILP/SLP distinction. And Bolinger (1967) discusses issues involving the placement of adjectives that may ultimately have bearing on this distinction.

Finally, I will mention briefly that Barss (1995:691) notes a contrast in the following examples:

(77) a. Who do you think's outside?
b. Who did you say's coming to the party?
c. Who do you think's available?
d. Who do you think's mortally wounded?
e. Who do you think's weary?
f. (out of Bill, Tom, and Karen) Which do you think's available?

(78) a. ?*Who do you think's altruistic?
b. ?*Who do you think's moral?
c. ?*Who did you say's tall?
d. ?*Who did you think's dreary?
e. ?*(out of *b,t,* and *k*) Which do you think's a labial?

Examples in (77) contain embedded SLPs, and the less acceptable examples in (78) contain embedded ILPs. Barss claims that contraction is possible only with embedded SLPs. Speakers I have consulted find this contrast very difficult to judge, particularly when the predicate is syntactically complex. Therefore, we will not use this as a diagnostic.

2. Structural Ambiguities

From the literature surveyed in this book, it has emerged that the coda of the existential construction and the embedded predicate in a perceptual report are grammatical only with SLPs. These two constructions have therefore been taken to be important diagnostics in work on the distinction. In each case, the syntactic environment that reveals a SLP/ILP distinction is a postverbal string consisting of a nominal constituent followed by a predicate phrase. The proper use of these diagnostics requires some care, however, because there is more than one syntactic structure that will yield such a string, and not all of these structures reveal an ILP/SLP contrast. In addition to the predication complement that is the environment needed for the diagnostic both constructions allow a simple nominal complement. For example, verbs of perception allow a simple nominal complement, as in (79a), in addition to the small-clause complement shown in (79b):

(79) a. Eric saw [NPToby].
b. Eric saw [SCToby leave].

Similarly, the dummy subject *there* can appear with a form of *be* (or other appropriate verb) and a single noun phrase, as shown in (80a):

(80) a. There was a book.
b. There was a book open.

At least two varieties of post-nominal modifier—depictives and reduced relatives—can appear in exactly the same linear position as the existential coda and the embedded predicate in a perceptual report. Interestingly, both modifier types have been claimed at one time or another to show a distinction in grammaticality that at least resembles the ILP/SLP contrast. We will see that these matters are not trivially straightforward, however, so we will need to exercise care in using these existential and perceptual report diagnostics.

2.1 Depictives

Depictives are predicates that describe a condition of one of the arguments in the clause to which they are adjoined. There is a substantial body of literature analyzing depictives, including Halliday (1967), Green (1973), Jackendoff (1990), McNally (1992), and Rapoport (1991). Examples of depictives are italicized in the sentences below:

(81)   a. Linda painted the barn *dirty*.
       b. Toby ate his lunch *cold*.
       c. Robin gave the book to Sandy *standing on the porch*.

These examples are ambiguous between subject and object control of the depictive adjunct. The sentences have the interpretation that the property denoted by the adjunct holds of one of the verb's arguments during the run time of the eventuality denoted by the verb. Thus, (81a) means that Robin painted the barn while either it or she was dirty. Because depictives can in principle be adjoined to the end of any clause, it is possible to confuse them with the existential coda or with the embedded predicate in a perceptual report. We will later consider ways of distinguishing depictives from embedded predicates, but first we will consider a claim that depictives show a contrast in interpretation depending on whether they contain an ILP or a SLP.

2.1.1 Depictives and the ILP/SLP Distinction

Rapoport (1991) makes the claim that only SLPs are grammatical as depictives, and she concludes that the ILP/SLP distinction in a depictive environment results in a contrast in grammaticality. McNally (1993) points out that ILPs are sometimes grammatical and describes the cases in which they are acceptable. Rapoport's claim that there is a contrast in grammaticality is supported by examples like the following (Rapoport's ex. 19):

(82)   a. Ayala sold the book used/*interesting.
       b. Mixa broke the glass new/*blue.
       c. Shuli ate the berries raw/*large.

McNally (1993) notes, however, that nominal phrases can appear comfortably as depictives with examples like the following:

(83)   a. Nancy returned home an Olympic silver medalist.
       b. Sean left the army a fervent noninterventionist.

Previous researchers all concluded that nominal predicates are always individual-level. McNally argues that ILP depictives are only grammatical when the main clause supports a reading of the depictive as a changed state. Although change-of-state predicates are SLPs due to the fact that they involve a state changing at a particular time, the result of a change of state is still a state. We have seen that stative predicates may be ILPs or SLPs, so a changed state could be rendered by either sort of predicate. A change-of-state eventuality is not stative itself, but the result of a change of state is. A change of state is an eventuality that involves a change in the truth value of a stative predication. Changing the truth of a proposition does not require the ILP/SLP status of the predicate to change. Thus, we conclude that a changed state (itself the result of a change of state) preserves the ILP/SLP status of the original predicate. Therefore, the predicative final NP in examples like (83) are ILPs, after all. So both SLPs and ILPs can appear in depictives.

We must note that many sentences with ILP depictives will be true only under bizarre circumstances or within the context of fantasy or science fiction:

(84) a. Alice left the room tall.
      b. The android returned to the spacecraft a living human.

We will consider more cases like these in the discussion of coercion and see what sort of interpretation for these would emerge if someone actually said them to you. Example (84a) clearly implicates that Alice was not tall at some point not too long before she left the room (the implicature can easily be defeated, however—*Yes, she left the room tall, but she had entered the room tall as well*); (84b) implicates that the android was not a human until recently before returning to the spacecraft. Any ILP for which it is hard to imagine a change in whether it holds of a particular subject will sound strange in this position. If such a predicate appeared following a noun phrase, the predicate could not be the embedded predicate of a perceptual report, or in the coda of the existential, because those positions require a SLP. What about a case in which a depictive has the interpretation of the result of a change of state? Can we conclude that the predicate is individual-level? If so, we could use this interpretation as a diagnostic for the ILP/SLP distinction. This hope, however, turns out not to be well founded: depictives that consist of a SLP may yield an interpretation similar to the resultant-state interpretation:

(85) a. Laurie returned home upset.
      b. Lou finished the exam in a sweat.

The conclusion is that there is no contrast in interpretation between ILPs and SLPs in depictive adjuncts. Because depictives do not show a clear contrast, it becomes very important for our purposes to find ways to distinguish them from the existential coda and the embedded predicate in a perceptual report.

2.1.2 Distinguishing Depictives from Other Predicates

First, we can note that bare verbs cannot be used as depictives (see ex. 86), and so (87) cannot be analyzed as having a depictive in it:

(86) Robin ate lunch driving/*drive.

(87) Leslie saw Robin drive.

Thus, the bare verb in (87) is clearly an embedded predicate. However, bare verbs are not acceptable in the coda of the existential construction, as (88) shows:

(88) There was a dog *walk/walking.

Moreover, other categories of predicates besides VPs can appear in perceptual reports, so we need a test that has broader applications.

It seems that no more than one depictive can be used to modify a single nominal expression. The following contains two depictives, but only one reading is possible for it:

(89) Robin painted the house dirty soaking wet.

This sentence has an interpretation in which Robin was soaking wet and the house was dirty, but not that either Robin or the house were both naked and dirty. This fact allows us the possibility of distinguishing depictives from small-clause predicates or from the existential coda: we can add a depictive after the predicate we are attempting to diagnose, and if the depictive can modify the subject of the predicate in question, the predicate must not be a depictive. Consider the following:

(90) a. I saw Robin throw the ball naked.
     b. Lynne saw Lyle leave upset.

Since the adjectives *naked* and *upset* can be predicated of *Robin* and *Lyle*, respectively, we are justified in concluding that *throw the ball* and *leave* are small clause predicates, and therefore that they are SLPs.

Another factor that must be controlled for is the possibility that one of the predicates is a reduced relative. This would nullify the test because depictives can appear with nominals modified by reduced relatives:

(91) Robin painted the house on the corner dirty.

Here, *on the corner* is a reduced relative, so only one depictive appears in the sentence, and it can modify either *Robin* or *the house*. We will take up the matter of reduced relatives in the next section.

It is somewhat disappointing to find that depictives are unacceptable with the existential construction:

(92) a. *There were people hungry tired.
     b. *There were people noisy upset.

If they were acceptable, we could tack them onto the end of the sentence, as we can with perceptual reports, to ensure that the predicate we are examining is in the coda. (See McNally 1992 for further relevant discussion.) McNally (1993) showed, as we saw above, that ILPs can appear as depictives, but only when the main clause supports the possibility of the depictive as the result of a change of state. Existentials clearly cannot do this.

Depictives can appear in the following sentences, which appear to be existentials; however, the first postnominal predicate can be analyzed as a reduced relative in each case:

(93) a. There were people on the porch upset with the election.
  b. There were people eating supper tired.

It is to these that we now turn our attention.

2.2 Other Postnominal Modifiers

Below are examples of reduced relatives, the other type of adjunct that could be confused for a SLP/ILP diagnostic environment:

(94) a. Sal hung the bucket *bought by Lou's father* on the wall.
  b. Several redwoods *displaying scars from past forest fires* are growing in the park.
  c. Bad teachers are sometimes threatened by students *knowing all the answers*.

Reduced relatives restrict the interpretation of the nominals in which they appear. Note that the reduced relative in (94c) is an ILP. Because perception verbs and the string *there be* can be followed by a simple nominal constituent, reduced relatives can be adjoined at the ends of such sentences, making them superficially like existentials and perceptual reports. (See Akmajian 1977 and Gee 1977 for discussion of the issues pertaining to perceptual reports.) As noted above, the fact that depictives are adjoined at the ends of sentences is a similar source of potential confusion; they may also be confused with reduced relatives.

It is standardly assumed that reduced relatives cannot follow full relative clauses within a single nominal phrase:

(95) a. A woman stacking boxes whose hair had been cut short stopped working when she saw Lyle.
  b. A woman whose hair had been cut short stacking boxes stopped working when she saw Lyle.

In the second sentence, *stacking boxes* cannot directly modify *a woman*; it can only appear as part of the *wh*-relative clause. This diagnostic is not fully robust, and contrasts in acceptability are sometimes quite subtle. I am grateful to an anonymous reviewer for pointing out that the following is not so bad:

(96) The men that I know sued by the government defended themselves successfully.

Nevertheless, in the earlier discussion of existentials I inserted full relative clauses before the predicate taken to be in the coda position. There may be some cases in which we will not be able to distinguish a coda or small-clause predicate from a reduced relative. However, there are other cases that can be distinguished reliably. For example, a reduced relative cannot consist of an uninflected verb phrase, and neither can a depictive; therefore, bare verbs will appear only as the main predicate of a small or infinitival clause.

Having been warned that structural ambiguity can mislead us into misinterpreting a diagnostic, we plunge boldly onward.

3. Summary

A general pattern has emerged from the survey of data in this chapter. It appears that English predicates that are not kind-level are partitioned into two natural classes: SLPs are grammatical as the coda of the existential construction; they also allow weak subjects, yield an existential reading for bare plural subjects, and are grammatical as the predicate in a perceptual report; but ILPs do not have any of these properties. Atemporal *when* and absolute adjuncts interpreted as quantifier restrictions yield bizarre readings for ILPs when no indefinite nominal is present in the adjunct. SLPs in the augmented absolute or free adjunct position are able to serve as the restriction of an operator, while the denotations of ILPs are entailed to hold in the world of discourse when they appear in these constructions. Finally, ILPs are often strange-sounding in the presence of temporal or locative modifiers.

It must be acknowledged that putting an ILP in an environment that is best suited for a SLP sometimes has the effect of causing the ILP to appear to be stage-level. This is particularly true with clever speakers and with adverbs of quantification, temporal and locative modifiers, the progressive, and *when* adjuncts, but these effects sometimes surface with perception verbs as well. In chapter 4, these issues and the relevant data will be examined in more detail, with the goal of establishing with greater precision the conditions under which these effects obtain.

A number of questions are posed by the array of data considered in this chapter. Foremost is the question of why these diagnostics should generally yield consistent results: what do they have in common, and are there ways in which they differ? All the data considered above, and most of the data examined in previous discussions of the ILP/SLP distinction, contain simple predicates. We will see that when complex predicates are considered, the results of the diagnostics diverge. This means that we will need to hone our understanding of what drives each of the diagnostics.

The diagnostics surveyed here arrange themselves into three groups when the function of the predicate in each is considered. First are the subject effects discussed by Milsark: the existential construction's refusal to accept ILP codas, and the prohibition against weak subjects with ILPs. The existential construction requires its pivot to be weak, but ILPs cannot have subjects with weak construals.

A second group reflects the ability of predicates to contribute to the construction of cases that can serve as a domain of quantification for an operator. Free and absolute adjuncts and *when* adjuncts are the constructions in which these effects are most striking. These adjuncts do not themselves introduce the operator—the operator appears in the main clause and can be a frequency or generic adverbial or a modal; the adjuncts serve as the restriction for the operator. Indefinite nominals can provide multiple cases for the restriction of a quantifier, but so can SLPs that are not once-only, even when no indefinite nominals are present; ILPs cannot. We saw that once-only SLPs also cannot do this, and this fact will lead us to see in chapter 5 that two slightly different factors are involved in the matter of restricting quantifiers.

Temporal and spatial modification constitute a group that can be thought of as overlapping with the second group. Kratzer's (1988) analysis, for example, proposes that SLPs provide variables, instances of which temporal and spatial modifiers can take as arguments. These variables also allow certain quantifiers to be restricted.

Perception verbs and *think* and *hold* with an infinitival complement appear to be in a group by themselves. It is not obvious that the preference for SLPs in perceptual reports, or the preference for ILPs with the other verbs, have anything to do with the weak/strong distinction, and they clearly have nothing to do with the restriction of quantifiers. What seems to be involved is a kind of selectional restriction.

The divisions laid out above are based mainly on the manner in which the predicate interacts with the construction in which it appears: the predicate can impose restrictions on its subject (as with the subject effects); some other constituent may impose restrictions on the kind of predicate that may appear (as with perceptual reports); and certain limitations of the interpretation of the predicate itself may prevent it from fulfilling certain functions (as is the case with ILPs that cannot be used to restrict a quantifier).

In the following chapter I will consider previous analyses of this range of data.

3

Traditional Explanations

1. Carlson (1977)

Carlson (1977) developed an account of the behavior of bare plurals using a sorted intensional logic. The set of entities is partitioned into three sorts: kinds, objects, and stages. Objects belong to the familiar sort of entity known from traditional logic. Names like *Jane Austen* and *Al Gore*, and common noun phrases like *that dog* are taken to have the set of objects as their denotation space. A stage is "a spatially and temporally bounded manifestation" (68) of an object. Carlson says that no constituent of natural language has the set of stages as its denotation space, but that, when we speak of Jane Austen or Al Gore in a particular situation, we are making claims about *stages* of those objects. Thus, an object may be said to "tie together" (69) the stages that are its instances at various points in space and time. Similarly, a kind is a type that ties together those objects that are tokens of it, along with the stages of those objects. Carlson claims that all ordinary bare plurals have kinds as their denotation space,[1] and, in fact, that they are *names* of kinds. Carlson offers the following simplified illustration (1977:69):

(1)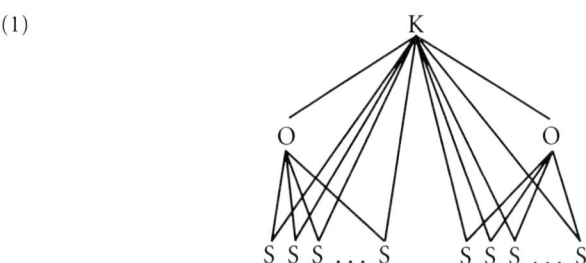

Here, *K* represents *kind*, *O*, *object*, and *S* represents *stage*. The simplification in the illustration is that most kinds referred to in natural language will have more than two objects ordered below them.

In addition to kinds, objects, and stages, Carlson declares individuals as a fourth sort: the union of the set of kinds and objects. These ontological distinctions are utilized in making a type-theoretic distinction among entities and then among predicates: stage-level predicates have stages as their arguments, individual-level predicates have individuals (objects or kinds) as arguments, and kind-level predicates have only kinds as their arguments. To set this up, Carlson augments Montague's intensional type theory with a set of subtypes. The basic idea is to create a subtype for each sort of entity, and then to allow the subtypes to distinguish SLPs, ILPs, and KLPs from one another.

Carlson defines *Type*, the set of types, and the set of denotations for the types as in PTQ (Montague 1973): let e, t, s be distinct objects that are neither ordered pairs nor triples; Type is the smallest set such that

$e \in$ Type

$t \in$ Type

If $\alpha, \beta, \in$ Type, then $<\alpha,\beta> \in$ Type

If $\alpha \in$ Type, then $<s,\alpha> \in$ Type

Carlson defines the denotation space $D_{\alpha AIJ}$ for each type α with respect to A, the set of entities, I, the set of possible worlds, and J, the set of moments of time, as follows (1979:141–142):

$D_{eAIJ} = A$

$D_{tAIJ} = \{0,1\}$ (falsity and truth, respectively)

$D_{<\alpha,\beta>AIJ} = \{x: x$ is a partial function with domain $D_{\alpha AIJ}$ and range included in $D_{\beta AIJ}\}$

$D_{<s,\alpha>AIJ} = \{x: x$ is a partial function with domain $I \times J$ and range in $D_{\alpha AIJ}\}$

Next, Carlson posits a set of sorts M that contains the elements st, o, k, and in, mnemonic for stage, object, kind, and individual, respectively. For each sort $m \in M$ there corresponds a function m' from the set of entities A to subsets of A, such that $st'(A)$ is the set of stages, $o'(A)$ is the set of objects, and $k'(A)$ is the set of kinds (where the intersection of any pair of these sets is required to be null), and $in'(A)$ is the set of individuals ($= o'(A) \cup k'(A)$). Carlson uses the sorts to define a set of subtypes, *SType*, and he uses their corresponding functions to fix their possible denotations. Carlson (1977:142) defines *SType* as the smallest set such that

$m(e) \in$ SType for all $m \in M$

$t' \in$ SType

If $\alpha, \beta \in$ SType, then, $<\alpha,\beta> \in$ SType

If $\alpha \in$ SType, then $<s,\alpha> \in$ SType

SType winds up looking exactly like *Type*, except that t' appears in *SType* where t does in *Type* (although they both have the same denotation space: $\{1,0\}$), and $m(e)$ appears in *SType* (for some sort $m \in M$) in place of e in *Type*. Thus, kinds are of subtype $k(e)$ (where e has its customary use as the type for entities), individuals are of subtype $in(e)$, objects are of subtype $o(e)$, and stages are of subtype $s(e)$. The denotation space for each subtype $m(e)$ is just the subset of entities picked out by $m'(A)$.

Carlson defines a relation between subtypes and their corresponding types as follows (1977:142):

(2) For any α ∈ SType and any T ∈ Type, α ⊆ T if α differs from T only in that every occurrence of t in T is replaced with t', and every e in T is replaced with m(e), for some m ∈ M.

With this relation defined, Carlson proceeds to define the denotation space $D_{\alpha'AIJ}$ for a sorted type α' with respect to A, I, and J as follows (1977:142):

$D_{m(e)AIJ}$ = m'(A) (where m ∈ M and m' is a function corresponding to m such that m'(A) ⊆ A)

$D_{t'AIJ}$ = {0,1}

$D_{<\alpha',\beta'>AIJ}$ = {x: x ∈ $D_{<\alpha,\beta>AIJ}$ (where α, β ∈ Type and α' ≤ α, β' ≤ β) and x has as its complete subfunction a function with domain $D_{\alpha'AIJ}$ and range included in $D_{\beta'AIJ}$}

$D_{<s,\alpha'>AIJ}$ = {x: x is a partial function with domain I×J and range included in α'}

These formal assumptions allow a type-theoretic distinction to be made among SLPs, ILPs, and KLPs. The effect of this is that any arbitrary predicate that one is "handed" can be classified instantly based on its type. Below, the second column shows the types assigned by Carlson's system to stage-, individual-, and kind-level predicates (from p. 146), and the third column shows the abbreviation he uses in his second fragment:

(3) SLP : $<st(e),t>$ $<e^s,t>$
     ILP : $<in(e),t>$ $<e^i,t>$
     KLP : $<k(e),t>$ $<e^k,t>$

Carlson uses superscripts to distinguish among entity type variables of different sorts: x^k, x^i, x^o, x^s are variables ranging over kinds, individuals, objects, and stages, respectively. Carlson omits superscripts after their first appearance in a formula "where no confusion will result" (1977:80).

In a semantic theory that does not make use of Carlson's sorted types, such as that of Montague (1973), (4a) has the interpretation shown in (4b) (disregarding tense), where *run"* is a set of individuals and *z* is the individual Zippy:[2]

(4)   a. Zippy ran.
      b. *run"* (z)

(5a) is translated similarly:

(5)   a. Zippy is intelligent.
      b. *intelligent'* (z)

Intelligent is also interpreted as a set of individuals. Carlson's system assigns the same interpretation to *Zippy is intelligent*: the predicate is individual-level, so its extension is a set of individuals. Carlson (1977:76) claims that sentences like (4a) are subtly ambiguous between expressing a claim about a particular happening and a claim about a characteristic of Zippy (in the past). During the development of his preliminary analysis (chapter 4), Carlson says that the source of this ambiguity is that *run* can function as either a SLP (yielding the "happening" reading) or an ILP (yielding the characteristic reading).[3] On this view, (4b) is a fine interpretation of the claim about a characteristic of Zippy, but it is ill-formed as a claim about a particular happening. Recall that Carlson claims that no nominal expression has the set of stages as a denotation space. But SLPs have sets of stages as their extensions, so the SLP variety of *run* is of the wrong type to compose with the individual that is the denotation of *Zippy*.

This is obviously a general problem which, unsolved, would prevent any stage-level predicate from ever composing with a subject. To deal with this, Carlson introduces a relation R (for "realizes") that holds between stages and individuals. $R(a,b)$ means that a is a stage of the individual b. The set of stages that run are taken to be *run'*. The stage-level reading of (4a) is as follows:

(6) $\exists y[R(y^s,z)\ \&\ run'(y^s)]$

This entails the existence of a stage of Zippy that is in the set of things that run. In Carlson's first fragment, the relation R is introduced into the translation in the translation of stage-level *run*, which is assumed to be $\lambda x^i \exists y^s[R(y,x)\ \&\ run'(y)]$. Whenever R is introduced by the basic translation of a predicate (it appears only with stage-level verbs), an existential quantifier is introduced as well. This creates the possibility of an existential interpretation for an indefinite subject—an inevitable result unless some other operator has wider scope. In all these cases, it is the existence of a stage of the denotation of the subject that is entailed, rather than a direct entailment that the individual denoted by the subject exists. This winds up entailing that the subject's denotation exists, but it does so somewhat indirectly.

In Carlson's second fragment, stage-level verbs do not include R or the existential quantifier as part of the basic translation of SLPs. This means that they cannot combine with any subject without additional help. Carlson introduces a rule to allow verbal SLPs to do this. (Other SLPs can combine with subjects by rule S13, which introduces be_2; see ex. 9 below). The following rule accomplishes this by introducing an existential quantifier, which will result in the reading that there is some stage of the subject that participated in the eventuality denoted by the SLP (Carlson 1977:252, 262):[4]

(7) S23. If $\alpha \in P_{IV}$ and α iotf $[\beta]_V(\delta)$, then $F_{21}(\alpha) \in P_{IV'}$, where $F_{21}(\alpha)=[\alpha]_{IV'}$.
    T23. If $\alpha \in P_{IV}$ and translates as α', then $F_{21}(\alpha)$ translates as $\lambda x^i \exists z^s[R(z,x)\ \&\ \alpha'(z)]$

In this notation, P_x is the set of sentential constituents of syntactic category X. Carlson's analysis distinguishes ILPs and SLPs on the basis of syntactic category. The categories IV' and IV are referred to in rule S23: IV' can combine with subjects and is thus the category corresponding to ILPs; IV cannot combine with subjects, so it corresponds to SLPs.

For those PPs and APs that are stage-level, Carlson introduces a form of the copula that he calls be_2. This copula is of a type to compose with a SLP to yield a predicate that composes with an individual. The R relation is introduced as part of the basic translation of be_2, and an existential quantifier is introduced along with it. Below is the translation for be_2:

(8) $\lambda Q \lambda x^i \exists y^s[R(y,x)\ \&\ ^\vee Q(y)]$

The following rule introduces be_2, which is a member of category IV'/IV (1977:251, 261):

(9) S13. If $\alpha \in P_{IV'/IV}$ and $\beta \in P_{IV}$ and β is not of the form $[\delta]_V(\gamma)$, then $F_{12}(\alpha,\beta) \in P_{IV'}$, where $F_{12}(\alpha,\beta) = [\alpha\beta]_{IV'}$.
T13. If $\alpha \in P_{IV'/IV}$ and $\beta \in P_{IV}$ and translate as α' and β' resp., then $F_{12}(\alpha,\beta)$ translates as $\alpha'(^\wedge\beta')$

Thus, the interpretation of be_2 introduces the existential quantifier that will entail the existence of a stage of the argument of the SLP. Carlson's rule of *There*-insertion requires be_2 to be present in the predicate being operated upon. Hence, the coda of the existential construction must contain a SLP; ILPs and KLPs are successfully banned from appearing in this position.

When an ILP has a bare plural (i.e., kind-denoting) subject, the relation R is not needed because ILPs are of a type that composes with a constituent of individual type, and objects and kinds are individuals. Below is the translation of *Dogs are intelligent*:

(10) $intelligent'(d)$

Recall that Carlson treats bare plurals as being names of kinds; hence, *dogs* is translated as $\lambda P^\vee P(d)$, the set of properties that hold of the individual kind d.

When a bare plural has a kind-level predicate, the translation is just as straightforward. Below is the translation of *Dogs are widespread*:

(11) $widespread'(d)$

Because *widespread* is a KLP, its type allows it to compose only with denotations of kinds, and this prevents it from having an object-level denoting expression as its syntactic subject. Thus, **John is widespread* is banned because of the sorted typology assumed by Carlson.

When a bare plural appears as the subject of a SLP, the relation R must be used. The following translation is given for *Dogs are available*:

(12) $\exists y[R(y,d) \ \& \ available'(y)]$

Here, y necessarily ranges over stages because it appears as the first argument of R. The second argument of R must be of individual type, and d is of kind type, so it is therefore also of individual type. This logical representation asserts the existence of a stage of the kind named by *dogs* that is available.

In chapter 5 of his dissertation, Carlson argues that a sentence like *Zippy ran* (on the habitual, characterizing reading) should not be treated as an individual-level predication but should be interpreted as a generalization over stages of the object Zippy. To accomplish this, and to account for the fact that English verbal SLPs have habitual interpretations in the simple present (e.g., *John smokes*), Carlson posits the existence of a phonologically vacuous, generic operator G. G is taken to be a VP operator of type $<<s,<e^s,t>>,<e^i,t>>$. It is introduced by the following rule (1977:252, 262):[5]

(13) S21. If $\alpha \in P_{IV}$ and α iotf $[[\beta]_V(\gamma)]$, then $F_{19}(\alpha) = [\alpha]_{IV'}$
T21. If $\alpha \in P_{IV}$ and translates as α', $F_{19}(\alpha)$ translates as $G^\wedge(\alpha')$

Note that this rule can apply only to SLPs that are headed by verbs (this is the effect of the condition in S21, "α is of the form $[[\beta_V(\delta)]]$"). "If this syntactic stipulation were not made, we would not be able to account for why it is that the non-verbal predicates over stages (e.g. adjectives and PP's) fail to exhibit generic/existential ambiguities" (1977:171). Thus, Carlson assumes that other SLPs do not allow generic readings on their own. Part of the motivation for this is that verb-headed SLPs have generic readings in the simple present, but other SLPs do not. This approach contrasts with more recent ones (e.g., Kratzer 1988, Diesing 1992) which assume that every SLP can have a generic reading (though not necessarily in the simple present).

The translation that results for the characterizing reading of *Zippy ran* (disregarding tense) is shown below:

(14)   G(^*run'*)(z)

Carlson notes that G, in effect, maps SLPs to ILPs. He has a separate generic operator, G' of type $<<s,<e^o,t>>,<e^k,t>>$, for mapping object-level predicates (OLPs) to KLPs. These two operators cannot be combined because G' applies to all OLPs, but Carlson wants G to apply only to V-headed SLPs. Carlson writes:

> The two G functions together in a sense serve the inverse purpose of the realization relation R (which could be split up into two similar functions, R and R'. Realization makes 'available' entities of a lower level from those of a higher level; generalization makes available predicates from a lower level to those of a higher level. (1977:172)

G' is introduced into Carlson's grammar by the following rule (1977:252, 262):

(15)   S22. If α ∈ P_{IV}, then $F_{20}(\alpha) \in P_{IV'}$, where $F_{20}(\alpha) = [\alpha]_{IV'}$
         T22. If α ∈ P_{IV} and translates as α', $F_{20}(\alpha)$ translates as G'(^α')

The translation of *Dogs are intelligent*, in Carlson's revised fragment, is as follows:

(16)   G'(^*intelligent'*)(d)

Carlson's account relies on a sorted typology of individuals. This allows him to make distinctions about the sort of object argument with which a predicate head composes as well as about the sort of the subject head. Because Carlson worked within Montague's framework, a syntactic category distinction between ILPs and SLPs was required along with the typological distinctions made among individuals.

2. Argument Structure Accounts of Subject Effects

Some more recent work has attempted to account for the subject effects by means of syntactic structure. In this section we will consider the most prominent of these attempts.

The proposals of Kratzer (1988) and Diesing (1988, 1992) are built on Diesing's modification of Heim's theory of indefinites. Heim (1982), building on work by Lewis (1975), proposes that indefinites be treated as follows:

> [A]   Indefinites are interpreted as restricted variables with no inherent quantificational force.

[B] Indefinites in the restriction of an operator are bound (unselectively) to that operator (unless they are bound by an operator with wider scope).

[C] Indefinites in the nuclear scope of an operator are bound by unselective existential closure (unless they are bound by an operator with wider scope).

[D] Indefinites that appear in a sentence containing no quantifier are existentially bound at text level.

Assumption [D], in Heim's theory, was originally needed to meet well-formedness requirements; it ensures that all variables will be bound at some point, making the formula containing them interpretable. In chapter 3 of her thesis, Heim shows that it is possible to interpret open formulas by requiring that there be a sequence of assignments which satisfy them. Thus, Heim eventually does away with [D] in favor of a systematic means for interpreting open formulas.

Since sentences containing free variables are interpretable following Heim's assumptions, with or without [D], the prediction is made that no sentence will be ungrammatical owing to the presence of an unbound indefinite.

The work of Diesing and Kratzer rejects this result. We have seen that weak indefinites sound odd as subjects of ILPs:

(17) a. *A sailor is tall.
     b. *Sm men are tall.

Diesing and Kratzer analyze the oddness of these sentences as arising from the indefinite subjects' being unbound. In Heim's analysis, these examples should be interpretable as existential statements because free variables are always bound by the assignment function.

Diesing (1988) proposes modifications of Heim's assumptions, and these modifications are adopted by Kratzer (1988). Diesing accepts assumptions [A], [B], and [C], but she does away with text-level closure and the assumptions that allow interpretations for open formulas. Instead, Diesing assumes that existential closure happens automatically at the VP node in a tree. This is taken to follow from her Mapping Hypothesis (Diesing 1992:15):

(18) *Mapping Hypothesis*
Material from the VP is mapped into the nuclear scope.
Material from the IP [exclusive of the material dominated by VP] is mapped into a restrictive clause.

Diesing intends this to characterize a "tree-splitting algorithm," or procedure, in which, evidently, the material is first moved from the VP, thus making it unnecessary to add my editorial comment, "exclusive of the material dominated by VP." For Diesing, existential closure is always the closure of a nuclear scope and the Mapping Hypothesis makes it so this always happens at the VP node. A true oddity of these assumptions is that there needs to be a nuclear scope even when there is no quantifier in the sentence. The interesting effect of these assumptions is that Heim's text-level closure has been pushed down a few nodes to allow the subjects of ILPs to escape it by appearing higher up in the syntactic structure. Of course, something must allow the subjects of SLPs to appear within VP if the necessary contrast is to be derived, and here Diesing's and Kratzer's accounts diverge.

2.1 Kratzer (1988)

2.1.1 The Basic Proposal

Kratzer (1988) accepts Diesing's strategy and seeks to reduce the difference between the interpretation of subjects of ILPs and SLPs to assumptions about argument structure and projection. Kratzer follows Carlson (1977) in noting that SLPs fundamentally need to be associated with a point in space and time in a way that ILPs do not. Thus, *Manon was dancing* is necessarily about some eventuality that took place somewhere and at some time, while *Manon was a dancer* is not. This distinction among predicates parallels Gawron's (1986) distinction between two kinds of facts. Gawron takes it that facts characterize situations: "Facts often obtain at particular locations, where locations are taken to be connected regions of space/time" (1986:429). The set theoretic construct that constitutes an abstract fact is an ordered n-tuple consisting of a location (possibly), a relation, its relata, and a polarity. The fact of Marc Antony addressing the Senate at some location l is represented thus:

(19) $f1$ = <l, Addressing, Marc Antony, Senate, 1>

Although this fact is located in space/time, Gawron notes that some facts are not, citing the following as an example:

(20) <man, Marc Antony, 1>

This fact would make the claim *Marc Antony was a man* true of it.

For Kratzer (1988), the association to space and time is the defining characteristic of SLPs, and it is taken to be the crucial semantic difference between ILPs and SLPs. Kratzer points out that SLPs tend to accept temporal and locative modification more easily than ILPs. This, she contends, indicates that SLPs have a logical argument that ILPs lack, and the argument must be the sort of thing that temporals and locatives can also have as arguments. Kratzer proposes that this argument is Davidsonian, recalling Donald Davidson's (1966) analysis of certain predicates and their modifiers. Kratzer writes, "At this point, I don't want to commit myself to a particular view with respect to the precise nature of the Davidsonian argument. It may not be an event argument. It may simply be an argument for spatiotemporal location" (1988:5).

It is important to note that only SLPs have a Davidsonian argument in Kratzer's analysis; ILPs and KLPs do not. This approach contrasts with approaches like that of Parsons (1985), in which all predicates have an eventuality argument. (Parsons makes aspectual distinctions between states, processes, and events by assuming that there are aspectual predicates *Hold* (atelic) and *Cul[minate]* (telic) which bind the eventuality arguments. He does not discuss the ILP/SLP contrast.)

The exact nature of the Davidsonian argument assumed by Kratzer remains in question. Kratzer uses an l, apparently borrowed from Barwise and Perry (1983), to represent the variable associated with the spatiotemporal argument in logical form. It is clear from the discussion of aspect in chapter 1 that this cannot simply be a nonstative argument: although all ILPs are stative, some SLPs are as well. The association to space and time seems correctly to differentiate the predicates, so we will take Kratzer's argument to be of this sort. The choice of representing both space and time in a single argument has the consequence of predicting that spatial and temporal modifiers should be uniformly acceptable with the entire set of SLPs. As we saw in chapter 2 (section 1.6), some SLPs (e.g., *on the lawn, kick over the trash can*) are associated to space more crucially than others (e.g., *drunk, bored*), and it may eventually be necessary to divide this argument in two. However, these issues become complex quite quickly, although they may make for fruitful study in the future.

Kratzer implements her proposal by taking the spatiotemporal argument of SLPs to be a thematic role in the sense of Williams (1981). Williams assumes that the lexical entry for a head includes a list of its arguments, and that at most one argument can appear outside the maximal projection of the head at deep-structure. That argument is called the "external argument," and all other arguments are projected internally, within the maximal projection. Kratzer assumes that a spatiotemporal thematic role will always be the external argument of the head. The effect of this is to prevent any other thematic role from being projected to the specifier of IP. This effect is realized by ranking the spatiotemporal role highest on a thematic hierarchy. Kratzer writes, "There may be some generalizations as to which argument of a lexical item will wind up as its external argument. Here are some candidates: If a predicate has a Davidsonian argument, it will always be its external argument. If a predicate has no Davidsonian argument, but an agent argument, the agent argument will be its external argument" (1995:135). It is clear that Kratzer assumes that the first candidate is a real generalization. Since at most one thematic role can be projected outside the maximal projection of a predicate, all other theta-roles must be projected internally. Thus, Kratzer assumes the older notion of "external argument" in which the theta-role is assigned outside the maximal projection for ILPs. Diesing (1992), discussed in the next section, assumes a more recent conceptualization of "external argument" by which the external theta-role is projected to the specifier of the predicate itself, external to X' rather than XP.

Since the *location* argument cannot be actually assigned to a nominal projected in the clausal subject position, all SLPs are "unaccusative" in the sense that all their nominal arguments will be projected within the predicate's maximal projection (the specifier of VP is taken to be a possible projection site). In (21), the (deep and surface) structure proposed for ordinary individual-level predications is shown; (22) shows the surface structure for stage-level predications:

(21)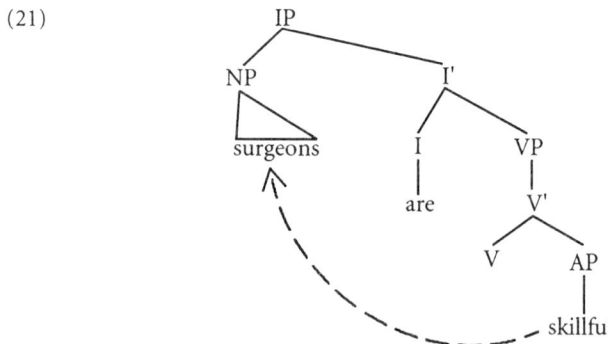

(22)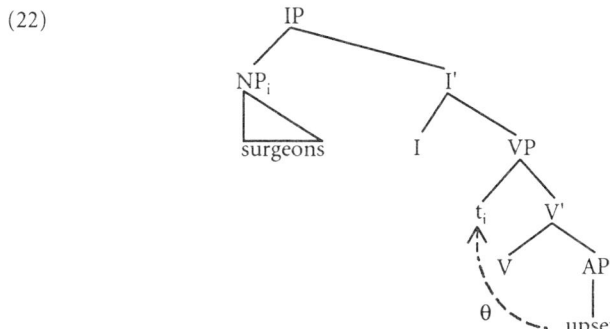

Kratzer does not discuss how VP-internal subjects receive case, although Diesing does, and there seems to be no reason why Kratzer would not assume the same. Diesing assumes that VP-internal subjects move to the specifier of IP to receive case. On the way to LF, this movement can be undone by reconstruction, allowing the NP to be caught up in the domain of unselective existential closure, that part of the tree that is dominated by VP.

Since ILPs do not have any spatiotemporal argument, some other thematic role can be projected outside the maximal projection of the predicate to the specifier of IP. For Kratzer, something must prevent a nominal projected at that position from moving inside VP on the way to LF: an existential reading would be incorrectly predicted for a nominal that could move to that position.[6]

The spatiotemporal thematic role has the effect of causing a spatiotemporal variable to appear in Kratzer's logical representations, as shown below (Kratzer's ex. 12):

(23) Manon is dancing on the lawn
      [dancing (Manon, l) & on the lawn (l)]

Kratzer has intentionally left this variable free. She writes, "These free occurrences of 'l' may become bound by quantifiers when the sentences appear as parts of more complex constructions. Or else they may be supplied with a value by the context of use" (1995:129). By "context of use," Kratzer cannot mean the assignment function, since allowing the assignment function to "rescue" a sentence containing free variables would eliminate Kratzer's explanation of the oddness of ILPs with weak indefinite subjects. This might be a suggestion that the spatiotemporal argument can be used deictically, or that it can pick up a referent from prior discourse; both these ideas will figure prominently later in this volume.

The spatiotemporal element in the argument structure needs to count as a thematic role for purposes of preventing any other thematic role from being projected to the specifier of IP. Kratzer gives sample argument structures which make it clear that the spatiotemporal argument has the same status as other thematic roles (Kratzer's exx. 25 and 26):[7]

(24) *Stage-level predicates that are not unaccusatives*
      hit   <*location*, agent, theme>
      dance   <*location*, agent>

(25) *Stage-level predicates that are unaccusatives*
       die <*location*, theme>
       fall <*location*, theme>

The spatiotemporal thematic role is unlike theta-roles previously assumed in the literature in that it does not project any syntactic constituent, and it is thus at odds with the Theta Criterion. Furthermore, as we have seen, NPs projected as VP-internal subjects must be able to move into the specifier of IP to receive case. But if the specifier of IP receives a spatiotemporal theta-role, any NP that was projected lower and that moves to the specifier of IP will form a chain that receives two different theta-roles from the same predicate. This is a violation of standard constraints on NP movement (Chomsky 1981, 1986, etc.). From this, we have to conclude that the spatiotemporal element in the argument structure of SLPs is present for purposes of the thematic hierarchy, but that it is a unique sort of theta-role that does not license the presence of any lexical item, and it is, by stipulation, invisible to the constraint on argument chains. Because the spatiotemporal thematic role is visible to argument structure constraints (i.e., for determining which arguments can be projected externally), we must assume that it behaves like a normal theta-role for lexical operations on argument structures. If we are willing to accept this, we can investigate some of the consequences this proposal has for lexical operations on argument structures.

2.1.2 "Unaccusative" ILPs

Kratzer's proposal predicts the existence of "unaccusative" ILPs. These are predicates which, like ILPs, cannot be comfortably modified by locatives, but which allow weak indefinite subjects and are grammatical as the coda of the existential construction. The unaccusative ILP category includes the class of passivized ILPs, discussed above. Diesing (1992) lists *be known to*, *belong to*, *be similar to*, and *be familiar to* as examples (Kratzer offers only the first two, so there may not be very many of these). All of these except *belong to* are actually passive forms of ILPs. Compare:

(26)   a. Counterexamples are known to Jorge.
       b. There are counterexamples known to Jorge.
       c. ??Counterexamples are known to Jorge in the next room.

Kratzer's story about these predicates is that they have no external arguments and they have no spatiotemporal argument. Their argument structures are as shown below (from Kratzer's ex. 28):

(27) belong <theme, goal>
      be known to <experiencer, theme>

Having these argument structures, "unaccusative" ILPs will project trees like the following deep-structure:[8]

(28)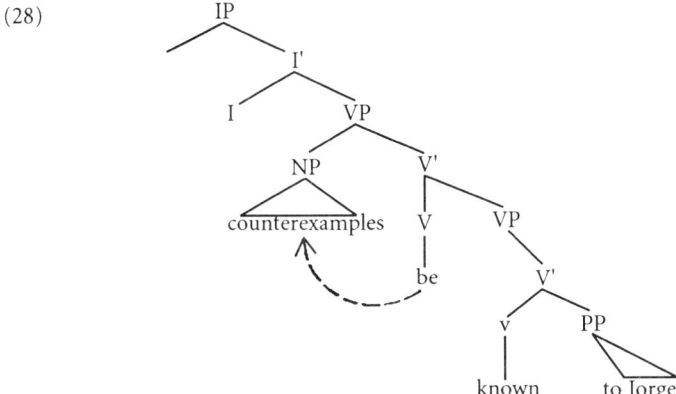

Because the subject receives its theta-role at the specifier of VP, it must move to the specifier of IP by surface-structure to receive case. Because no theta-role was assigned to the specifier of IP, two logical forms are possible: one with the subject in the specifier of IP, and one with the subject in the specifier of VP. In the former case, a generic reading will result in the usual way; in the latter, an existential reading will result because the subject is within VP at logical form where it gets caught up in existential closure. Thus, Kratzer predicts the existence of predicates that are ILPs (by virtue of lacking any Davidsonian argument), but that allow an existential interpretation for bare plural subjects.

2.1.3 Passives

Because Kratzer's proposal is driven by argument structure, we should expect it to make some predictions about the readings available for passivized verbs. Presumably the passive argument structure is derived by a lexical rule that internalizes the external argument of the active argument structure (see Levin and Rappaport 1986). Because ILPs have no location argument for the active form, there is none for the passive. The only change in the argument structure is that the subject of the passive, in contrast to the active form, is projected internally. Below are some examples:

(29) Active: know <*experiencer*, theme>
     Passive: known <experiencer, theme>

(30) Active: own <"*owner*", theme>
     Passive: owned <"owner", theme>

The argument structures for the passive forms are exactly like those for unaccusative ILPs (cf. ex. 27). This means that passivized ILPs are predicted to behave exactly like unaccusative ILPs. That is, they should continue to seem ungrammatical with temporal or locative modification, but they should be acceptable with weakly construed subjects and in the coda of the existential construction. This fairly subtle prediction is successful:

(31)   a. ??Stores are owned by Tom on Sunday.
       b. There are stores owned by Tom.

48 Predicates and Temporal Arguments

      c. Stores are owned by Tom. (existential possible)
      d. Sm stores are owned by Tom.

(32) a. ??Ballads are known by Kipling on Sunday.
      b. There are ballads known by Kipling.
      c. Ballads are known by Kipling.
      d. Sm ballads are known by Kipling.

These examples are a challenge for Milsark's analysis, which relies on two conditions to account for the general ungrammaticality of ILPs as the coda: ILPs require their subjects to be strong, and the existential construction requires its pivot to be weak. If passivized ILPs really are ILPs, this analysis incorrectly predicts the examples in (31) and (32) to be ungrammatical. If we assume that *there*-insertion is permitted in Kratzer's analysis wherever there is no theta-role assigned to subject position, her analysis will make the correct prediction for these challenging cases.

What should we expect about passivized SLPs? If we simply internalize the external argument we will internalize the spatiotemporal theta-role and leave the rest of the argument structure unaffected. Passive must work differently, given Kratzer's assumptions about argument structure. Let us modify Kratzer's suggestion that internal agent arguments are projected to the specifier of VP, and add to Williams's assumption about argument linking (that at most one argument is projected externally), by saying that exactly one internal argument may be projected outside the c-command domain of the head. We will continue to identify the external argument by using italics; the upper internal argument will be identified by capital letters. Passive will now pick out an argument either in italics or in capital letters (but the chosen argument cannot be the location argument), and rewrite it in lowercase letters, and move it to the right end of the theta-grid. The consequence of this is that when passive applies to a SLP, the capitalized argument will be demoted; when it applies to an ILP, the italicized argument will be demoted. Note that, once again, it is necessary for the spatiotemporal theta-role to be treated differently from all other theta-roles: all other theta-roles are visible to this formulation of the passive lexical rule, but the spatiotemporal role is not. Below is a SLP example with *build* and *be built*:

(33) a. build   <*location*, AGENT, theme>
      b. be built <*location*, theme, agent>

The passive form still has the spatiotemporal location as its external argument, so SLP subject effects are predicted, and again the prediction is successful.

2.1.4 Scrambling

Kratzer's assumptions make the prediction that indefinites that appear within VP at LF should have an existential interpretation and, in particular, should not be able to have a generic reading. Kratzer points out that this prediction is justified for some cases but not for others. It is false for the following:

(34) a. Tom likes movies.
      b. These assignments are too hard for students.
      c. Lisa prefers blondes.

Kratzer's story is that the objects in these cases can scramble out of the VP at LF. She notes that scrambling transformations are now frequently assumed to happen on the way to surface-structure for Japanese (Saito 1989) and German (Webelhuth 1985, 1989; von Stechow and Sternefeld 1988). Kratzer proposes that English is similar to these languages but that in it scrambling is not overt, happening only on the way to LF. Kratzer argues that generic readings for English indefinite objects are possible exactly when overt scrambling is possible in German; however, a general prediction about which objects will be able to scramble in German remains elusive.

Jäger (1997), however argues that German scrambling follows from principles independent of the ILP/SLP contrast, and shows, among other things, "that strong quantifiers may very well occur VP-internally as subjects of individual level predicates... [and that] there is evidence that a VP-external bare plural subject can bind a VP-internal trace" (1997:238).

2.1.5 Conclusion

Kratzer's proposal successfully captures a subtle nonuniformity in the ILP/SLP effects, namely that unaccusative and passive ILPs yield SLP subject effects (but see de Swart 1991 and Chierchia 1992 for additional challenges facing this proposal). The proposal distinguishes SLPs from ILPs on the basis of spatiotemporal locatedness, and this seems to be quite intuitive. Perhaps the most troubling feature of this account is the treatment of the spatiotemporal location as a theta-role. This argument counts as a theta-role only for the purpose of preventing any other theta-role from being an external argument. It does not count as a theta-role for purposes of the Projection Principle or the Theta Criterion, for passive formation, or for *there*-insertion. Diesing's account attempts to capture the same set of facts without treating the location as a theta-role.

2.2 Diesing (1992)

2.2.1 The Basic Proposal

Diesing (1992) takes a strategy similar to that of Kratzer (1988). Diesing assumes that indefinite nominals are variables, following such works as Lewis (1975), Kamp (1981), and Heim (1982). In order for a sentence to be well-formed, some operator must bind any variable found in the sentence. Diesing follows Heim (1982) and others in assuming that syntax creates tripartite quantificational structures, specifically positing the Mapping Hypothesis, repeated from (18) above:

(35) *Mapping Hypothesis*
Material from the VP is mapped into the nuclear scope.
Material from the IP [exclusive of the material dominated by VP] is mapped into a restrictive clause.

Following Heim, the nuclear scope must be quantificationally closed: any variables not found in the restriction are bound by unselective existential closure. Diesing differs from Heim in that Diesing disallows existential closure at text level but allows essentially the same thing at the VP node of any sentence. Given these assumptions, every root VP of every sentence will be mapped at LF to a nuclear scope, and everything else in the sentence will be mapped to a restriction. Because the nuclear scope gets closed existentially, any indefinite dominated by VP will receive an existential interpretation (unless the same variable appears in the restriction).

Diesing puts these results to use in her theory of the interpretations of bare plurals. Since she assumes bare plurals are indefinites (contra Carlson 1977), it follows that if one is dominated by VP at LF, it will receive an existential interpretation. One appearing outside VP (e.g., in the specifier of IP) cannot be bound by an existential operator because there is no text-level closure. Because all variables must be bound by something in order for the sentence in which they appear to be well-formed, some other operator must rescue the sentence. Following Farkas and Sugioka (1983) and others, Diesing posits the existence of a null, generic adverb of quantification to bind variables in this position. We have seen that bare plural subjects receive an existential interpretation only when the predicate is stage-level, and that generic readings are usually possible with either kind of predicate.

Diesing follows the VP-internal subject hypothesis in assuming that all predicates project their subjects to the specifier of VP (rather than IP, as assumed in earlier versions of GB), and that overt subjects must move to the specifier of IP on the way to surface structure to receive Case. This proposal thus differs from Kratzer's, which assumed that only SLPs project their subjects internally. The correct readings for bare plural subjects will be predicted if subjects of SLPs can appear in the specifier of either IP or VP at LF, and if the subjects of ILPs are restricted to the specifier of IP at LF. The correct readings follow from Diesing's assumptions, since no existential reading is possible for any indefinite outside VP at LF. To derive this result, Diesing posits that there are two kinds of Infl: one assigns a theta-role to the specifier of IP, and the other does not. Since verbs assign what used to be their external arguments to their specifier positions, the following two structures are possible:

(36)

(37)

In (36), Infl does not assign a theta-role to the specifier of IP. V assigns its theta-role to its specifier, and the NP projected in that position moves to the specifier of IP to receive Case. (37) contains the Infl that assigns a theta-role to the specifier of IP (this theta-role means "has the property x"). Since V also assigns a theta-role to its specifier, two NPs will be projected; but since the NP in the specifier of VP cannot receive Case, it must be a PRO.[9] Thus, (36) is a raising structure and (37) is a control structure. It will be convenient to follow Diesing in referring to the Infl in (36) as "raising Infl" and to the other as "control Infl." In both sentences, the subject is in the specifier of IP at surface structure. An indefinite in this position at LF would be outside the domain of existential closure. In such a case, the null generic operator binds the variable, and the sentence is given a generic interpretation. Because of these assumptions, a generic reading is predicted to be available for an indefinite subject in either structure.

Diesing makes the additional assumption that an NP can optionally reconstruct to the position at which it received its theta-role on the way to LF, as shown below:[10]

(38)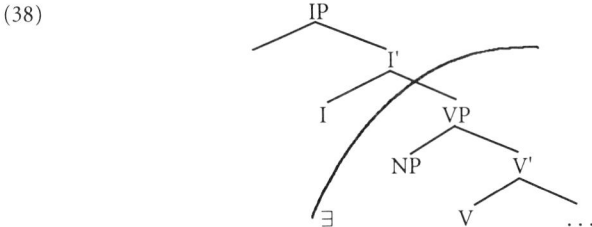

This allows the subject in (36), the raising structure, to appear inside VP at LF, but this is not possible for (37), the control structure, since the theta-role is assigned to the specifier of IP. Because material dominated by VP at LF is closed by an unselective existential quantifier, an existential reading is made available for a subject appearing in the raising structure, but not for one appearing in the control structure. The raising structure also allows a generic reading, which results when the subject is not reconstructed but remains at the specifier of IP at LF.

As we have seen, bare plural subjects can usually be interpreted generically or existentially when they appear with SLPs, but they have only a generic interpretation when they appear with ILPs. Thus, if Diesing can force ILPs to appear only in the control structure in (37) and not in the raising structure in (36), the correct results will be obtained. (Note that it does not matter whether SLPs appear in the control structure, as long as they can appear in the raising structure: a SLP in the control structure will simply duplicate the generic reading generated by the raising structure.) Diesing is inexplicit about what prevents ILPs from appearing with the raising Infl. She simply states that SLPs "have" a raising Infl (1992:24) and that ILPs "have" a control Infl (1992:25). Diesing does not state whether this association between Infl and the predicate is supposed to follow from category selection, or from semantic selection—the two well-established ways for heads to impose restrictions on their complements—or from some other grammatical mechanism that has yet to be defined. If the dependency is due to category selection, Diesing would have to posit that ILPs and SLPs are distinguished by some syntactic category feature. If the distinction were to be made by semantic selection, the restriction imposed on VP by Infl would have to follow from the assignment of a particular theta-role to VP, rather than simply the presence or absence of a theta-role assigned by Infl to the specifier of IP. This would mean that the ILP/SLP distinction would need to be something that could be semantically selected by a head. Diesing discusses none of these possibilities for making the association between Infl and VP explicit.[11]

If the copula is assumed to be a verb, the dependency between Infl and VP must also be reflected in the dependency between the copular verb and its predicate complement. To account for adjectival predicates in copular sentences (formal accounts of nominal and prepositional predicates are not discussed, but there is no reason why they should be treated differently), Diesing follows Stump (1985) in assuming that

> there are (at least) two verbs *be*. The first is a predicative *be* that selects an individual-level adjective and forms an individual-level predicate (Stump's be_2, p. 75). The second *be* selects a stage-level adjective to form a stage-level predicate (Stump's be_4, p. 79). The individual-level *be* takes the individual-level Infl, and the stage-level *be* takes the stage-level Infl. (1992:27)

Diesing notes that these copulas may correspond to *ser* and *estar* in Spanish.

Stump's implementation assumes Carlson's (1977) sorted intensional logic, which distinguishes individuals from stages of individuals. An ILP is then a predicate that combines with an individual, and an SLP is a predicate that combines with a stage. Stump's be_2 combines with any individual-level predicate (not just an adjective) to yield something of individual-level, intransitive VP type, and his be_4 combines with a SLP to yield an object of stage-level, intransitive verb type.

I am not sure that Stump's copulas will suffice for Diesing's larger goal of providing support for her Mapping Hypothesis. For Diesing to adopt Stump's copulas, she would need to adopt Carlson's ontology as well. But it seems that her proposal comes close to allowing us to do away with at least the distinction between objects and stages by allowing the subject effects to follow from assumptions about the Mapping Hypothesis. In the quote from Diesing above, *be* is said to "select" an individual- or stage-level complement, and to "take" an Infl with the appropriate theta grid.

As we saw earlier, Kratzer's (1988) proposal predicts the existence of "unaccusative" ILPs, which, like ILPs, cannot comfortably be modified by locatives, but which are like SLPs in allowing weak indefinite subjects and in appearing grammatically as the coda of the existential construction. These predicates clearly are a challenge for Diesing's attempt to account for the ILP/SLP distinction in terms of the Infl that c-commands the predicate: if these predicates really are individual-level, as Kratzer and Diesing assume, then they should appear with the control Infl, and it should be impossible for the subject to reconstruct inside VP and receive an existential reading.

Diesing assumes with Kratzer (1988) that SLPs have event arguments that ILPs lack. For Kratzer, this was the only difference; Diesing also takes this to be an essential difference, and she adds the distinction between Infls to allow all subjects to be

VP-internal. Diesing suggests that the "apparent mismatch [shown by 'unaccusative' ILPs] is resolved if the properties that distinguish stage- and individual-level predicates (the event argument and θ-role assignment to [Spec, IP] in [Deising's] account) are allowed to vary independently" (1992:47). Diesing does not pursue this provocative line. If there really are two determining characteristics of the ILP/SLP distinction, and if those two characteristics are permitted to vary independently, we ought to find that there is a four-way distinction rather than a binary distinction. Diesing continues, however, to write of the distinction as a binary one.

From Diesing's analysis of unaccusative ILPs it becomes clear that she assumes that the fundamental distinction between ILPs and SLPs is not, after all, determined by the kind of Infl associated with each sort of predicate. Rather, Diesing assumes with Kratzer that SLPs have an argument that ILPs do not have (Diesing calls it an "event" argument, while Kratzer remains agnostic on this point). Unlike Kratzer, Diesing assumes that this argument is not realized as a theta-role. In the end, Diesing must assume that some ILPs can appear with raising Infl. This seems to violate the requirement that "individual-level predicates . . . have an Infl that assigns a θ-role to [Spec, IP]" (1992:25–126). If an ILP does appear with control Infl, its subject is prevented from reconstructing to the specifier of VP and hence cannot be caught up in existential closure. SLPs are said to have raising Infl (although no ungrammaticality would result from allowing them to appear with control Infl). This allows their subjects to appear at LF in the specifier of IP—where they must be interpreted in the restriction of some quantifier—or in the specifier of VP, where they will be caught up by existential closure.

For concreteness in extending Diesing's analysis, it is desirable to assume that the dependency between Infl and VP is either syntactic or semantic selection. Everyone who has worked on the ILP/SLP distinction has assumed that there is some semantic distinction between the two classes. The distinction remains elusive, but Carlson's and Kratzer's idea about a spatiotemporal distinction seems to be on the right track. Suppose Infl and the copula can assign two different theta-roles to their predicate complements. One theta-role (assigned by the raising Infl) somehow requires the predicate to have a spatiotemporal argument, and the other (assigned by the control Infl) requires the predicate not to have one. This approach, clunky as it may be, will suffice for the ordinary cases, but it is derailed by the assumption that unaccusative ILPs appear with the raising Infl. We would need to assume that the raising Infl can assign either kind of theta-role to its predicational complement, but this would not prevent ordinary ILPs from appearing in that position, resulting in ungrammatical existential readings for their bare plural subjects. The only way to salvage this attempt would be to posit that unaccusative ILPs and regular ILPs are somehow distinct semantically. If we could do this, we could have one theta-role for SLPs, one for regular ILPs, and one for unaccusative ILPs. The obvious problem with this tack is that there seems to be no semantic difference between unaccusative and regular ILPs; a semantic similarity between them was one of the primary reasons for claiming that the unaccusative cases were ILPs in the first place. Hence, the only theta-theoretic analysis that is compatible with most of Diesing's assumptions undermines the assumption that unaccusative ILPs are in fact ILPs.

The same problem arises with syntactic selection. Let us suppose, as Carlson and Stump do, that ILPs and SLPs belong to distinct syntactic categories. They can be distinguished by positing the existence of [ilp] and [slp] as (independently unmotivated) syntactic features. Let SLPs belong to the set of categories schematized by XP[slp] (where X ∈ {A,N,P,V}), and let ILPs belong to the set schematized by XP[ilp]. Now we can assume that raising Infl syntactically selects complements of category XP[slp], and that control Infl selects complements of category X[ilp]. But here we are again confronted by unaccusative ILPs, which are assumed to be the complements of raising Infl. We have just stipulated that raising Infl requires its complements to bear the feature [slp]. If we allow raising Infl to appear with complements bearing either feature, we will again generate ungrammatical readings for sentences containing ILPs that are not unaccusative. To create a system that is empirically adequate, we need to posit a third category feature to distinguish unaccusative ILPs as a category. Call it [u-ilp]. Now, raising Infl can select complements bearing the category features [slp] or [u-ilp]; control Infl remains as it was, selecting complements with the [ilp] feature. To take this approach is to concede that unaccusative ILPs are exceptional, and, indeed, they seem to be just that. Although this way of formalizing Diesing's suggestions seems uninsightful, it appears to be the only empirically adequate analysis, given the assumptions that Diesing wishes to maintain.

Given this way of formalizing Diesing's suggestions, we can attempt to extend the analysis to some additional cases.

2.2.2 Generics in Embedded Clauses

The basic assumptions of Diesing's analysis predict that generic readings should not be possible for bare plurals in object position. Diesing notes, however, that there are some problems with this prediction. Carlson (1977) pointed out that complements to *like, hate, fear,* and *loathe* tend to have generic interpretations. Diesing gives the following examples (her ex. 23):

(39)   a. Cellists hate boring bass lines.
       b. Contrabassoonists love chocolate chip cookies.

Diesing appeals to Kratzer's (1988) proposal that the objects in these sentences scramble outside VP on the way to LF, allowing them to be caught up in the restriction where they will be bound by the generic quantifier. Aside from this class of exceptions, bare plurals are expected to have generic interpretations only when they appear outside the root VP node.

Diesing does not systematically investigate what happens with bare plural subjects of non-root clauses, although in a footnote (1992:140, fn. 17), there is a brief discussion of small clause complements of *consider* and infinitival complements of *believe*. Diesing notes that postverbal bare plurals have no existential reading in the following sentences, contrary to what her theory predicts (1992:140):

(40)   a. I consider firemen available. (generic only)
       b. I consider firemen intelligent. (generic only)

Diesing also notes that the following allow generic readings:

(41) a. I believe firemen to be available. (both generic and existential)
b. I believe violists to be intelligent. (generic only)

Diesing does not claim to have an account for these sentences, but she suggests that an "embedded tripartite logical representation" might be the answer (Diesing 1992:140). Indeed, when a broader range of clausal complements is considered, it seems that embedded structures are routinely necessary.[12] The examples below contain finite complement clauses, and generic readings are clearly available for the bare plural subjects:

(42) a. Lisa believes that surgeons are intelligent.
b. Sandy used to think that dogs were scary.
c. Leslie said that ball-peen hammers have numerous uses.

Clearly, no adequate theory can maintain that indefinites receive a generic interpretation only if they appear outside the VP node of the root clause.

So let us follow Diesing's suggestion and make her Mapping Hypothesis recursive, so that every VP can be mapped to a nuclear scope and so that all material between CP and VP for every clause can be mapped into a restriction. A generic operator will be available to bind any restriction that lacks an overt quantifier. Let us consider the sentence in (43a), which has two embedded clauses and has the surface structure shown in (43b):

(43) a. Sandy thought that surgeons believed that dogs were scary.
b.

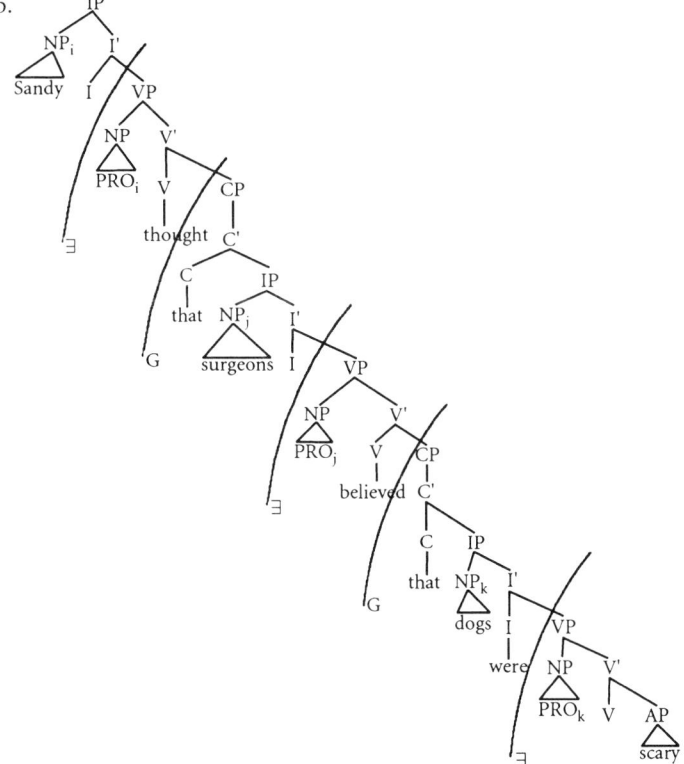

A generic reading is required for each of the bare plurals in this sentence. As long as the bare plurals remain in the specifier of some IP, they will be in a restriction rather than a nuclear scope, and the modified Mapping Hypothesis will predict the correct reading. Note that both embedded Infls must be of the control variety to prevent the bare plurals from (optionally) moving inside VP on the way to LF.

The examples in (42), which contain ILPs in the embedded clauses, contrast with those below, which have SLPs:

(44) a. Lisa believes that surgeons are in the next room.
b. Sandy used to think that dogs were chasing him.
c. Leslie said that ball-peen hammers were in the bottom drawer.

The embedded bare plurals have existential readings. Since the embedded predicates are stage-level, we expect these readings, given our modification of the Mapping Hypothesis. The following extraposition cases show the same effects:

(45) a. It seems that there are bears in the next room.
b. It seems that bears are in the next room. (existential)

(46) a. *It seems that there are bears intelligent.
b. It seems that bears are intelligent. (generic only)

Thus, the effects of the ILP/SLP distinction on the interpretation of bare plurals are not restricted to root clauses. By allowing the null generic operator to bind any variable that appears in any subject position, we will allow generic interpretations for the cases seen here.

Once Diesing's proposal is modified in this fashion, all the root clause effects of the ILP/SLP distinction are predicted to hold in embedded clauses.

3. Previous Accounts of *When* Adjuncts and Adverbs of Frequency

3.1 Previous Accounts of Absolutes: Stump's Analysis

In the previous chapter, we saw that SLPs can restrict modals and generic adverbial quantifiers, but that ILPs in general are unable to. Stump (1985) develops a formal account of the behavior of free and absolute adjuncts, borrowing Carlson's (1977) sorted ontology in which entities are kind-, object-, individual-, or stage-denoting. However, Stump rejects Carlson's idea that generic operators apply to predicates (1985:195 ff.), treating them instead as adverbs of quantification which denote relations between two sets of time intervals. In a manner similar to Carlson's, Stump provides syntactic categories for predication over individuals and stages (e.g., IV^s, IV^i, for verb phrases; ADJ^s, ADJ^i, for adjective phrases, etc.). Stump also creates two supercategories, $PRED^s$ and $PRED^i$, to include all SLPs and ILPs, respectively.

Noun phrases are assumed to denote individual-level property-sets. Any SLP, then, must be converted into an individual-level VP before it can combine with a subject. Carlson's R relation is needed to relate stages to individuals.

Stump provides four versions of the copula: one seeks a SLP complement and yields a SLP; one goes from SLP to ILP; one goes from ILP to SLP; and one goes from

Traditional Explanations   57

ILP to ILP. (For the translation of *John is being obnoxious*, be_3 is used to combine with the ILP *obnoxious* to yield a SLP. Since all subjects are individual-level property-sets, the VP must be turned back into an ILP before it can combine with the subject.)

Stump points out that not all ILPs can be converted into SLPs by combining with the copula be_1. (There is no need to prevent any SLPs from being converted into ILPs by a copula because these SLPs display ILP effects.) Thus, certain ILPs (e.g., *a blonde*) are "inherently individual-level" (1985:87) and appear unable to have weak interpretations. Stump points out that when *as* combines with a NP, a SLP results (Stump's ex. 132):

(47)   Twenty years ago, we saw John as a young man.

Hence, *as* "has an intimate semantic connection" (1985:89) to be_1. Stump also notes that *as* and *with* can combine with an ILP to create a weak adjunct (one capable of restricting a modal) (Stump's exx. 134 and 138):

(48)   a. As a blonde, Mary might look something like Jane.
        b. With green eyes, Mary might look something like Jane.

Stump shows that SLP free adjuncts can serve as the restriction of a modal, but that ILP free adjuncts cannot (without *as* or *with*). Stump proposes an analysis of these sentences assuming Kratzer's (1977, 1979) theory of conditional modality. The analysis allows SLPs to serve as the restriction of a modal, but prevents ILPs from doing so. Thus, (49a) is interpreted as (49b):[13]

(49)   a. Standing on a chair, John can touch the ceiling.
        b. can' (D(cb)(^John-stands-on-the-chair')) (^John-touches-the-ceiling')

Stump notes that "for any modal α, $\alpha'(D(cb)(p)(q))$ fails to entail either $^\vee p$ or $^\vee q$." Thus, there is no entailment that the condition expressed by the adjunct holds of the subject. This is a direct consequence of the semantics assumed for modals. Since ILP adjuncts denote conditions that are entailed, it is clear that they cannot appear within the scope of the modal. Stump says that the roles of ILP free adjuncts are inferred, and generally have an interpretation similar to a *because* adjunct (cf. *Because John has unusually long arms, he can reach the ceiling*).[14] Stump proposes that SLP free adjuncts are of category t', the category Kratzer (1977, 1979) proposes for antecedents of conditionals. For free adjuncts, he offers Montague-style rules that convert a predicate into a "temporal abstract." Rules S1 and T1 turn a SLP into an adjunct that is marked with the feature [+Weak] (1985:163–164):

(50)   S1. If $\alpha \in P_{PRED}s$, then $F_{1,n}(\alpha) \in P_{TAB'}$[–Tense, +Adjunct, +Weak, –Perfect], where $F_{1,n}(\alpha)$ is α.
        T1. If $\alpha \in P_{PRED}s$ and α translates as α', then $F_{1,n}(\alpha)$ translates as $\lambda t[AT(t, \exists x^s[R(x^s, x^i_n) \& \alpha'(x^s)])]$.

Rules S2 and T2 turn an ILP into an adjunct bearing the feature [–Weak] (1985:164):

(51)   S2. If $\alpha \in P_{PRED^i}$, $\notin P_{ADJ^i}$, then $F_{2,n}(\alpha) \in P_{TAB'}$ [–Tense, +Adjunct, –Weak, –Perfect], where $F_{2,n}(\alpha)$ is α.
        T2. If $\alpha \in P_{PRED^i}$ and α translates as a', then $F_{2,n}(\alpha)$ translates as $\lambda t[AT(t, \alpha'(x^o_n))]$, $\lambda t[AT(t, \alpha'(x^k_n))]$, or $\lambda t[AT(t, \alpha'(x^i_n))]$, according as α' is of sorted type <o,t'>, <k,t'>, or <[o,k],t'>, respectively.

S10 and T10 allow a [+Weak] temporal abstract to become constituents of category t', the only category that can appear as the antecedent of a conditional (and thus serve as the restriction of a modal on Kratzer's analysis) (1985:165):

(52) S10. If $\alpha \in P_{TAB}$, [+Adjunct, +Weak, −Perfect], then $F_{10}(\alpha) \in P_{t'}$, where $F_{10}(\alpha)$ is α.
T10. If $\alpha \in P_{TAB}$ and α translates as α', then $F_{10}(\alpha)$ translates as $\exists t[\alpha'(t)]$.

Strong adjuncts are taken to belong to the syntactic category MTA ("main tense adverbs"). S11 and T11 convert TAs that are either [+Weak] or [−Weak] into MTAs (1985:167, 170):[15]

(53) S11. If $\alpha \in P_{TAB}$, [+Adjunct, −Perfect], then $F_{11,m,n}(\alpha) \in P_{MTA}$, where $F_{11,m,n}(\alpha)$ is α.
T11. If $\alpha \in P_{TAB}$ and α translates as α', then $F_{11,m,n}(\alpha)$ translates as
$\lambda P^t \lambda t[K(L_m)(^\wedge \exists t_1[M_n(t,t_1) \& \alpha'(t_1)])(^\wedge P^t\{t\}])]$.

This allows ILPs or SLPs to have strong interpretations. There is no formal problem with this, but it points out that the [+Weak] feature really does not indicate that the adjunct will end up having a weak interpretation; it means that the adjunct contains a SLP. Hence, Stump's proposal requires the existence of a syntactic feature to indicate that a constituent contains a SLP or an ILP. (In the case of free adjuncts, this feature is not required to percolate very far, but Stump will make use of it to distinguish among augmented absolutes—those that consist of *with* followed by a small clause. In such cases, the feature will need to be triggered by the predicate (as above), and it will appear on the small clause node and percolate up to the PP node that dominates the adjunct.)

The rules combining frequency adverbs with TABs require the presence of the feature [+Weak] on the adjunct. Rules S9 and T9 accomplish this (1985:185, 186):

(54) S9. If $\alpha \in P_{TAB}$, [+Adjunct, +Weak, −Perfect], then $F_{9,n}(\alpha) \in P_{TA'}$ [+Adjunct], where $F_{9,n}(\alpha)$ is α.
T9. If $\alpha \in P_{TAB}$ and α translates as α', then $F_{9,n}(\alpha)$ translates as $\lambda t \exists t_1[M_n(t,t_1) \& \alpha'(t_1)]$.

There are two chief shortcomings to Stump's analysis. The first is that it offers no explanation of why absolutes should need to be augmented in order for the ILP/SLP effects to be realized. Stump introduces *with* syncategorematically in the rule that composes the subject with the predicate (1985:278):

(55) S5. If $\alpha \in P_T$ and $\beta \in P_{PREDS}$, then $F_{5a}(\alpha,\beta)$, $F_{5b}(\alpha,\beta) \in P_{TAB}$, [−Tense, +Adjunct, −Perfect], $F_{5a}(\alpha,\beta) \in$ [−Weak], and $F_{5b}(\alpha,\beta) \in$ [+Weak], where $F_{5a}(\alpha,\beta)$ is CON (α,β) and $F_{5b}(\alpha,\beta)$ is CON (with, CON(OBJ(α),β)).
T5. If $\alpha \in P_T$, $\beta \in P_{PREDS}$, and α, β translate as α', β', then $F_{5a}(\alpha,\beta)$, $F_{5b}(\alpha,\beta)$ translate as $\lambda t[AT(t, \alpha'(^\wedge \lambda x^i \exists x^s[R(x^s,x^i) \& \beta'(x^s)])])]$.

The second shortcoming is that Stump's analysis ignores the internal constituent structure of the adjunct.

3.2 Kratzer (1988)

Kratzer (1988) proposes that adjuncts can serve as operator restrictions only when occurrences of a single variable appear in the adjunct and in the main clause. If this condition is not met, the quantification will be vacuous, and ungrammaticality will result. This led Kratzer to conclude that SLPs contain a variable that ILPs lack. The presence of the variable makes it possible for SLPs to appear in quantifier adjunct structures even when no other variables (e.g., due to indefinite nominals) are present. ILPs do not have this capacity, and this accounts for the contrast shown below (Kratzer's exx. 15a and 15d):

(56) a. *When Mary knows French, she knows it well.
      b. When Mary speaks French, she speaks it well.

Kratzer assumes (following Lewis 1975, Kamp 1981, and Heim 1982) that indefinites and the pronouns they bind are interpreted as variables, but that definites are not, and that the pronouns bound by definites are not. Kratzer gives the following examples and interpretations (Kratzer's exx. 15c, 15'c, 15d, and 15'd):

(57) a. When Mary knows a foreign language, she knows it well.
      b. Always$_x$ [foreign language(x) & knows (Mary, x)] [knows-well (Mary, x)]

(58) a. *When Mary speaks French, she knows it well.
      b. *Always$_l$ [speaks (Mary, French, l)] [knows-well (Mary, French)]

(58) is ruled out because there is no variable in the consequent. (57) is predicted to be grammatical because the pronoun and its indefinite antecedent are interpreted as variables. In Kratzer's theory, the *when*-adjunct diagnostic is sensitive only to the presence of a bindable variable. Absolute adjuncts have the same requirement.

3.3 De Hoop and de Swart (1989)

De Hoop and de Swart (1989) point out that data related to those discussed by Kratzer cannot be accounted for by appealing to the presence or absence of variables. They argue that the ungrammaticality of examples like (59) stems from the fact that a particular individual can be killed only once, and so it is not an indication that the antecedent does not contain a variable:

(59) *When a Moroccan kills Fido, she kills him quickly.

De Swart writes:

> There are two ways out of this dilemma. Either we ignore the similarity just noted, that is, we maintain Kratzer's account of the stage-level/individual-level contrast and we formulate an additional rule for 'once-only' predicates or we try to reformulate the stage-level/individual-level contrast as an instance of a more general phenomenon. This will make it possible to develop a unified analysis of the 'once-only' predicates and the stage-level/individual-level contrast. I will pursue the latter approach here. (1991:59)

De Hoop and de Swart's approach is to require the cardinality of the domain of quantification to be greater than one. The ungrammaticality of (59) follows from the fact that it has the structure of a generalization, but there is only one instance of the eventuality type being generalized over.

De Hoop and de Swart assume that all predicates have a Davidsonian argument, and that the ILP/SLP effects that involve the ability to restrict a quantifier follow from whether there is a uniqueness presupposition associated with the eventuality denoted. Describing their proposal, de Swart writes, "What individual-level and 'once-only' predicates have in common is that their application to a particular individual is felicitous only once. The situation the proposition describes has a unique location in the life of an individual (cf. Verkuyl 1972:117,118 for similar observations)" (1991:59). The idea is that ILPs hold for a single, very long period of time, and in this sense, like once-only SLPs, they hold only once. Their uniqueness presupposition is formulated as follows:

(60) *Uniqueness presupposition on the Davidsonian argument*
The set of spatiotemporal locations that is associated with an individual-level or a 'once-only' predicate is a singleton set for all models and each assignment of individuals to the arguments of the predicate. (1991:59)

This presupposition interacts with the following condition on "Q-Adverbs" (adverbs of quantification):

(61) *Plurality condition on quantification* (revised version)
A Q-adverb does not quantify over a set of situations if it is known that this set has cardinality less than two.
A set of situations is known to be a singleton set if:
(1) the predicate contained in the sentence satisfies the uniqueness presupposition on the Davidsonian argument, and
(2) there is no (in)definite NP in the sentence which allows indirect binding by means of quantification over assignments. (de Swart 1991:118)

De Swart notes that a stronger version of the plurality condition would allow Q-adverbs to quantify only over sets with cardinality greater than two. De Swart does not opt for this since

> there does not seem to be a reason to block quantification when, with respect to a particular model and a certain assignment function, the set of locations which corresponds to a normal stage-level predicate happens to be empty or contains just one element. It is the fact that a unique location is associated with individual-level and once-only predicates with respect to all models and each assignment function that makes quantification unfelicitous in the absence of (in)definite NPs. (1991:60)

Thus, de Swart assumes the association of a unique location to individual-level and once-only predicates as a well-formedness condition on models. Despite the desire expressed to do away with the ILP/SLP distinction (at least where quantifier restrictions are concerned), it winds up being crucial in her uniqueness presupposition statement in (60) because of the concern about models expressed in the paragraph above.

De Hoop and de Swart discuss the interaction of the ILP/SLP distinction with adverbs of quantification, focusing primarily on *when* adjuncts. The same contrast can be seen in the examples below:

(62) a. Sam is often asleep.
  b. Sarah seldom sits on the porch.
  c. Bob frequently makes guitars.

(63) a. ?Sue is sometimes tall.
  b. ?Karen is often German.
  c. ?Max is sometimes intelligent.

The restriction for these quantifiers is not specified in these sentences and comes from context. The material in the clause, exclusive of the quantifier itself, supplies the nuclear scope.

Interestingly, the once-only predicates pattern with ILPs in these cases as well as in the *when* and absolute adjunct cases. De Hoop and de Swart's cardinality condition constrains possible restrictions. The data above show the same empirical effects, but they involve supplying the nuclear scope rather than the restriction. Clearly, more needs to be said. Both the restriction and the nuclear scope must have the potential to denote multiplicities. It was clear why there should be a plurality condition on restrictions: a generalization over a single case is no generalization. The nuclear scope apparently must be able to contribute something for each case in the restriction. Fernald (2000) discusses this issue and related ones in more detail.

In chapter 5 we will again take up the issues raised by de Hoop and de Swart in response to Kratzer. We will conclude that both the plurality condition and the prohibition against vacuous quantification are necessary.

4. Chierchia (1995)

The proposal of Chierchia (1995b) takes a different view of the ILP/SLP contrast. It will not figure prominently in our discussion, but it deserves to be mentioned.

Chierchia (1995b) proposes that ILPs are a sort of predicate that can appear only within the scope of a generic quantifier. In this account, every predicate has a Davidsonian argument. His analysis is exactly the standard analysis given for negative polarity items (see Ladusaw 1979) applied to ILPs. The story is that ILPs have an abstract habitual morpheme *Hab* in the lexicon. This morpheme carries the feature [+Q], which must be locally licensed by the generic operator *Gen*. Many of the standard facts about the distribution and interpretation of ILPs follow from this assumption quite elegantly.

One consequence of this analysis is that ordinary ILPs are interpreted as involving generic quantification over situations in which the subject is present. Thus, *John is intelligent* is interpreted as a claim that in general a situation involving John will be a situation in which John is intelligent. The formal representation is shown below:

(64) a. John is intelligent.
   b. Gen s [$in'(j,s)$][$intelligent'(j,s)$]

The variable s is Davidsonian. (64a) is thus taken to express a generalization over situations in which John appears. Chierchia's assumptions make fairly successful predictions about locative modification, perceptual reports, existential sentences, and bare plurals. However, the interpretation of (64a) strikes me as counterintuitive: (64a) seems to be more the attribution of a property to an individual than a generalization about situations in which that individual appears.

An issue that is not addressed by Chierchia (1995) is the question of why *Gen* is the only adverb of quantification that is semantically compatible with ILPs:

(65) a. That is a tree.
   b. ??That is often a tree.
   c. ??That is always a tree.

With SLPs, there is no such limitation:

(66) a. Lyle smokes.
b. Lyle often smokes.
c. Lyle always smokes.

Chierchia's account of *when* adjuncts relies on the Plurality Condition of de Hoop and de Swart (1989): with adverbs of quantification "it seems plausible to maintain that not only do variables have to be there but also that they must in principle be satisfiable by more than one entity" (Chierchia 1995b:216). ILPs, he says, cannot meet this requirement because they are tendentially stable and thus not naturally iterable. I am inclined to agree with this, but I do not understand why ILPs are compatible with *Gen*, which is assumed to be a null adverb of quantification. It may be possible to lay out semantic differences between *Gen* and the other adverbs of quantification that would account for this discrepancy. However, Chierchia (1995b) crucially assumes that all adverbs of quantification, including *Gen*, quantify over situations, thus eliminating an attempt to claim that *Gen* quantifies over something else.

In the development of the analysis, Chierchia rejects the possibility that ILPs contain *Gen* in the lexicon. If that analysis could have been maintained, (65b) and (65c) could perhaps be ruled out on the grounds of vacuous quantification. However, Chierchia had good grounds for rejecting that analysis. It predicts that *Sheep are black or white* means only 'Sheep are black or sheep are white'. And Chierchia concluded that it could not produce acceptable readings for reflexives.

The intuitive motivation for treating ILPs as inherent generics is that ILPs often denote properties that hold of an individual for a significant period of time and thus could perhaps be said to be generally true of that individual. In Kratzer's typology, SLPs have an implicit spatiotemporal argument and ILPs do not. I think that this captures the intuitive distinction between ILPs and SLPs at least as well: ILPs denote properties by themselves, but SLPs need to have their spatiotemporal argument provided before they denote properties, thus emphasizing their dependency on time.

4

The Distinction and Its Slipperiness

1. Views of the Basis of the Distinction

Now that we have considered the traditional accounts of the ILP/SLP distinction, I would like to consider two leading views of what the distinction is really all about. I have complaints to make against both of them.

Researchers agree, for the most part, that SLPs are associated with time and/or space in a way that ILPs are not. So when one encounters a sentence that suggests that the subject only intermittently has a property denoted by an ILP, it is reasonable to imagine that the predicate has become stage-level, or that the speaker is using it, somehow, as a SLP, or is pretending that it is a SLP. We have seen examples of this before:

(1) a. John is a goalie this morning.
 b. When Bo is an American, he is a capitalist.
 c. Robin is a villain in this evening's production.

I would like to point out that simply because a property ceases to hold of an individual, that does not mean that the property had anything to do with space or time. Entities regularly acquire and shed properties as they proceed through their existence. I think the reason that many researchers have been inclined to believe that ILPs are temporally stable is that for some ILPs, it is very unlikely that they will ever be shed by an individual. For example, if a chair is wooden, it will remain so, except for materials used in repairs, until it falls apart. I agree with most researchers that many ILPs denote properties that tend to hold of their arguments for a considerable length of time; but the mere fact that a sentence suggests that a property holds for a short duration should not mean that the predicate in the sentence is stage-level. Indeed, an analysis of the contrast would have to go through contortions to preclude models in which an ILP sometimes holds of a particular individual and sometimes does not.

Next I would like to argue against another popular theme: that the ILP/SLP contrast is mainly pragmatic. Kratzer (1988) notes that *having brown hair* is an ILP, but she asserts, "If I dyed my hair every other day, my property of having brown hair would be stage-level. Usually we think of having brown hair as an individual-level property, though, since we don't think of persons dyeing their hair capriciously" (1988/1995:126). Chierchia (1996) expresses the same view, using the following sentence as an example:

(2) John was intelligent on Tuesday, but a vegetable on Wednesday.

First, Chierchia notes that the sentence has the reading that we take *was intelligent* to mean 'behave intelligently'. This is a case of what I will call "evidential coercion" in section 2.1 of this chapter. Chierchia continues to note, however, that there is another reading true in case "John has a double personality which involves switching his mental capacities on and off in an abnormal manner" (1995b:178). Then Chierchia asserts, "If we all were like him, *intelligent* would be s[tage]-level."

Although my view is outvoted, I am not convinced by these assertions. I am not sure that we can have reliable intuitions about what sentences would be grammatical if the world differed from its current condition in certain specific ways. Let us assume a world in which people dye their hair capriciously and in which everyone has a multiple personality disorder such that certain personalities are intelligent and others are not. I agree that it would then be perfectly natural to use temporal modifiers with predicates about intelligence and hair color. But I do not think we can have trustworthy intuitions about perceptual reports and the existential construction, or even about readings for bare plural subjects. Thus, my view is that the ILP/SLP distinction is a more idiosyncratic one than what Kratzer and Chierchia seem to believe (cf. *I saw John tower over his friends* vs. **I saw John taller than his friends*). Surely the language could change over time, but I do not think it necessarily will in the way suggested here. Greg Carlson pointed out to me the following contrast:

(3) a. Whenever I land in New York lights are on.
     b. ??Whenever I land in New York buildings are tall.

(3a) sounds perfectly fine, even though lights are always on in New York. Of course, it is not necessary for lights always to be on in New York, but neither is it necessary for buildings to be tall. This leads me to believe that the ILP/SLP distinction is not simply a matter of pragmatics: it is a true grammatical distinction.

Kratzer writes, "If a distinction between stage-level and individual-level predicates is operative in natural language, it cannot be a distinction that is made in the lexicon of a language once and for all" (1988:126). I disagree, except that I will leave open for discussion in the following chapters the possibility that the sort of predicate one has can be composed, and so not everything is determined in the lexicon. And, of course, I would not want the phrase "once and for all" to rule out the possibility of diachronic change.

Rather than these two views, I prefer the idea behind Kratzer's proposal that SLPs occur or hold crucially in space and time but that ILPs do not—or, in terms compatible with work on the thetic/categorical distinction (e.g., Kuroda 1972, Sasse 1987, Ladusaw 1994, McNally 1998), the idea that ILPs are properties of individuals and SLPs are descriptions of the world, or perhaps a spatiotemporal slice of it. How else can we explain the difference in meaning between *tower over* and *taller than*?

2. Coercion

The diagnostics for the ILP/SLP distinction that we have seen are notoriously slippery—some more so than others. In some cases, simply putting an ILP in a necessarily SLP environment forces the predicate to take on certain SLP characteristics. The sentence may be grammatical with the reading typically associated with sentences containing a SLP, but the ILP might seem to be used in a slightly unusual way. In such cases, the diagnostic depends on a very subtle and subjective judgment. Because of this slipperiness, it is not unusual to find, in the literature on the ILP/SLP distinction, comments to the effect that a particular individual-level predicate is "being used" as a SLP. Such a claim should have consequences and make predictions about how the interpretation of the predicate is affected, but past work has rarely pursued these consequences. This chapter gives theoretical teeth to such claims by examining the systematic changes in interpretation that accompany such usage.

If the ILP/SLP distinction really is a grammatical classification, why is there any slippage at all between levels? That the diagnostics seem slippery no doubt has to do with the cleverness of language users in concocting an interpretation for anything thrown at them that looks like a sentence. I take it to be a common assumption of semantics and pragmatics that hearers are very resourceful in their efforts to interpret whatever is said to them when they assume that someone is trying to communicate with them. So, when there is a violation of one of the rules of semantics, hearers try to make what sense they can of the utterance they perceive. When possible, a minor adjustment will be made in the interpretation of the offending portion of the utterance to bring it in line with the requirements of the grammar. This kind of coercion allows some sense to be made of what was said. When the violation is serious, the hearer is also led to wonder why the speaker chose to violate the rule, and this may lead to a conclusion that the speaker intends to be humorous or poetic. The less obvious the violation, or the more frequently a particular sort of violation occurs, the more likely it is that an adjustment in interpretation will be made without the hearer's noticing.

Previous discussions of coercion have centered on the interaction of aspect, Aktionsart, and tense. Moens and Steedman (1988) and de Swart (1998) examine in detail cases of coercion involving Aktionsart; Smith (1995) also touches on it. In a discussion directly relevant to the ILP/SLP distinction, Krifka et al. (1995) appeal briefly to coercion. In arguing that *John (usually) has pink hair* is not a counterexample to the claim that there are no lexical characterizing sentences with an object-referring, specific subject, they write, "One could argue that in [this example] the basically stative predicate *have pink hair* is 'coerced' into an episodic meaning" (1995:18).

This capacity of hearers to make sense of marginal data has the adverse effect of making the diagnostics needed for our investigation less clearcut than we would like them to be. In this section, we will investigate the ways in which predicates of one level are able to exhibit the characteristics of predicates from a different level, when they appear in a particular kind of environment. It will turn out that their interpretations are coerced in ways that, in some cases, are quite predictable, and in any case that conform to certain well-differentiated patterns of interpretation. These patterns can, in turn, be helpful in classifying predicates because they allow us to predict the changes in meaning made possible by coercion. We will also see that certain ILPs are more resistant to coercion than others, and we will try to explain why that is.

2.1 Evidential Coercion

Many of the standard diagnostics for the ILP/SLP distinction yield quite clear results, but others are less clear. The sentences below contain ILPs, as indicated by the ungrammaticality of the existential construction in (4), and by the lack of an existential interpretation in (5):

(4) a. *There is a man clever.
 b. *There is a man pedantic.
 c. *There is a man a bore.
 d. *There is a man intelligent.
 e. *There is a man a child.
 f. *There is a man Bohemian.

(5) a. People are clever.
 b. People are pedantic.
 c. People are bores.
 d. People are intelligent.
 e. People are children.
 f. People are Bohemian.

However, these same predicates are surprisingly good with adverbs of quantification:

(6) a. Nancy is rarely clever.
 b. Laura is often pedantic.
 c. Sam is sometimes a bore.
 d. Max is sometimes intelligent.
 e. Carlos is frequently a child.
 f. Karen is often Bohemian.

The conventional wisdom is that one is at least expected to feel a bit of a twinge whenever an ILP is used in an environment that "prefers" SLPs. The problem posed for the diagnostic by data like those in (6) is that the twinge we are supposed to feel is quite subtle, and sometimes we cannot really tell whether we felt one at all. However, by carefully examining the meanings of these sentences, we will find that we no longer need to hang our hopes on detecting the subtle twinge we allegedly feel. A predictable change has occurred in the interpretations of the ILPs in these sentences. These examples all entail that the subject is behaving, in some situation, in a manner consistent with having the property denoted by the ILP. This change in interpretation is due to what I will call "Evidential Coercion," since it involves the subject giving behavioral evidence for having the property named by the ILP.

We begin our discussion assuming Carlson's (1977) framework for concreteness; then we will see how it would work for the assumptions of Kratzer (1988) or Diesing (1992). We would like to understand what it means for a SLP to be used as an ILP. Carlson, as we have seen in chapter 3, assumed that SLPs have stages as their arguments, and ILPs have individuals. To use an ILP as a SLP, a variable must fill the individual-sort argument, and there needs to be an abstraction over a stage-sort entity, and that entity variable must be related by the realization relation R to the individual-sort variable. Further, some quantifier will be needed to bind the individual-sort variable. Below is a first try at an informal statement of the idea, using Carlson's assumptions about the ILP/SLP distinction:

(7) Evidential Coercion (first try): Let α be an ILP with interpretation α'. α can be used as a SLP with the following interpretation:
$\lambda x^s \exists Q, y^i [R(x,y) \& Q(x) = $ 'x behaved in a manner supporting the judgment of α'(y)']

Notice that (7) does not result in an entailment that the subject actually has the ILP property—only the subject's behavior is consistent with having it. This is in fact just what we want. Consider (6e). We would not want to predict that this means that Carlos is actually judged to be a child from time to time—only that he frequently acts like one. The effect of (7) is to entail that evidence supporting the inference has been given, allowing all the while that the judgment might not turn out to be valid. The following version of (7) is more formal:

(8) Evidential Coercion [Carlson-style]: Let α be an ILP with interpretation α'. α can be used as a SLP with the following interpretation:
$\lambda x^s \exists Q [Q(x) \& G_{y^s, z^i}(Q(y) \& R(y,z)) [\alpha'(z)]]$

Here, G is the generic operator. The coerced predicate denotes a set of stages for which there is some stage-level property Q that holds of the stage, and in general, having Q predicated of a stage entails that the individual associated with the stage has α, the ILP, predicated of the corresponding individual. By this formulation, *?Laura is often pedantic* will be coerced into expressing the claim that often there is some stage-level eventuality, in which Laura participates, and one would generally judge the individual who participates in such eventualities to be "pedantic." The success of coercion in this case depends on the hearer's ability to imagine there being stage-level evidence of having the ILP property, which is not difficult in the case of *pedantic*. The idea that stage-level property Q must be a *behavior* is not explicit in (8), but at least the property is required to be one that holds of stages.

Before considering the consequences of (8), we will pause to see how evidential coercion can be formulated in terms of Kratzer's and Diesing's proposals. On these accounts, SLPs have a spatiotemporal argument and ILPs do not. To convert an ILP to a SLP, we have somehow to add a position for a spatiotemporal argument and abstract over it. Below is a formulation that parallels (8):

(9) Evidential Coercion [Kratzer-style]: Let α be an ILP with interpretation α'. α can be used as a SLP with the following interpretation:
$\lambda l_j \lambda x \exists Q [Q(x, l_j) \& G_{y,l}(Q(y,l))[(\alpha'(y)]]$

For Kratzer's account, the thematic grid in the lexical entry for the predicate would need to have a location argument added to it as the external argument. By either formulation, (8) or (9), the output of Evidential Coercion is a stage-level predicate. This story predicts that ILPs should be usable in any stage-level environment provided that coercing can take place. We have already seen in (4) and (5) that the existential construction does not induce coercion, and neither do bare plural subjects. (Without these judgments, we would not have considered the relevant predicates ILPs in the first place.) What about perceptual reports? Compare:

(10) a. I have seen Lyle clever (on several occasions).
      b. We have seen Laura pedantic (on several occasions).
      c. *Robin has seen Sam a bore (on several occasions).
      d. You have seen Max intelligent (on several occasions).
      e. *Leslie has seen Carlos a child (on several occasions).
      f. Robin has seen Karen Bohemian (on several occasions).

With the exception of cases in which the predicate in the perceptual report is nominal, these sentences (helped along by perfect aspect in the matrix and by the frequency modifier) are not so bad. So if we assume that nominal predicates are independently ruled out in this environment by subcategorization, then we conclude that evidentially coerced predicates are stage-level because they are grammatical in the perceptual report. In fact, if we add a form of *be* to turn the nominal predicate into a verbal one, the results are grammatical with an evidential coercion interpretation:

(11) c'. Robin has seen Sam being a bore (on several occasions).
      e'. Leslie has seen Carlos being a child (on several occasions).

Our analysis captures a subtlety of interpretation that is worth dwelling on for a moment. Ordinary perceptual reports are said to be veridical: that is, they entail that the perceived eventuality held or happened, unless the perceiver was hallucinating. However, veridicality does not hold for the ILPs in (10) and (11), but only for the SLPs derived by coercion. For example, as we saw with (6e), (11e') does not entail that Carlos was a child when Leslie saw him—only that he behaved like one. Our account makes exactly the correct distinction.

Of course, aspectual information is being added in (11), in addition to simply changing the predicate into a VP. In fact, a coerced reading is possible in simple sentences with *be* in the progressive:

(12) a. Nancy is being clever.
      b. Laura is being pedantic.
      c. Sam is being a bore.
      d. Max is being intelligent.
      e. Carlos is being a child.
      f. Karen is being Bohemian.

This is also noted by Stump (1985:76–79), building on Partee (1977) (and see Smith 1991:43). Stump refers to this form of *be* as be_3 and says that it "has a meaning something like that of **act** (**like**) (1985:77)." It seems odd that a particular lexical item like be_3 should trigger coercion: coercion is what happens when the rules of the grammar are violated in a fairly minor way, so how could a lexical item require a coerced reading rather than a basic one? On the other hand, the progressive needs to combine with an eventuality description that is non-stative. If an ILP stative is inserted into the progressive, the aspectual coercion that is triggered would result in a SLP.

We must ask what the limits are on coercion. I take it that evidential coercion is a pragmatic effect, since it is triggered by a mismatch in the grammar. Being pragmatic, coercion is constrained by the imagination of the hearer. It would be nice if we could nail down hard and fast rules, but we are discussing phenomena that are outside the grammar which is the domain of hard and fast rules. Despite this concern, we can identify what is involved in successful applications of evidential coercion by examining cases where coercion is more difficult.

Not all ILPs are equally coercible. The ones we have been examining thus far are easily coerced. But now that we have a precise idea of at least one thing that is meant by saying that an ILP is being used as a SLP, we can get an idea of why some ILPs are more easily coerced than others. The following are not as easily coerced as the ones we have seen:

(13) a. ?Sue is sometimes tall.
 b. ?Karen is often Norwegian.
 c. ?Nancy is rarely a human.
 d. ✓/?Francis is occasionally blond.

These do seem to allow metaphorical readings for the predicates, however. For example, *tall* might be taken to mean something like 'highly respectable' or 'above the fray'. Thus, if we first take the predicate to indicate a set of stereotypical properties, then a reading is possible in which the subject exhibited behaviors consistent with those stereotypes. This can be seen by comparing (13b) with (6f), *Karen is often Bohemian*: (13b) is likely to be meaningful only for people with stereotypical ideas about Norwegians. Similar stories can be told, I think, about the other examples in (13). Note that (13d) is ambiguous between a stereotypical evidential coercion reading, and a reading in which sometimes Francis's hair is actually blond. We will discuss the latter reading in the following section. In sum, evidential coercion is possible when standard behaviors are associated with a certain property described by an ILP, and when the subject potentially has control over those behaviors. In each case, the success of evidential coercion depends on the availability of stereotyped behaviors associated with the property.

2.2 Inchoative Coercion

Moens and Steedman (1988) point out that use of a stative predicate in a position that requires a non-stative often results in a change-of-state reading for the predicate. In the examples below, the stative predicates are interpreted as a changes of state:

(14) a. Suddenly, Lynne knew the answer.
 b. After six years of hard work, Leslie knew Italian.

A change of state is a telic event and is thus stage-level. Stative predicates, of course, can be individual- or stage-level. So, although inchoative coercion is not triggered by an environment sensitive to the ILP/SLP contrast, it is relevant to it, because any ILP that is coerced in this manner will become stage-level.

2.3 Interruption

Some ILPs can appear with frequency adverbials without an evidential coercion reading. Adding a quantificational adverb to these induces a reading by which sometimes the property holds of its subject and sometimes it does not. Schubert and Pelletier (1989) and Krifka et al. (1995) discuss this as a kind of coercion, and I will call it "interruption." The interruptions in the intervals over which the ILP is true of the subject allow a plurality of cases for the nuclear scope of a quantificational adverb. Below are some cases in which this occurs:

(15)   a. Max is sometimes a California resident.
          b. Francis is occasionally blond.
          c. Alice is sometimes tall.
          d. Karen is sometimes Norwegian.

(15a) and (15b) sound quite natural since these ILPs can easily be interrupted. (15c) and (15d) do not fit well with the way we typically think of the world, but in spite of this pragmatic interference, the sentences clearly indicate that the predicate holds of its subject intermittently. Interruption fails if the hearer cannot imagine the truth-value of the proposition changing. To get a reading for (15d), we either have to think of Karen changing her citizenship from time to time, or we have to think of Karen being reincarnated repeatedly, sometimes as a Norwegian.

It is important to notice that interruption is not really coercion in my terms. Taking Carlson's (1977) approach, the predicates still have arguments that are of the individual sort. In Kratzer's (1988) terms, there is no need to suppose that the predicates in (15) describe eventualities that are spatiotemporally located. The only interesting thing about the sentences in (15) is that they are interpreted as formulas that fluctuate in truth-value over evaluation times. Thus, while evidential coercion actually produces a SLP, interruption does not. From (4) and (5), we see that evidential coercion is not triggered by the existential construction or by bare plural subjects.

2.4 Going the Other Way

We have seen how a SLP can be coerced from an ILP. It is worth contemplating what it would be like to coerce a SLP *into* an ILP. For a SLP to become an ILP, in Kratzer's terms, the predicate would need to lose its strong connection to space and time, and to become an atemporal property of individuals. Something would need to supply the spatiotemporal argument for the predicate and bind it. There are at least two ways in which this might happen. First, the SLP could receive a habitual interpretation. This appears to be what happens when a non-stative SLP is employed in the simple present:

(16)   a. Sam goes jogging after work.
          b. Hakeem plays basketball for a living.

The habitual interpretation is also involved in what Carlson originally treated as an individual-level reading for sentences like *Zippy ran*. What is involved (for Kratzer's analysis) is clearly the binding of the spatiotemporal argument by a generic quantifier, along with the assertion that the subject generally has the relevant property. This can be formalized as follows:

(17) [for Kratzer's theory] Let α be a SLP with interpretation α'. α can be used as an ILP with the following interpretation:
$\lambda x G_l[\alpha'(x,l)]$

Also, the thematic grid must have its location argument removed, and possibly one of the other arguments would be promoted as the new external argument.

In Carlson's terms, what happens is that the stage-sort argument of the SLP needs to be supplied and bound by an operator. Then it must be related to an individual-sort entity which is bound by a lambda operator. Since Carlson assumes that no natural-language nominal has the set of stages as its denotation space, he has already built into his system various mechanisms for doing just what we have been talking about. Every time a SLP composes with its subject, it must already have been, in effect, converted into an ILP. Below is the counterpart of (17) in Carlson's terms:

(18) [for Carlson's theory] Let a be a SLP with interpretation α'. α can be used as an ILP with the following interpretation:
$\lambda y^i G_{xs}[R(x,y) \& \alpha'(x)]$

We should note that (18) is not really a coercion rule in the same sense that evidential coercion is. For the latter, coercion is the result of forcing a predicate of one level into an environment that requires a predicate of a different level. We certainly do not wish to say that SLPs are coerced into ILPs when they appear in the simple present; we have seen that stative SLPs retain their ordinary readings in that environment. (17) and (18), then, express a way in which a located description can come to denote an atemporal property. This takes place in an environment that permits both ILPs and SLPs to appear, so it differs in kind from evidential coercion.

The second way to derive an ILP from a SLP would be to bind the spatiotemporal location, in Kratzer's terms, or the stage-sort argument, in Carlson's, with an existential operator. It seems that the past perfect is an environment in which some kind of shifting could occur from SLP to ILP status. Once a stage of an individual has done something, it becomes an eternal property of that individual that one of its stages has done whatever it is. This does not result in a generalization, but in an existential quantification over the stage and the location at which the eventuality took place.

2.5 Consequences

I would like to comment on four consequences of my inquiry into coercion. First, unless the ILP/SLP distinction is subject to some additional sort of coercion not noted here, this analysis supports McNally (1993), arguing against Rapoport (1991). Recall from chapter 2 that Rapoport claims depictive adjuncts are required to be stage-level. McNally cites examples like (19) below (repeated from chapter 2) as counterexamples, noting that ILPs can be used as depictives when the main clause supports a reading of the depictive as a changed state:

(19) a. The neighbor's girls entered the Army enthusiastic advocates of U.S. interventionism. (McNally's ex. 8a)
b. Nancy Kerrigan returned from Lillehammer an Olympic silver medalist.

The present argument makes it unlikely that these ILPs are "being used" as SLPs because these examples do not display evidential coercion. They also do not display interruption or change-of-state readings; they simply implicate that the depictive *is* a changed state, as McNally claims.

The second consequence is related to depictives. I have claimed that interruption does not change ILPs to SLPs. This claim makes the prediction that ILPs with an interruption interpretation should not be acceptable in perceptual reports. The following examples suggest that this prediction is incorrect:

(20) a. Robin has seen Max a California resident (on several occasions).
b. I have seen Francis blond (on several occasions).
c. We have seen Sue tall (on several occasions).
d. Pat has seen Karen Norwegian (on several occasions).

Interruption is clearly induced here by the perfect aspect in the matrix, even though it is operating on the perceiving event. I think it is possible that the ILPs in these examples are depictives rather than reports of perceived eventualities. If so, following McNally, I would have to claim that a report of perception in past perfect is an environment supporting the inference that the depictive is a changed state.

If we add a form of *be* in the progressive to the examples in (11), we get the following:

(21) a. ?Robin has seen Max being a California resident (on several occasions).
b. ?I have seen Francis being blond (on several occasions).
c. ?We have seen Sue being tall (on several occasions).
d. ?Pat has seen Karen being Norwegian (on several occasions).

As we have seen, the progressive *be* induces evidential coercion. The examples are odd only to the degree that it is difficult to imagine behavioral evidence that supports the inference of having the described property.

Third, the view of coercion proposed here is clearly distinct from one that says that an ILP has become a SLP whenever it becomes the case that the truth of a proposition containing an ILP is not constant over time. Such a view seems at times to be held by Kratzer (1988) and Diesing (1992). This view seems to derive from the intuitive characterization of ILPs as tendentially stable, immutable properties. Researchers always hasten to acknowledge that the truth values of certain propositions based on ILPs necessarily or potentially change over time (e.g., *Rose is a child*, *Tom is a novice*), and that others, although they do not change out of necessity, change freely as the result of volitional acts (e.g., *Janet is a resident of Idaho*, *Tim has blond hair*). Despite acknowledgments of this sort, many researchers persist in reasoning that seems to be based on the assumption that ILPs denote constant sets over time (at each world).

This kind of reasoning may be behind Kratzer's (1989) discussion of the following, her ex. (73):

(22) Henry was French.

Kratzer notes that (22) can be taken to implicate that Henry is no longer alive (but that he was French when he was alive), or that Henry has changed his national allegiance and is no longer French. Kratzer asserts that the difference between these construals is due to the former being derived from an ILP and the latter from a SLP. Kratzer writes, "The past tense is an effective tool for turning individual-level predicates into stage-level predicates" (1989:41f.), and from this it seems clear that she has something like coercion in mind. Kratzer does not provide arguments for the claim that the construals line up in the manner she proposes. Presumably, the idea is that if the truth conditions of a proposition containing an ILP vary over time, the ILP has been coerced into acting like a SLP. Above, however, we have seen several ILPs (and there are many more) that are not necessarily constant over time.

As de Swart (1991) notes, *be French*, even in the past tense, passes all the diagnostics for classification as an ILP:

(23) Brain surgeons were French.

(23) does not have an existential interpretation. Neither is the existential in (24) grammatical:

(24) *There were brain surgeons French.

What I offer to this debate is the observation that evidential coercion is not involved here. Something much more like interruption is involved, and, as I have argued, there is no reason to believe that this results in a SLP.

Finally, we should pause to note an important fact. We recall that frequency adverbials are subject to the plurality condition, and it has long been established that a plurality of cases can be obtained from ordinary indefinite nominals or from stage-level predicates that are not once-only. We have now found that a plurality of cases can be obtained by interruption. In such cases, the frequency adverbial quantifies over the evaluation time of the formula that is the interpretation of the sentence built on the ILP. We shall have more to say about evaluation time in chapter 7.

2.6 Conclusions

I have argued that evidential coercion derives a SLP from an ILP. Coercion needs to be induced by something, and some syntactic/semantic environments are better at inducing it than others. Adverbs of quantification are very good at getting a plurality of cases for their restrictions. Perceptual reports do not seem to induce evidential coercion, but they accept coerced predicates as descriptions of the perceived event. The progressive induces it strongly, but the existential construction and weak construals of indefinite subjects do not induce coercion at all.

This analysis offers a new diagnostic for determining when ILPs are being used as SLPs. It gives theoretical teeth to such a claim by showing precisely what change in interpretation is predicted. This is a significant contribution because it extends the domain of interpretation that is subject to empirical testing. In addition, I hope that these considerations contribute to dispelling the notion that simply because there is an interruption in the temporal interval over which an ILP holds, the predicate is being used as a SLP.

5

Taking Stock

Having surveyed the previous accounts of the ILP/SLP distinction, and having seen ways in which slippage is possible between the sorts of predicates, we now will consider what is required of an adequate analysis. This chapter will make three main points that, along with the conclusions of chapter 6, will serve as the basis for the analysis in chapter 7. First, it will be established that, given considerations of syntax, the ILP/SLP distinction must be visible after the predicate has composed with its subject argument, at least in infinitival and small clauses. Evidence supporting this conclusion comes from the analysis of perceptual reports and augmented absolutes as containing small clauses. Second, although the Plurality Condition of de Hoop and de Swart is part of the larger story, it does not eliminate the need for a logical distinction along the lines of Diesing's and Kratzer's proposals that will appeal to the Prohibition against Vacuous Quantification. This is evident in the fact that free adjuncts containing once-only predicates have a conditional interpretation when a modal is present in the sentence. Third, and related to the above, we will see evidence that SLPs are anaphoric in a way that ILPs are not. In fact, as will be shown, SLPs exhibit the characteristics of donkey pronouns.

1. A Clause-Level Distinction

1.1 Perceptual Reports

In this section we will see that current syntactic assumptions force us to conclude that there is a clause-level contrast based on the ILP/SLP distinction, rather than simply a predicate distinction. A small clause analysis of perceptual reports forces us to conclude that the ILP/SLP distinction is still evident after the predicate has composed with its subject. In Carlson's (1977) analysis, the ILP/SLP distinction is realized in the arguments the predicate takes, and the distinction is neutralized at the clause level. However, a feature of Diesing's and Kratzer's analyses can be exploited to allow a compositional account to be developed.

Semantic compositionality is a fundamental assumption of the syntax–semantics interface. It is the assumption that the interpretation of each syntactic node is composed of the interpretations of its immediate constituents (the nodes it immediately dominates), and the structure in which they appear, and nothing else. Once an interpretation is composed, it cannot be decomposed.

In Carlson's (1977) analysis of perceptual reports, *see* first combines directly with the predicate of the complement and then combines with the postverbal NP. Carlson gives the following translation (1977:126):

(1) $see_2 \Rightarrow \lambda Q \lambda P x^{iv} P(\hat{y}^i \exists w^s \exists u^s [R(w,x) \& R(u,y) \& see^+(w,u) \& {}^\vee Q(u)])$

Since the argument of Q is u, and since u is the first argument of R (defined as a position for a stage), Q can only be a stage-level predicate. The syntactic structure assumed is tripartite—that is, the V' no de dominates three constituents:

(2)
```
        V'
      / | \
     V  NP  PRED
```

Given this structure, the sort of predicate that appears in the sentence is evident when an interpretation is composed for the V' node. ILPs cannot be generated in this position because ILPs and SLPs belong to different syntactic categories, and the syntactic rule that generates (2) accepts only the category to which SLPs belong.

Since the time of Carlson's (1977) theory, it has become standard to analyze the postverbal nominal and predicate as a single, clausal constituent (see, e.g., Pollard and Sag 1994, Higginbotham 1983). This means that the predicate will not be a sister to the perception verb but will be dominated by the sister:

(3)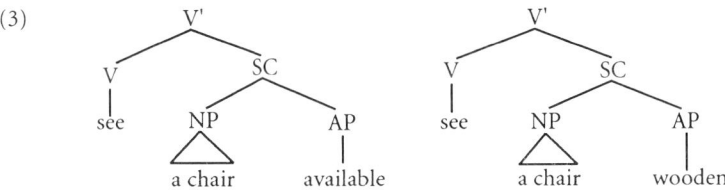

Many syntacticians today take binary branching as an assumption (see Kayne 1984, and much work in Government & Binding and the Minimalist Program); that is, they assume a theory that requires every mother node to have exactly two daughters. Any such theories would adopt the structures shown in (3) rather than those in (2). The syntactic assumption that perception verbs have small clause complements poses a compositionality challenge. How is the effect of the ILP/SLP distinction among perceptual reports to be encoded in the grammar in a way that makes it evident at the small clause node?

Carlson's (1977) type-driven analysis distinguishes predicates on the basis of the sort of entity that saturates them. Once the predicate is saturated, a proposition is the result regardless of the predicate's level; there is no distinction at the clause level. These assumptions mean that a Carlsonian analysis cannot treat *see a chair available* as a construction involving a small clause complement. Once *a chair* composes with *available*, the fact that a SLP is present will no longer be reflected in the type of the complement. The effect is that *see* will not be able to distinguish between complements that contain ILPs and those that contain SLPs. Given Carlson's typological assumptions, the complement of *see* cannot be a small clause without drastically weakening the principle of compositionality.

What is needed for a small-clause account to be successful is to find a way to make the ILP/SLP distinction visible at the small clause node. Within Government & Binding, it is a standard assumption that heads impose two kinds of restrictions on their complements: category selection and semantic selection (see, e.g., Pesetsky 1982,1994).

Various issues pertaining to possible structures of small clauses are relevant to the possibility of category selection. For example, see the debate between Stowell (1981, 1989) and Williams (1980, 1983), and see Svenonius (1994) for a more recent consideration of these issues. Stowell's (1981) assumption was that the mother node of a small clause matches the category of the clause's predicate. If SLPs and ILPs were of different syntactic categories, syntactic selection for the predicate category would be possible. Williams offers a number of counter-arguments, however, and current work in extensions of GB assume that the root of a small clause is some sort of functional projection. Hence, for most likely analyses of the structures of small clauses, the predicate is not in a position to be syntactically selected even if a syntactic distinction between ILPs and SLPs could be maintained. A clausal, syntactic distinction, if independently motivated, would allow syntactic selection to work.

Raposo and Uriagereka (1995) adopt Diesing's distinction between control and raising Infl into an exploded Infl framework and have a sub-Infl functional head making Diesing's control/raising distinction. This functional head is taken to be the head of small clauses. Since heads share (some) features with their maximal projections, by standard GB assumptions, the small clause node will bear different features depending on whether its predicate is individual-level or stage-level. This syntactic feature is assumed to be visible to syntactic selection. Recall that Diesing proposes that "unaccusative" ILPs appear with the raising Infl, which is otherwise associated exclusively with SLPs. Raposo and Uriagereka's account makes the prediction that "unaccusative" ILPs should be grammatical in perceptual reports. This prediction turns out to be incorrect, however:

(4) a. *We saw this bicycle belong to Greg.
　　b. *Betsy saw Michael own a house.
　　c. *Jorge heard Peter know French.

I will argue in chapter 6 that the eventuality described in the perceptual report must be perceivable in the manner indicted by the verb. This is likely to be the reason that (4a) and (4b) are unacceptable. However, exactly why (4c) is unacceptable is not entirely clear. Note that we can say:

(5) Robin saw Steve drunk.

Since drunkenness cannot be established simply by inspection, we must allow indirect evidence to be sufficient in the perceptual report; see chapter 6 for more on this. Even if the examples in (4) can be explained by lack of perceptibility, I do not know whether Raposo and Uriagereka would like to appeal to this. They write:

> In the minimalist model that we are assuming, it is axiomatic that semantics has no place in the derivational history of these matters, contra some recent work on the distinction of concern here [i.e., the ILP/SLP distinction]. Our approach, thus, is blind to semantic motivation, although it is not immune to semantic consequence. (1995:180)

Semantic selection in the Government & Binding framework is done by the assignment of theta-roles from a functor to its arguments. If *scene* were taken to be a theta-role assigned to descriptions of events—the latter being Higginbotham's (1983) suggestion—then semantic selection might suffice for these cases. We would need to understand *event description* in such a way as to include stative SLPs. Perceptual reports do not play a central role in the analyses of Kratzer and Diesing. However, requiring the complement of *see* to be spatiotemporally located would allow a treatment to be developed. The spatiotemporal argument that SLPs have will provide the means for the type-theoretic account of this developed in chapter 7.

1.2 Absolutes

The challenge posed by perceptual reports is potentially compounded in the cases of absolute adjuncts. Recall that Stump's (1985) analysis is similar to Carlson's analysis of perceptual reports in that a tripartite syntactic structure is assumed. The preposition *with* is introduced syncategorematically, allowing the predicate distinction to have an effect on the interpretation and the syntactic category of the adjunct.

With current syntactic assumptions, absolutes are most plausibly analyzed as small clauses:

(6) Augmented Absolutes

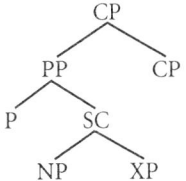

Stump's analysis will have the same difficulty that Carlson's had for perceptual reports. Selectional restrictions are of no help either, since both ILPs and SLPs are grammatical in this position. Thus, neither the theta-theoretic idea of Higginbotham nor the category distinction of Raposo and Uriagereka will be of help.

The account I will pursue in the next chapter will allow SLPs to compose with arguments to yield a different sort of object from that resulting from ILPs composing with their arguments. This idea is probably compatible with Higginbotham's proposal, and it uses a piece of the proposals of Diesing and Kratzer to achieve its aim.

Even with a semantic distinction at the small clause node, a challenge remains with the augmented absolutes. The challenge, as we have seen, is that the ILP/SLP distinction affects the interpretation of the root clause just in case the absolute is "augmented" by the preposition *with*. When an unaugmented small clause is adjoined, the effect is neutralized; although the material in the adjunct is presupposed, it cannot appear in the restriction of an operator. This fact is surprising because, ordinarily, material in the restriction can come from just about anywhere, including nonlinguistic discourse context. The fact is also surprising because it means that information about the predicate must be "visible" at the PP node, which is higher in the syntactic tree than the small clause node which immediately dominates unaugmented absolutes.

I will make a tentative suggestion about this. Manfred Krifka pointed out to me that free adjuncts and augmented absolutes can freely occur before or after the main clause and still retain their ability to restrict an operator:

(7) a. Standing on a chair, John can touch the ceiling.
    b. John can touch the ceiling standing on a chair.

(8) a. With the truck in first gear, we would coast gently downhill.
    b. We would coast gently downhill, with the truck in first gear.

However, unaugmented absolutes can appear after the main clause only with very flat intonation, and they can just as easily appear within the main clause:

(9) a. The children being asleep, Mary might watch TV.
    b. ?Mary might watch TV, the children being asleep.
    c. ?Mary might, the children being asleep, watch TV.

The unaugmented absolutes in (9b) and (9c) seem to have the status of parenthetical comments. These observations can be taken as evidence that the free and augmented adjuncts are base-generated within the main clause but the unaugmented absolutes originate outside it. The adjuncts that are generated within the main clause can be interpreted as constituents of the proposition that the main clause denotes. Thus, they can provide material for the restriction of a main clause operator (although nothing requires them to do so). Unaugmented absolutes cannot do this because they are base-generated outside the clause.

Why should there be these differences at deep structure? The unaugmented absolute is a small clause, not a full clause, but still a clause. It relies on the main clause for its evaluation time, but other than that it is a complete proposition on its own. The free adjunct is just a predicate on its own. It relies more heavily on the main clause because it must find its controller there. Finally, the augmented absolute is nothing like an independent clause: the adjunct provides one of the relata for the comitative *with*, but the other must come from the main clause.

2. The Plurality Condition and Vacuous Quantification Again

In our earlier discussion, we saw that Kratzer (1988) argued that the sentences below should be interpreted as shown:

(10) a. *When Mary knows French, she knows it well.
 *G [knows (Mary, French)] [knows well (Mary, French)]
 b. When a Moroccan knows French, she knows it well.
 G_x[Moroccan(x) & knows (x, French)] [knows well (x, French)]
 c. When Mary knows a foreign language, she knows it well.
 G_x[foreign language(x) & knows (Mary, x)] [knows well (Mary,x)]
 d. When Mary speaks French, she speaks it well.
 G_l[speaks (Mary, French,l)] [speaks well (Mary, French, l)]
 e. *When Mary speaks French, she knows it well.
 *G_l[speaks (Mary, French,l)] [knows well (Mary, French)]

This motivated the argument structure distinction between ILPs and SLPs, and it motivated the Prohibition against Vacuous Quantification. Then, we saw that de Hoop and de Swart (1989) argued against this analysis on the basis of "once-only" stage-level predicates, which do not allow generic quantification of the sort shown in (10d):

(11) a. *When a Moroccan kills Fido, she kills him quickly.
 b. *When Anne makes the film "Dangerous Liaisons," she is happy.

The observation that these sentences are unexpectedly bad motivated the plurality condition on adverbial quantification and the uniqueness presupposition on the Davidsonian argument. De Hoop and de Swart suggest that their analysis removes the motivation for Kratzer's argument structure distinction.

Let us consider whether this is so. In the analysis of *when* adjuncts that contain SLPs, I will assume that the possibility of a generic conditional reading is due to the presence of a null or overt adverb of quantification of which the adjunct is interpreted as the restriction (always with the possibility that context can also contribute to the restriction). I assume that null generic operators are routinely available whenever an adequate restriction and nuclear scope can be formed. I take it that the fact that *when* adjuncts containing ILPs do not have a generic, conditional interpretation is due to a failure of these adjuncts to form adequate restrictions for the generic operator. Following de Hoop and de Swart, I assume that a condition on restrictions of generalizations is that they must denote a set with cardinality greater than one.

Recall that the restriction of the generic operator can be supplied by augmented absolute and free adjuncts as well:

(12) a. Standing on a chair, Lisa's head touches the ceiling.
 b. With her children asleep, Mary watches TV.
 c. With his work done, John goes straight to bed.

We have seen that once-only SLPs do not allow *when* adjuncts to restrict a generic operator. Since this is accounted for by a condition applied to the generic operator, it is not taken to be a peculiarity of *when* adjuncts. Therefore, we expect that once-only SLPs should not allow a generic interpretation for free adjuncts or augmented absolutes either. Indeed, this is the case:

(13)   a. Killing Fido, John seems like a thug.
       b. Making "Dangerous Liaisons," Anne is contented.
       c. With the White House burning down, the Clintons need a place to spend the night.

In each sentence, the adjunct eventuality is presupposed to hold in the world of discourse. This is exactly the same effect seen with *when* adjuncts.

Recall, however, that free adjuncts and augmented absolutes reveal ILP/SLP effects not only when the operator is a generic adverbial, but also when the operator is a modal. This is a significant fact because modals, not being adverbial quantifiers, are not subject to the plurality condition. Examples with modal operators are shown below:

(14)   a. Killing Fido, John might seem like a thug.
       b. Making "Dangerous Liaisons," Anne might be contented.
       c. With the White House burning down, the Clintons might need a place to spend the night.

In stark contrast to the examples in (13), we find that conditional readings are possible for these even though the adjunct predicate is once-only. And of course, as we have seen, ILP adjuncts do not allow conditional readings even when the operator is a modal:

(15)   a. Having unusually long arms, John can touch the ceiling.
       b. With his mother being a doctor, John would know the way to the Med Center.

The insight of de Hoop and De Swart is that ILPs differ from most SLPs in that only the latter are able to denote a multiplicity of cases, without the presence of an indefinite nominal, to form an adequate restriction on adverbs of quantification. They showed that once-only SLPs do not have this capacity. It is now clear from the contrast between (14) and (15) that ILPs and SLPs show a contrast in their ability to form a restriction at all, and that the Plurality Condition cannot account for these cases.

But neither can Kratzer's Prohibition against Vacuous Quantification account for the once-only cases. We must conclude that both conditions are necessary: Kratzer's spatiotemporal variable predicts that SLPs will be able to delimit at least one case; and de Hoop and de Swart's Plurality Condition concerns the ability to delimit multiple cases.[1]

Finally, let us try to see whether the cardinality restriction is really an effect of the ILP/SLP distinction. Above, I quoted de Swart as follows: "What individual-level and 'once-only' predicates have in common is that their application to a particular individual is felicitous only once. The situation the proposition describes has a unique location in the life of an individual" (1991:59). There is a problem with this line of reasoning. Stative predicates in general yield an implicature of temporal persistence whether they are individual-level or stage-level. And there is only a *tendency* for ILPs to hold of an individual exactly once; as noted in chapter

4, many ILPs are interruptible, routinely holding for periods of time, ceasing to hold, and then holding once again (e.g., hair color, place of residence, nationality, religion, or likes and dislikes), and the world does not have to be too bizarre for other ILPs to fluctuate in a similar manner.

These interruptible ILPs constitute a crucial set of data. It turns out that they seem fully grammatical when they restrict an adverb of quantification:

(16) a. When Sam is a California resident, he is usually optimistic.
b. When Marty is an American, he always approves of capitalism.
c. When Melanie's hair is red, she resembles Alexi Lalas.

The conclusion is that the phenomenon captured by the plurality condition is orthogonal to the ILP/SLP distinction. Thus, the plurality condition does not allow us to do without a separate ILP/SLP distinction in accounting for the facts about restricting operators. The diagram below characterizes the interaction of these effects:

(17)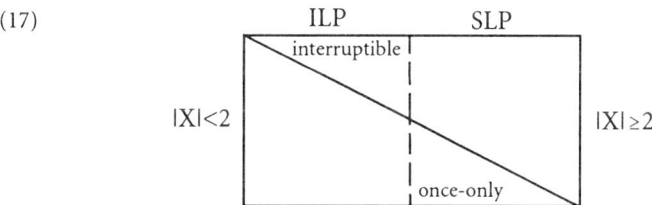

The vertical line in the center divides ILPs from SLPs. The diagonal line divides those predicates that denote a set of eventualities with cardinality greater than two (located to the upper right) from those which do not (located to the lower left).

Finally, it is significant for our investigation to note that if we apply the tests carefully by controlling for once-only predicates, generic quantification can be a reliable diagnostic for the ILP/SLP distinction.

3. The Anaphoric Nature of SLPs

A classical challenge for theories of semantics in the 1980s and 1990s has been to provide an account of a phenomenon called "donkey anaphora." We will see in this section that the interpretation of SLPs shows the same characteristics. First, we will consider the classical donkey sentences, reviewing the challenge they pose, and then we will discuss the leading analyses of donkey anaphora. Finally, we will note the relevance of these phenomena to SLPs, following Fernald (1999).

3.1 History of donkey anaphora

The term "donkey anaphora" comes from a series of sentences due to Geach (1962):

(18) a. Every farmer who has a donkey beats it.
b. If a farmer has a donkey, he beats it.

A rich body of literature has developed to deal with problems posed by these and related sentences. The problem posed by the examples in (18) is that the pronoun *it* is understood to be interpreted as a donkey, but its antecedent, the expression *a donkey*, appears in a position that does not allow the pronoun to be bound. Montague (and many others) assumed that pronouns are interpreted with variables, and that an indefinite description is interpreted as an existential quantifier binding a variable that is the argument of the descriptive content of the nominal. Thus, *a donkey* has the interpretation $\lambda P \lambda x \exists x [donkey'(x) \& P(x)]$. The problem presented by (18) is that the indefinite description appears within the scope of a universal quantifier in (18a), and it appears in the antecedent of a conditional in (18b). This means that the existential quantifier that is part of the interpretation of *a donkey* cannot bind the variable introduced by the interpretation of *it*. The formulas below illustrate the problem:

(19) a. $\forall y \, [farmer'(y) \& \exists x [donkey'(x) \& own'(y,x)] \to beat'(y,x)]]$
b. $\exists y \, [farmer'(y) \& \exists x [donkey'(x) \& own'(y,x)]] \to beat'(y,x)$
c. $\forall x \forall y \, [(farmer'(y) \& donkey'(y) \, own'(y,x) \to beat'(y,x)]$

In (19a), the *x* in the consequent is unbound, and in (19b), neither variable in the consequent is bound. Thus, neither formula is well-formed. The problem is not that it is impossible to produce an interpretation for these sentences in Tarskiian logic—(19c), which uses two universal quantifiers captures the most obvious reading for the examples in (18)—the problem is that this cannot be done compositionally using the traditional tools.

Other constructions have been shown to pose the same challenge, including the generic *when*-adjunct sentences that have been so significant for us so far:

(20) When a farmer has a donkey, he beats it.

In fact, a sequence of sentences shows a similar problem when an individual introduced in one sentence is referred to by a pronoun in a subsequent sentence:

(21) A dog came into the room.
It flopped down.

This kind of discourse anaphor was mentioned by Strawson (1952) as a problem for Bertrand Russell's analysis in which indefinites are treated as having an existential quantifier as part of their interpretation. If a classical quantifier binds the variable restricted by *dog* in the first sentence, it cannot bind the variable introduced by the pronoun in the second sentence. Additional related phenomena are discussed by Karttunen (1976). It is not necessary for our purposes to delve deeply into this rich area, but see especially Chierchia (1992) for a summary of relevant work.

3.2 Dynamic Semantics

There are two major traditions of research that have made substantial progress in the analysis of donkey sentences. One is Discourse Representation Theory (DRT), building on Kamp (1981) and Heim (1982). See Kamp and Ryle (1993) for an introduction to this theory. The other tradition builds on the Dynamic Montague Grammar of Groenendijk and Stokhof (1990, 1991). For an introduction to this theory and a summary of work in it, see van Bentham (1996) or Chierchia (1995).

Both approaches interpret utterances as context change potential, rather than as propositions. This allows information to be tracked through a discourse in a way that is not possible with classical logic. Both approaches provide a way to enter discourse referents into the common ground of a discourse, to keep track of them, and to allow nominal expressions to refer to them. Utterances containing indefinite descriptions will introduce discourse referents along with information about them. Utterances containing definite descriptions or pronouns will change the context by adding information about previously identified referents. Groenendijk and Stokhof (1990) formalize this by taking sentential interpretation to be a change from one set of "states" to another set of states. A state is an assignment of values to discourse referents. A conversation can be thought of in Stalnaker's (1978) way as an effort to narrow down the set of states under consideration. As an example, consider the sequence of sentences noted above:

(22) A dog came into the room.
      It flopped down.

In a dynamic analysis, the nominal expressions will all include discourse referents as part of their interpretations. The definite description *the room* will be identified with a previously established discourse referent, but *a dog* will introduce a new one. The first sentence will thus be interpreted as a function from a set of states, in each of which a referent is already identified with a room, to a set of states in which a dog is identified with a new referent, and it came into the referent identified as the room. The pronoun in the second sentence must be identified with a previously established referent; the referent identified with the dog is one possibility. Thus, the second sentence will take the output of the first sentence and map it to states in which a previously established referent flopped down. The point that the output set of states from the first sentence serves as the input to the second sentence is crucial. It is what allows the pronoun *it* to pick up the discourse referent that was introduced by *a dog*.

This approach will work for donkey sentences as well as for the discourse anaphoric case shown in (22). In (18), repeated below, *a donkey* introduces a discourse referent that can be picked up by a subsequent pronoun:

(23) a. Every farmer who has a donkey beats it.
      b. If a farmer has a donkey, he beats it.

In Groenendijk and Stokhof (1990), indefinite nominals are interpreted with a dynamic existential quantifier $\mathcal{E}$ which binds a discourse marker. They define this in terms of the classical, static (i.e., non-dynamic) existential quantifier, as follows:

(24) Dynamic Existential Quantifier $\mathcal{E}d\Phi = \lambda p\, \exists x\, \{x/d\}\, (\Phi(p))$

The expression $\{x/d\}$ is called a state-switcher. What it does is assign the value x to any instances of the discourse marker d occurring within $\Phi(p)$. The effect of λp is to absorb the interpretation of the subsequent sentence and pull it inside the scope of the classical existential quantifier. A proposition can be made dynamic by applying the "uparrow" operator to it; it can be made static by applying the "downarrow" operator. These are given the following definitions:[2]

(25) Uparrow $\uparrow\phi = \lambda p\,[\phi \wedge {}^\vee p]$, where ϕ is an expression of type t, p a variable of type $<s,t>$ which has no free occurrences in ϕ.

(26) Downarrow $\downarrow\Phi = \Phi\,({}^\wedge\text{true})$, where Φ is an expression of type $<<s,t>,t>$.

The effect of the downarrow is to saturate a dynamic proposition with a tautologous static proposition **true**, which will have no effect on the interpretation of the larger proposition.

We have seen that indefinite descriptions usually allow pronouns in subsequent utterances to refer to the discourse referents they introduce. Negation, however, is generally assumed to eliminate this possibility:

(27) a. It is not the case that a man is walking in the park. He is whistling.
b. No man is walking in the park. He is whistling.

In neither of these discourses can the pronoun *he* be taken as the discourse marker introduced by *man*. Hence, negation (~) is normally taken to be static. It is defined as follows:

(28) Static Negation $\sim\Phi = \uparrow\neg\downarrow\Phi$

The inner downarrow closes off the dynamics of Φ, $\neg$ is the classical negation operator ($\neg\phi$ is true with respect to a model, state, and assignment function just in case ϕ is false with respect to the model, state, and assignment function), and the outer uparrow allows the interpretation to compose with any subsequent utterances.

The behavior of universal quantification with respect to donkey anaphora is somewhat unusual. We see in the classic donkey sentences that an indefinite within the restriction of a universal quantifier can bind a variable in the nuclear scope. However, no pronoun in any subsequent sentence is able to refer to it:

(29) Every farmer who has a donkey beats it. He is unhappy.

Thus, the universal quantifier is dynamic within the sentence in which it appears, but static with respect to subsequent sentences. These properties are captured by the definition of the static universal $\mathcal{A}$:

(30) Static universal quantifier $\mathcal{A}d\Phi = \sim\mathcal{E}d\sim\Phi$

We should note that the state-switcher is not used as a formal device in every dynamic framework, but that the same effects are achieved by taking propositions to be context-change potential (see Dekker 1993, for example). It must also be noted that the treatment of dynamic and static operators here reflects generalizations that are widely but not universally accepted. Groenendijk and Stokhof (1990) go into some detail in discussing exceptions to the generalizations their analysis is designed to capture. For our purposes, it is enough to stop here and return to the ILP/SLP distinction.

3.3 Anaphoric Predicates

Partee (1989)—summarizing earlier work by Bäuerle (1979), von Stechow (1982), Hinrichs (1981), Partee (1984), and Cooper (1986)—points out that temporal and locative implicit variables behave like overt anaphora in having deictic, discourse anaphoric, and bound variable behavior. She illustrates this with the following examples (Partee's exx. 1–3 and 4–6):

(31) a. Deictic or demonstrative: Who's he?
b. Discourse anaphoric: A woman walked in. She sat down.
c. Bound variable: Every man believed he was right.

(32) a. Deictic past reference time: I didn't turn off the stove.
b. Discourse anaphoric reference time: Mary woke up sometime in the night. She turned on the light.
c. "Bound variable" past reference time: Whenever John wrote a letter to Mary, she answered two days later.

Partee argues that tense is an implicit anaphor. Significantly, all the relevant examples in Partee's work—and in Hinrichs (1986), which develops this idea further—involve stage-level predicates. ILPs seem to have none of these pronominal characteristics:

(33) a. Sam was smart.
b. Sam was a professor. He is altruistic.
c. ??Whenever Sam was a professor, he was altruistic.

All these sentences have tense in them, but they do not show the anaphoric effects seen in (32). (33a) has a deictic use like (32a) only if the predicate is coerced into being stage-level through Evidential Coercion. On such a reading, *was smart* is taken to mean 'gave evidence at a spatiotemporal location of having the property denoted by the ILP *smart*'. But the uncoerced ILP reading of (33a) is not deictic in the way that (32a) is. Similarly, the uncoerced readings for the (33b) lack the discourse anaphoric reading possible with the SLPs in (32b). Finally, (33c) has the same status as *When Mary knows French, she knows it well*. These sentences usually appear in the literature with an ungrammaticality star before them, although I usually think this is a bit too strong. I take it, however, that to the extent that (33c) is acceptable, it is not quantifying over event time, but the time at which the proposition in each clause is to be evaluated. All the sentences in (33) have tense in them, but they lack the similarity to pronouns of the examples in (32) which contain SLPs. We conclude that tense is not anaphoric or deictic except when it appears with SLPs. Dynamic semantics was designed to deal with cases of discourse and bound variable anaphora like (32b) and (32c). Thus, an analysis needs to be developed in which SLPs have dynamically-interpreted implicit arguments.

A significant consequence of this analysis will be that the implicit temporal arguments will be expected to pattern exactly with donkey anaphora. This prediction appears to be successful:

(34) a. When a woman$_i$ speaks$_t$ French, she$_i$ speaks$_t$ it well. (Kratzer 1988)
b. A woman$_i$ woke$_t$ up sometime in the night. She$_i$ turned$_t$ on the light.
c. No one$_i$ walked in. *He$_i$ turned on the light.

d. No one walked$_t$ in. *Sam turned$_t$ on the light.
e. If a farmer$_i$ has a donkey, he$_i$ beats it. *He$_i$ is upset.
f. If a farmer has$_t$ a donkey, he beats$_t$ it. *Robin is upset$_t$ about this.

(34a) is a classical donkey sentence3. (34b) shows that the implicit argument in the second sentence can pick up the discourse referent used in the first sentence. The temporal argument in the second sentence of (34c) cannot be interpreted as referring to locations of walking in. This parallels the inability of the overt pronoun *he* in the second sentence of (34d) to pick up a referent from the first sentence.

Finally, consider the pair in (34e) and (34f). (34e) shows that, while the conditional connective is internally dynamic, it is externally static. That is, an indefinite description contained in the antecedent of a conditional introduces a discourse referent that can be picked up by an expression in the consequent (hence the connective in dynamic within the sentence in which it appears); but the referent cannot be picked up by any pronoun in a subsequent sentence (contrasting with the simple case in (34b)). Now we see in (34f) that the temporal argument of SLPs works exactly the same way. (34f) is an acceptable discourse, but not on an interpretation in which Robin's being upset coincides with each instance of a farmer seeing and beating a donkey.

In chapter 7, we will develop a dynamic analysis of SLPs which predicts that SLPs can be used deictically or anaphorically, and ILPs cannot.

6

Nonuniformity

In this chapter we will investigate the ILP/SLP effects seen with syntactically complex predicates. We will find that the effects seen in a matrix clause sometimes depend on the sort of predicate that appears in an embedded clause. We will also see the perceptual report diagnostic diverge from the others.

Next, we will consider the consequences of these two observations. First, we will consider ways to extend an analysis involving the Mapping Hypothesis. I will argue that no such extension is reasonable within the assumptions of the framework. Second, we will need to explain the deviation between perceptual reports and the subject effects. Two reasonable possibilities are considered. One possibility is that the status of a predicate as individual-level or stage-level is determined compositionally; if this is the case, an added constraint will need to be placed on perceptual reports. The other reasonable possibility is that contextual factors are involved in the subject effects. Both hypotheses have merit. To decide the issue, we will turn to the ability of SLPs to delimit cases for quantification. The vote will be cast in favor of the additional condition on perceptual reports. This will not, however, rule out the possibility that context may play a role in the subject effect interpretations in some instances.

1. Syntactically Complex Predicates

Previous discussions of the ILP/SLP effects have almost always focused on predicates that consist of a single lexical item, or a verb followed by a nominal object. In this section we will see that the subject effects do not depend entirely on a classification of the head of the predicate. The data we will consider include sentences that have embedded clauses. In particular, we will look at predicates with raising and control heads, and at those that take clausal complements. In each case, we will see that embedded clauses can determine whether the matrix clause shows ILP or SLP subject effects. At the same time, we will see that predicates of this variety are not acceptable within perceptual reports.

To begin this investigation, we assume with Kratzer that certain heads (e.g., *hit* or *dance*) require the predicate in which they appear to be located in space or time, and that certain heads (e.g., *own* or *know*) do not. If all that is needed in order for a predicate to display stage-level effects is for the predicate to be located, might it be that the locatedness could arise by some constituent other than the head? In this discussion, we will examine data involving unlocated heads that appear with SLPs in adjunct or complement positions.

1.1 Subject Effects

1.1.1 Raising

Carlson (1977:118f.) briefly notes the following contrast (his ex. 106):

(1) a. Bears seemed to like to eat meat. (Generic)
    b. Bears seemed to be in the next room. (Existential)

Seem is a raising verb. It has long been established that the subjects of raising sentences behave logically as if they were the subjects of the embedded predicates. Jacobson calls this the *inheritance* property: "Any syntactic category restrictions imposed by the embedded VP on the category of its subject must be satisfied by the raised constituent" (1990:429). Raising verbs and adjectives are analyzed in the Government & Binding literature as assigning no theta-role externally. They also lack the ability to assign Case to nominals in embedded positions. Since the Case Filter requires all nominal arguments to receive Case, a nominal in the complement must raise to become the subject of the root clause where it can receive Case from the finite inflectional head I^0. The effect is that the root subject will have the thematic role assigned by the embedded predicate, and the denotation of the subject will be interpreted as a participant in the eventuality denoted by the embedded clause. Similarly, if the embedded predicate assigns no theta-role externally, an expletive will appear as the root subject at surface structure.

Since a raising verb or adjective allows its subject to inherit restrictions imposed by the complement predicates, we would expect the effects of the ILP/SLP distinction to be inherited by the root VP in the raising construction. Indeed, this expectation is well received by the data. The following examples show the raising adjective *likely* with embedded SLPs:

(2) a. Workers are likely to be in the field. (existential possible)
    b. Sm workers are likely to be in the field.

The examples below have embedded ILPs:

(3) a. Workers are likely to be pedantic. (generic only)
    b. *Sm workers are likely to be pedantic.

We find that the ILP/SLP effects on the subject of the root clause are consistent with the classification of the embedded predicate. This is just what we would expect from an analysis of the ILP/SLP contrast that is based on argument structure (although Diesing's and Kratzer's accounts will need to be extended a bit—see below) or on Carlson's sorted typology. Next we consider the raising verbs *seem* and *appear*.

(4) a. There seemed to be bears in the next room.
    b. Bears seemed to be in the next room. (existential possible)
    c. Sm bears seemed to be in the next room.

(5) a. *There seemed to be students intellectual.
    b. Students seemed to be intellectual. (existential possible?)
    c. Sm students seemed to be intellectual.

(6) a. There appeared to be bears in the next room.
    b. Bears appeared to be in the next room. (existential possible)
    c. Sm bears appeared to be in the next room.

(7) a. *There appeared to be students intellectual.
    b. Students appeared to be intellectual. (existential possible?)
    c. Sm students appeared to be intellectual.

The existential construction shows the contrast that we should expect: it is acceptable exactly when the embedded predicate is stage-level. On the assumption that the subject *there* has risen from the embedded subject position, the existential sentences shown simply diagnose the embedded predicate rather than the raising predicate together with its complement. To diagnose the latter, we would need to form an existential sentence with a verbal predicate. Our best attempt is the following:

(8) a. There are students seeming to be intellectual.
    b. There are bears seeming to be in the next room.

(9) a. There are students appearing to be intellectual.
    b. There are bears appearing to be in the next room.

Perhaps surprisingly, these do not show an ILP/SLP contrast. In (4–7), the indefinite subjects with embedded SLPs are affected in exactly the way we would expect: the reduced form of *some* is acceptable, and the bare plural subject has an existential reading. However, although the indefinite subject cases perhaps show a contrast in acceptability with the two kinds of predicates, the contrast is less striking than usual. It seems to me that existential readings are possible in the right context with an embedded ILP, and that *sm* sounds better with *seem* and *appear* than it did with *likely*.

The explanation for all this lies with the difference in meanings between *seem* and *appear* on the one hand, and *likely* on the other. All three heads entail a judgment about the subject and the predicate. With *seem* and *appear*, the individual filling the role of judge can be expressed in the syntax by an adjunct:

(10) a. Students seemed to me to be intellectual.
     b. Students appeared to me to be intellectual.

This logical argument, which is syntactically optional for *seem* and *appear*, cannot appear as an overt argument of *likely*:

(11) *Students are likely to me to be intellectual.

Thus, the judge in a sentence headed by *likely* is determined by discourse context and by default is taken to be the speaker.

All three heads entail that the judge is uncertain whether the individual denoted by the subject has the property denoted by the predicate. *Seem* and *appear* differ truth-conditionally from *likely* in that they entail that the subject has given some perceivable evidence for having the described property. *Likely* has no such entailment.

I would like to consider a decompositional analysis of *seem* and *appear* for purposes of seeing better the effect of embedded ILPs and SLPs. A fair approximation of the interpretation of *John seemed to be available*, using Carlson's sorted typology, is as follows:

(12) a. John seemed to be available.
      b. $\exists Q, x^s [R(x, j)\ \&\ Q(x)\ \&\ Gy^s(Q(y))\ [\text{available}'(y)]]$

This formula entails that there is some stage-level property that John has, and it is generally true that if one has this property, then one is available. An approximation of the interpretation of *John seemed to be intelligent* is shown below:

(13) a. John seemed to be intelligent.
      b. $\exists Q, x^s [R(x, j)\ \& Q(x)\ \&\ Gy^s, z^i(Q(y)\ \&\ R(y,z))\ [\text{intelligent}'(z)]]$

This entails that there is a stage-level property that John has, and that in general if one has this property, one is intelligent. The interpretations in (12b) and (13b) decompose the meaning of *seem*.

Now compare these interpretations to the formulation of Evidential Coercion developed in chapter 5:

(14) Evidential Coercion [Carlson-style]: Let α be an ILP with interpretation α'. α can be used as a SLP with the following interpretation:
      $\lambda x^s \exists Q[Q(x)\ \&\ G_{y^s, z^i}(Q(y)\ \&\ R(y,z))\ [\alpha'(z)]]$

The similarity to the proposed decompositional meanings is clear. Once again, I am not arguing that lexical decomposition is always a fruitful enterprise; I attempt it here only to make precise the way in which *seem* and *appear* are truth-conditionally like the result of Evidential Coercion. (13b) is straightforwardly like the formulation of Evidential Coercion. But (12b) resembles it as well. (12b) differs from (13b) only in that R is not needed because the embedded predicate is stage-level. The reason for including the existentially quantified Q in (12b) is that John's availability is not entailed to be directly perceived, nor does veridicality hold with *seem* or *appear*. Further support for this point of view comes from the fact that (12a), in the right context, can conversationally implicate that John is in fact not available. For these reasons, I take it that (possibly indirect) evidence of having a stage-level property is sufficient to satisfy the truth conditions of a *seem* or *appear* sentence containing an embedded SLP. Thus, *seem* and *appear* have an effect on an embedded predicate that is very much like Evidential Coercion. The embedded predicate must express something perceivable. SLPs are ideal for this, but ILPs that can undergo Evidential Coercion work well also.

I have not included the judge argument in the interpretations in (12b) and (13b), and it is not obvious how to do it. A difficulty with lexical decomposition as a research strategy is finding arguments in favor of doing things in one way rather than another. To plunge boldly forward, we could add the entailment that the judge perceives the eventuality $Q(x)$, which is the stage-level property that gives evidence of having the individual-level property described in the sentence. This would give us the following in place of (12b) and (13b):[1]

(15) $\exists Q, x^s$ [$R(x, j)$ & perceive' (speaker, $Q(x)$) & $Gy^s(Q(y))$ [available'(y)]]

(16) $\exists Q, x^s$ [$R(x, j)$ & perceive' (speaker, $Q(x)$) & $Gy^s, z^i(Q(y)$ & $R(y,z))$ [intelligent'(z)]]

These representations clearly emphasize the idea that the subject was involved in an eventuality perceivable by the judge. (15) and (16) also make an implicit connection to perceptual reports. However, the following contrast in acceptability:

(17) a. John seemed intelligent.
      b. (?)I saw John intelligent.

On my account, the latter involves coercion and thus receives the interpretation shown below, and the former does not:

(18) $\exists Q, x^s[R(x,j)$ & see' (speaker, $Q(x)$) & $Gy^s, z^i(Q(y)$ & $R(y,z))$ [intelligent'(z)]]

This interpretation is nearly identical to (16). If I am to account for the contrast in (17), I must claim that the fact that coercion has taken place in one case is responsible for the difference. That is, I could not claim (even if I wanted to) that there is any semantic incompatibility between the meaning of *intelligent* and the rest of the formula in (18), since the same incompatibility would obtain in (16). Such a proposal would predict that both (17a) and (17b) would be awkward.

Instead of claiming that the *meaning* arrived at by coercion is degraded, I propose that (17b) is degraded because coercion was needed to arrive at its interpretation. That is, in the absence of coercion there is a straightforward mapping between syntax and semantics. Coercion is necessary when no straightforward mapping is possible. Thus, there is nothing degenerate about the coerced meaning, but rather it is the mapping between syntax and semantics that is degenerate when coercion is needed; identifying the right meaning for sentences like (17b) requires extra work because the syntax does not simply hand us the meaning.

The lexical interpretations for *seem* and *appear* that are needed for the sentential interpretations in (15–16) are shown below:

(19) a. *seem$_1$ / appear$_1$* $\Rightarrow \lambda T \lambda x^s \exists Q[$perceive' $(Q(x))$ & $Gy^s(Q(y))$ [$T(y)$]]
      b. *seem$_2$ / appear$_2$* $\Rightarrow \lambda P \lambda x^s \exists Q[$perceive' $(Q(x))$ & $Gy^s, z^i(Q(y)$ & $R(y,z))$ [$P(z)$]]

The first interpretation is for SLPs in the complement, and the second for ILPs. (Here the variable T ranges over SLPs, and P and Q range over ILPs.) Two interpretations are needed for each verb because ILPs and SLPs are of different types, given Carlson's assumptions.

Let us briefly examine the interpretation of *likely*, focusing on the following examples:

(20) a. Sarah is likely to be available. (SLP)
b. Sarah is likely to be intelligent. (ILP)

At first glance, (20b) seems to be a bit odd. However, it is fully acceptable if the speaker doesn't know very much about Sarah. There is nothing odd about (20a). According to (20a), the speaker does not know whether Sarah will be available at the relevant time, but the speaker does know something about Sarah, from which it is plausible to surmise that Sarah will be available then. But now we can see that the interpretation of (20b) works in exactly the same way, omitting the overtly stage-level part about the relevant time. (20b) conversationally implicates (by Quantity and perhaps Manner) that the speaker does not know whether Sarah is intelligent: it entails that there is something the speaker does know about Sarah, from which it is plausible to surmise that Sarah is intelligent. (20b) is a less useful sentence than (20a) because the combination of its truth conditions with the proposition it implicates are not likely to be satisfied very often; but there is nothing more here than the ordinary ILP/SLP contrast inherited from the embedded predicate. Since perception is not overtly involved with *likely* the way it is with *seem* and *appear*, there is no need for evidence to be inferred from the description of the embedded predicate, and so *likely* does not result in anything like a coerced reading. Thus, we interpret (20a) and (20b) as impersonal propositional attitudes (following Klein and Sag 1985), as follows:

(21) a. $\exists x\ [R(x,s)\ \&\ likely'\ (available'(s))]$
b. $likely'\ (intelligent'(s))$

Since we are assuming Carlson's sorted typology in this discussion, we have two different interpretations for *likely*:

(22) a. $\lambda x^s \lambda P\ [R(x,y)\ \&\ likely'\ (P(y))]$
b. $\lambda x^i \lambda Q\ [likely'\ (Q(x))]$

Because the meanings of *seem* and *appear* play such a prominent role in the interpretation of an embedded ILP, they are not typical, pristine raising cases which are completely transparent to the syntactic and semantic requirements of the embedded predicate. *Likely* is much closer to the pristine case in which, because the matrix subject is an argument of the embedded predicate and not of the raising head, we find subject effects in the matrix that are consistent with the sort of predicate found in the embedded clause.

1.1.2 Controlled Complements

Control heads differ from raising heads in that a single overt nominal expression serves as an argument both to the control head and to the embedded predicate. Hence, it might be surprising to find a control head that is "transparent" to the level of its embedded predicate in the way that raising heads can be.

Want is a control verb which allows complements that are individual-level or stage-level. Naïvely, we might think that wants are not the sorts of things that have spatiotemporal locations, so we would not expect the lexical item *want* to require the predicates in which it appears to be located. The examples in (23) and (24) have SLPs in the infinitival complement to *want*:

(23) a. People want to eat supper. (N.B. *Hurry it up will you? People want to eat!* This clearly has existential import.)
   b. Sm people want to eat supper.

(24) a. Children want to be picked up after school.
   b. Sm children want to be picked up after school.

A fair amount of contextualization is needed to make the existential reading for the bare plural sound natural, but the existential reading clearly needs to be made available by the grammar, and there is a clear contrast between the (b) examples above and those below with embedded ILPs:

(25) a. Doctors want to be skillful. (generic only)
   b. *Sm doctors want to be skillful.

(26) a. Scholars want to be athletic. (generic only)
   b. *Sm scholars want to be athletic.

Weak subject construals are disallowed in these cases, and this is what we expect to find with ILPs. *Want* is a case of a control head that is transparent to the level of the predicate in its complement as far as the indefinite subject effects are concerned.

Other raising heads are located in their own right. Below are some examples Diesing (1992) gives (her ex. 18):

(27) a. A unicorn is anxious to damage the walls.
   b. Unicorns are anxious to damage the walls.

Fernald (1994) claims that ILPs are generally unacceptable in this position:

(28) a. *A unicorn is anxious to be intelligent.
   b. *Unicorns are anxious to be intelligent.

However, others are not so bad:

(29) a. Robin is anxious to be an American.
   b. Kyle is anxious to know French.

To my ear, all these sentences would be better with *eager* in them than with *anxious*, but I find those in (29) acceptable on a change-of-state reading. Indeed, this inchoative reading is also found with atelic stage-level predicates:

(30) a. Marian is anxious to be on the porch.
   b. Sam is anxious to be available.
   c. Robin is anxious to run.

I take it that *anxious* heads a stage-level predicate and that it requires the predicate in its complement to have an inception time. The latter is needed because the thing one is anxious about is for the eventuality named by the complement to begin. If the embedded predicate does not have an inherent inception time, then one must be coerced. The explanation for the contrast between (28) and (29) is that it is hard to coerce an inchoative reading for *intelligent*, but inchoative coercion is relatively easy to apply to predicates for citizenship and competence in French. So Fernald (1994) was partly correct in claiming that *anxious* composes with a SLP and results in one after composition: the result of inchoative coercion is a SLP. However, if we analyze *anxious* as including an inchoative operator in its translation, there would be no reason to prevent ILPs from composing with it.

Thus, we see a fair amount of lexical idiosyncrasy among control predicates with respect to what kinds of eventualities their complements can denote, and what sort of predicate is obtained after the control head composes with its complement. *Want* was seen to be ambiguous or else transparent to the sort of predicate in its complement. *Anxious*, on the other hand, can compose with any predicate that has an inception time, and the result is stage-level.

1.1.3 Controlled Modifiers

Too and *enough* modifiers are also control constructions. In *Sam was happy enough to dance a jig* and *Lisa was too tired to move*, the infinitival adjuncts are controlled by the subject. Such modifiers can adjoin to heads that appear as ILPs in simplex expressions. Let us see what happens when a SLP adjoins to one of these heads.

Skillful, clever, and *clumsy* head ILPs when they are unmodified, as shown by the following subject diagnostics, shown in the past tense:

(31) a. *There were clowns that I knew in high school skillful.
 b. Clowns were skillful. (generic only)
 c. *Sm clowns were skillful.

(32) a. *There were surgeons that I knew in high school clever.
 b. Surgeons were clever. (generic only)
 c. *Sm surgeons were clever.

(33) a. *There were lab technicians that I knew in high school clumsy.
 b. Lab technicians were clumsy. (generic only)
 c. *Sm lab technicians were clumsy.

When the same predicates are modified by a *too* or *enough* adjunct that contains a SLP, the result passes the subject tests for SLP status:[2]

(34) a. Clowns were skillful enough to please most any audience. (existential possible)
 b. Sm clowns were skillful enough to please most any audience.

The diagnostics involving subject effects all behave as if the main predicate were stage-level:

(35) a. Surgeons were clever enough to perform delicate operations. (existential possible)
 b. Sm surgeons were clever enough to perform delicate operations.

The examples are even more convincing if we use a definite nominal in the adjunct:

(36) a. Clowns were skillful enough to please the audience. (existential possible)
 b. Sm clowns were skillful enough to please the audience.

(37) a. Surgeons were clever enough to perform the operation (last night). (existential possible)
 b. Sm surgeons were clever enough to perform the operation (last night).

Below are cases in which *too* modifiers contain SLPs:

(38) a. Negotiators were too clever to sound convincing. (existential possible)
b. Sm negotiators were too clever to sound convincing.

(39) a. Clowns were too clumsy not to fall from the tightrope. (existential possible)
b. Sm clowns were too clumsy not to fall from the tightrope.

All the modifying phrases contain SLPs, and we have SLP subject effects even though the head of the predicate appears to be individual-level when it is unmodified. This seems to be just what we observed with the raising and controlled complement cases. To test this, we would like to find some *too* and *enough* modifiers that contain ILPs. It is difficult to find ILPs that are acceptable with *enough* modifiers, however. The following is clearly degraded:

(40) *Surgeons were clever enough to be intelligent.

The following, however, is somewhat surprising:

(41) a. Students were tall enough to be basketball players. (existential possible)
b. Sm students were tall enough to be basketball players.

These examples suggest that *enough* will turn whatever it modifies into a SLP. However, I do not fully understand why so many ILPs are unacceptable with *enough*, so my conclusion is quite tentative.

Test cases with ILPs are easy to find for *too* adjuncts. With *too*, it is possible for the lack of one property to depend on the presence of another:

(42) a. Politicians are too clever for their own good. (generic only)
b. *Sm politicians are too clever for their own good.

The adjunct here is a *for* purpose clause, but it has the same effect as the infinitival one shown below:

(43) a. Barges were too bulky to be fast. (generic only)
b. *Sm barges were too bulky to be fast.

From these examples it is clear that *too* converts an ILP that it modifies into a SLP just in case a SLP is contained in the adjunct. This conversion happens in (38) and (39), but not in (42) and (43). It is clear that an *enough*-SLP modifier will convert an ILP that it modifies into a SLP; however, we only tentatively conclude that *enough* converts the predicate it modifies into an SLP even if the adjunct contains an ILP. Semantically, *too* and *enough* denote relations between the adjunct predicate and the predicate to which they are adjoined. Thus, semantically they are the heads of the larger predicates in which they appear. A syntactic analysis that mirrors the semantic relations would allow one to maintain that the classification of the root predicate depends only on a lexical classification of the head (*too* and *enough*, in these cases). However, we have already seen other kinds of cases (e.g., with *want*) that show this cannot be maintained. In the next section, we find still more evidence to support this conclusion.

1.1.4 Full Clause Complements

We have seen that embedding an ILP or a SLP under raising and control heads can affect the interpretation of the root subject. Moreover, we have seen that both kinds of predicates show lexical idiosyncrasies about which variety of predicate they are compatible with as a complement. We will find both of these phenomena with full clause complements as well.

Raising and control both involve a dependency between the matrix and embedded subject positions. Analogous to these cases is pronominal binding into a full clause complement. We will begin with cases like these, and then we will consider those in which there is no overt binding between the embedded and matrix clauses.

Propositional attitudes are verbs like *think, believe, doubt*, and so on, which have proposition-denoting complements. Dowty (1979) notes that many cognitive verbs with propositional complements are ambiguous between being statives and being achievements. Achievements, of course, are stage-level, and statives can go either way. Therefore, we will want to try to set aside the achievement readings as we consider these cases. *Believe* is fairly difficult to interpret non-statively, so we will begin with it. Below, an ILP appears in the embedded clause:

(44) a. Surgeons believe that they are intelligent. (generic only)
b. *Sm surgeons believe that they are intelligent.

Only a generic reading is possible for (a), and weak subjects are ungrammatical, suggesting that the predicate is individual-level. The examples below have embedded SLPs:

(45) a. Surgeons believe that they are ready (for tonight's operation). (existential possible)
b. Sm surgeons believe that they are ready (for tonight's operation).

The same contrast holds with *doubt* and *think*:

(46) a. Politicians doubt that they are honest. (generic only)
b. *Sm politicians doubt that they are honest.

(47) a. Politicians doubt that they will win. (existential possible)
b. Sm politicians doubt that they will win.

(48) a. Politicians think that they are honest. (generic only)
b. *Sm politicians think that they are honest.

(49) a. Politicians think that they will win. (existential possible)
b. Sm politicians think that they will win.

In each of the examples in (44–49), the embedded clause contains a pronoun that has an antecedent in the matrix clause. These are clear cases in which the predicate embedded in a full clause complement determines the subject effects seen in the matrix. However, we will see that there are other full clause examples in which an embedded predicate determines the subject effects seen in the matrix. This is exemplified by the following:

(50) a. Surgeons believe that there is a fire in the operating room. (existential possible)
b. Sm surgeons believe that there is a fire in the operating room.

Here, a SLP appears in the embedded clause and the matrix subject is sensitive to it. Here is another example:

(51) a. Republicans think that Clinton was lying at the hearing. (existential possible)
b. Sm Republicans think that Clinton was lying at the hearing.

Contrast these with the following:

(52) a. Voters think that Clinton is crafty. (generic only)
b. *Sm voters think that Clinton is crafty.

What seems to be happening in (50) and (51) is that the embedded propositions describe eventualities that are pinned down to very specific times. An embedded ILP with a coerced reading can show similar effects. Consider the following as comments about a particular hearing:

(53) a. Republicans doubt that Clinton was honest. (existential possible)
b. Sm Republicans doubt that Clinton was honest.

At issue here is whether Clinton spoke honestly at the hearing, rather than whether he has honesty as a characteristic property. The examples below contrast with (53):

(54) a. Democrats doubt that Nixon was honest. (generic only)
b. *Sm Democrats doubt that Nixon was honest.

By applying the ILP to an individual who is deceased, and by not pinning the embedded proposition down to a specific time, we reduce the likelihood of getting a coerced reading for the ILP.

We conclude that even predicates embedded within full clauses can determine the subject effects found in the matrix clause, and that this does not happen only when there is pronominal binding between the clauses. What does seem to be required is that the embedded clause refer to a specific time. An embedded SLP can do this automatically, but a coerced ILP works also.

When we examined cases with raising and control heads, we also saw lexical idiosyncrasies related to the sorts of predicates that are acceptable within the complements, and related to the sort of predicate that results from composing the head with the complement. Heads that have full clause complements show similar idiosyncrasies. We have seen that several propositional attitudes are transparent to the sort of predicate that appears in the embedded clause. *Say* and *declare*, however, always express SLPs after composing with their complements. Like the attitudes, they impose no restrictions on their complements with respect to the ILP/SLP distinction. Sometimes these verbs express direct quotes, and sometimes not, but they always head predicates that display the characteristics of SLPs:

(55) a. Senators said the bill would cause problems. (existential possible)
b. Sm senators said the bill would cause problems.

(56) a. Scientists declared that the moon is uninhabitable. (existential possible)
b. Sm scientists declared that the moon is uninhabitable.

Other verbs denoting some sort of vocalization or other expression or emission of noise display SLP characteristics as well. This is unsurprising, given the notion that SLPs necessarily take place at a particular spatiotemporal location. We conclude that these verbs require the predicates in which they appear to be located.

1.1.5. Specificity Effect

There are a number of cases in which definite nominals seem to cause what we would otherwise interpret as a ILP to act like a SLP. The following contrast is from Fernald (1994) and is discussed in Glasbey (1997):

(57) a. Monkeys live in trees. (generic only)
b. *Sm monkeys live in trees.

(58) a. Monkeys live in that tree. (existential possible)
b. Sm monkeys live in that tree.

Own ordinarily heads a stative predicate, and it is usually assumed to be individual-level (Diesing 1992, Kratzer 1988). The head itself, of course, is not the entire predicate. Here we will see that it is capable of heading a predicate that displays stage-level subject effects. The contrast between (59) and (60) is striking:

(59) a. Tycoons own banks. (generic only)
b. *Sm tycoons own banks.

(60) a. Tycoons own that house. (existential possible)
b. Sm tycoons own that house.

Own banks has all the characteristics of an ILP. On the other hand, *own that house* looks like a SLP. We must conclude that the nominal object of *own* plays a crucial role in determining possible readings for indefinite subjects.

It would seem that the definiteness of (60) makes the stage-level interpretations possible. However, compare (60) with the following:

(61) a. Tycoons own the world. (generic only/existential possible)
b. ✓/*Sm tycoons own the world.

These sentences are ambiguous. *Tycoons own the world* is ordinarily not taken to mean that tycoons actually hold the deed to this entire planet, but that tycoons own so much of the means of production that people must answer to their bidding, or something to this effect. Thus, *own the world* can be used as an idiom. On this reading, *the world*, though definite, does not actually refer to the world, and the predicate seems to be individual-level. The other reading for the sentences in (61) is that tycoons hold an actual deed to the planet. For this reading, it seems to me that the judgments coincide with those in (60). Thus, a definite description is not sufficient to license SLP subject effects, but a deictic is. This suggests that a specific location is sufficient to license the SLP subject effects. Below is an additional example, with another pair provided for contrast:

(62) a. Presidents are similar to these senators. (existential possible)
b. Sm presidents are similar to these senators.

(63) a. Presidents are similar to senators. (generic only)
b. *Sm presidents are similar to senators.

We should note at this point that deictic temporal modifiers also display this effect:

(64) a. Surgeons were clever last night. (existential possible)
b. Sm surgeons were clever last night.

(65) a. Politicians were neurotic yesterday. (existential possible)
    b. Sm politicians were neurotic yesterday.

These have evidential coercion readings, apparently triggered by the use of a temporal modifier of short duration.

2. Consequences for the Mapping Hypothesis

We have seen a number of sentence types which show that a lexical classification by the head of a predicate alone is not adequate to predict the ILP/SLP subject effects. We will take these as grounds for rejecting the semantic partition analysis of Kratzer (1988) and Diesing (1992). In this section we will see why.

In the raising, control, and clausal complement cases considered above, we found what may be described in Diesing's and Kratzer's terms as follows: when the head of the matrix predicate does not require the predicate to be located, a SLP in the adjunct can provide the locating necessary to obtain subject effects consistent with SLPs. What is happening in the raising case is that the root subject can receive an existential interpretation if its trace is in a position to receive an existential interpretation. The control and pronominal binding cases are structurally similar—in both cases the root subject binds an anaphoric element in an embedded clause—but in these cases, the subject cannot be interpreted as if it were in the embedded clause because it must also serve as an argument in the matrix clause. Moreover, we found examples with clausal complements in which the matrix subject had no anaphoric element in the embedded clause, and still the embedded predicate influenced the interpretation of the matrix subject. The raising case should come as no surprise for theories that assume the Mapping Hypothesis, and it seems that such theories can be extended straightforwardly to account for raising sentences: the subject has only to be interpreted in the clause at which it received its theta-role. If the embedded predicate is a SLP, the subject can receive an existential interpretation by getting caught up in existential closure at the embedded VP. In these theories, however, it will be impossible to treat the subject of *want* or *believe* in the same way because it will receive a theta-role in the root clause. Even when the embedded predicate is stage-level, the subject cannot be caught up in existential closure because the variable in the embedded clause is already bound to the overt subject outside the domain of closure.

It should be fairly clear that, although the Mapping Hypothesis can be extended to handle some of the data considered here, it cannot deal with all cases in which bare plurals have existential readings. However, we will consider Deising's analysis in some detail, since one mechanism that will be required might be useful for data on sequencing of tense, not considered here.

In Diesing's theory (prior to modification to account for generic interpretations of subjects embedded under propositional attitudes), an existential reading for a bare plural subject is available if it is caught up in the nuclear scope of some operator, or if it ends up within the root VP at LF. To avoid an existential reading, an indefinite must avoid all nuclear scopes and must manage to remain higher than the root VP at LF.

2.1 The Raising Cases

Recall that VPs headed by raising verbs exhibit the characteristics of the complement predicate with respect to the subject effects:

(66) a. Students seem to be intelligent.
b. *A student seems to be intelligent.

(67) a. Students seem to be standing on chairs.
b. A student seems to be standing on a chair.

Diesing's original set of assumptions was not designed to deal with raising verbs. These assumptions predict that any predicate headed by a particular raising head should always behave in the same way with respect to the behavior of indefinite subjects, regardless of the level of the complement predicate. By assumption, the null generic operator appears only in the root clause. Because the root VP node is assumed to be the point at which existential closure can occur, no variable dominated by the root VP can be outside the domain of unselective binding. From these assumptions, it follows that no variable dominated by the root VP node can be bound by the null generic operator. Diesing proposed that (most) ILPs appear with a null "control" Infl that assigns a theta-role to its specifier, and that SLPs appear with a null "raising" Infl that does not. In order to get off the ground with an analysis of infinitival complements, we have to assume that there are two more Infls that have the phonological shape *to*—one of the raising variety, and one of the control variety. Although Diesing was not specific about the nature of the dependency between the predicate and Infl (that is, whether it is c-selection, s-selection, or something else), we would surely want it to be a fairly local relationship. Presumably, then, for the raising cases in (66) and (67), it is the embedded Infl that must match the embedded predicate.

But given this combination of assumptions, no matter which kind of Infl is assumed to appear with raising verbs, the data in (66) and (67) will pose a problem. If we assume that control Infl always appears with raising verbs, the subject will not be able to have an existential interpretation, but the subject in (67a) clearly has one. On the other hand, if raising verbs always take raising Infl, subjects should always be allowed to be interpreted existentially, but this is clearly not possible for (66a). It would work if we could somehow force the root Infl to match the embedded Infl with respect to the ability to assign a theta-role to its specifier. The following constraint will suffice:[3]

(68) **Infl-to-Infl Agreement:** Every non-finite Infl must agree with the Infl of its matrix clause with respect to the (Boolean-valued) feature [control].

We will require, further, that every Infl bearing the feature [+control] must assign Diesing's 'is-a-property-of' theta-role to its specifier, and that no other Infl can assign any theta-role to its specifier. Some heads that have clausal complements (e.g., *anxious* and *eager*) are listed in the lexicon as "taking" Infl[−control], and others (e.g., *seem*, *appear*, and *likely*) are not specified in the lexicon. If a head is specified, its complement must agree with the head's specification; but if a head is not specified, it can appear with either kind of Infl that results from agreement.

With this added machinery, we can account for the contrast seen with the raising heads that are transparent to the level of the predicate contained in their complements. The structures below would result from this "Infl-to-Infl Agreement":

(69) Students seem to be intelligent.

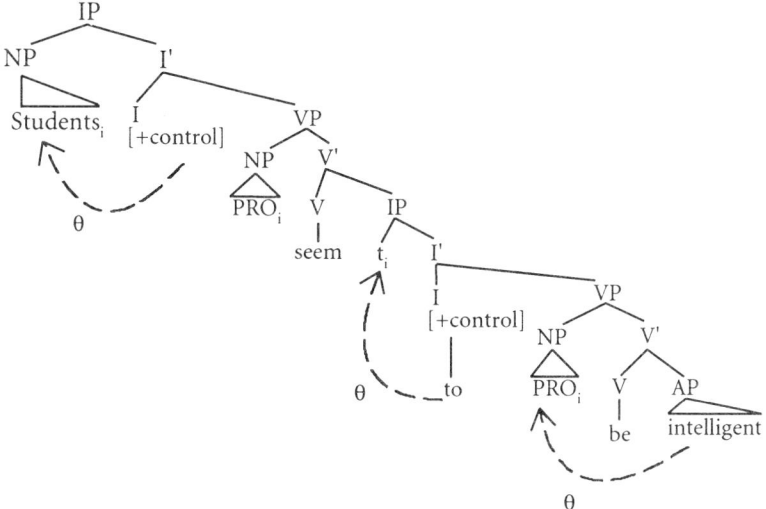

(70) Students seem to be standing on chairs.

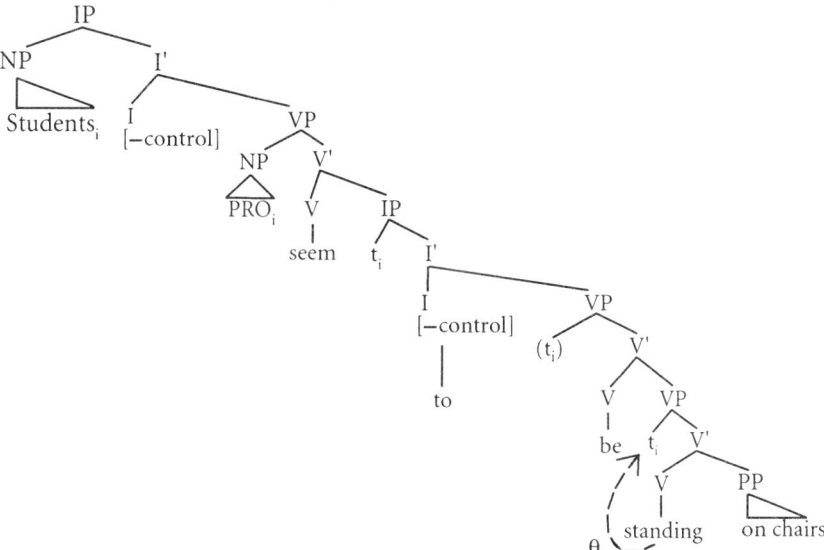

With the ILP case in (69), the subject is generated at the specifier of the matrix IP because it is assigned a theta-role by the root Infl. As long as reconstruction is not permitted to move a nominal lower than the point at which it was projected, *students* will be unable to move down inside the root VP, and therefore it will be unable to receive an existential interpretation. For (70), the subject is generated at the specifier of the embedded VP because that is the only position that receives a theta-role of the appropriate sort. From this position, the subject moves up to the specifier of the root IP to receive Case (and to satisfy the Extended Projection Principle by providing a subject for the root clause). Because the subject originated in the specifier of the embedded VP, it can reconstruct to that position on the way to LF. This position is dominated by the root VP node, so the variable introduced by the subject can be caught up in unselective closure.

This proposal makes the necessary predictions for the raising data, but we cannot be very happy about the lack of locality involved in the Infl-to-Infl Agreement requirement. In the next section, we will see that the raising cases can be handled, without Infl-to-Infl Agreement, by mechanisms we already introduced in chapter 3 to provide an account of generic readings for subjects of complements to propositional attitudes. However, when we attempt to account for the effects of the ILP/SLP complements to *want*, we will find that we cannot maintain Diesing's assumptions without adding Infl-to-Infl Agreement.

In the discussion of how Diesing would handle generic readings for subjects embedded under attitude verbs, we had to assume that null generic operators could appear in embedded clauses and bind variables in the specifier of the embedded IP. This made it possible for a variable to escape existential closure at any specifier of IP (or CP), and not just in the root clause. With this modification of Diesing's assumptions, we can provide an account of the raising cases. We still must make an assumption about what sort of Infl appears in the root clause. Because raising verbs acquire the ILP/SLP flavor of their embedded predicates, we are not likely to have reliable intuitions, a priori, about whether raising verbs should be classified as ILPs or SLPs, and so we might not have accurate expectations about which sort of Infl should dominate raising verbs. However, it is easy to see that if raising verbs appear with the control Infl, an existential interpretation will be predicted no matter what the embedded predicate is.

Raising Infl is the only alternative. Given this assumption, let us see what structures are assigned to raising sentences that have embedded ILPs and SLPs. First, one with an embedded ILP:

(71)

```
              IP
            /    \
         NP_i     I'
          △     /   \
       students I    VP
              (t_i)  V'
                   /    \
                  V      IP
                  |    /   \
                seem  t_i   I'
                           /  \
                          I    VP
                          |   /  \
                         to  NP   V'
                             △   / \
                           PRO_i V   AP
                                 |   △
                                 be  intelligent
```

Compare this with a SLP substituted for the ILP:

(72) Students seem to be available.

(71) has only a generic reading for the bare plural subject, but (72) has an existential reading as well.

There are two locations in each of these trees at which the bare plural has a chance of avoiding an existential reading: the specifier of the matrix IP, and the specifier of the embedded IP. Because *students* is base-generated in the specifier of the embedded VP in (72), it can reconstruct to that position at LF (or, possibly, it could reconstruct only as far as the specifier of the root VP) and thereby be caught up in existential closure at the embedded VP (or the matrix VP, in the other case), and the correct reading will be generated. If it remains at the specifier of the root IP, a generic interpretation will result. For (71), *students* is generated in the specifier of the embedded IP, because the embedded Infl assigns a theta-role to that position. Thus, if the subject does not reconstruct, or if it reconstructs to the position at which it was projected, it will have a generic reading. The obvious difficulty is that the subject ought to be able to reconstruct to the specifier of the matrix VP as well; in this position, it cannot be bound by any null generic operator, since, by assumption, null generic operators can bind only variables that appear in the specifier of some IP (or possibly CP). If reconstruction is permitted only to the position at which a theta-role was assigned, this problem will be solved, since the specifier of the root VP is not a possible reconstruction site in (71).

2.2 The Control Cases

In the discussion in chapter 4, we saw inheritance effects, with respect to indefinite subjects, with the control verb *want*. The following examples show that an existential reading is possible for a bare plural subject just in case the embedded predicate is stage-level, and a weak subject is grammatical in the same case:

(73) a. Children want to be tall. (generic only)
 b. *Sm children want to be tall.

(74) a. Children want to go for a ride. (existential possible)
    b. Sm children want to go for a ride.

Let us see how the Mapping Hypothesis proposal fares with these cases.

Because *want* is a control verb, the denotation of its subject must play two roles: it must be the wanter, and it must control the embedded predicate. This, of course, distinguishes it from raising cases in which the denotation of the subject plays the single role as the controller of the embedded predicate. This means that the solution (which did not involve Infl-to-Infl Agreement) we reached for the raising cases will not work here, however. We cannot simply allow *want* to appear with the "raising" Infl and let the different properties of ILPs and SLPs follow from the positions at which the subject was projected in the embedded clause: the subject cannot be projected in the embedded clause because it must receive a theta-role from *want*.

There are two nodes at which the subject can receive a theta-role from *want*: the specifier of IP, and the specifier of VP. The effect of this requirement is that *want* must assign a theta-role to the specifier of IP just in case the complement of *want* contains an ILP, and it must assign a theta-role to the specifier of VP just in case its complement contains a SLP. No ordinary mechanism of GB can offer a way out. The only recourse Diesing's proposal has at this point is to adopt Infl-to-Infl Agreement. With the assumption that *want* is unmarked in the lexicon with respect to the Infl that it "takes," the following surface structures are generated for (73a) and (74a):

(75)   Children want to be tall.

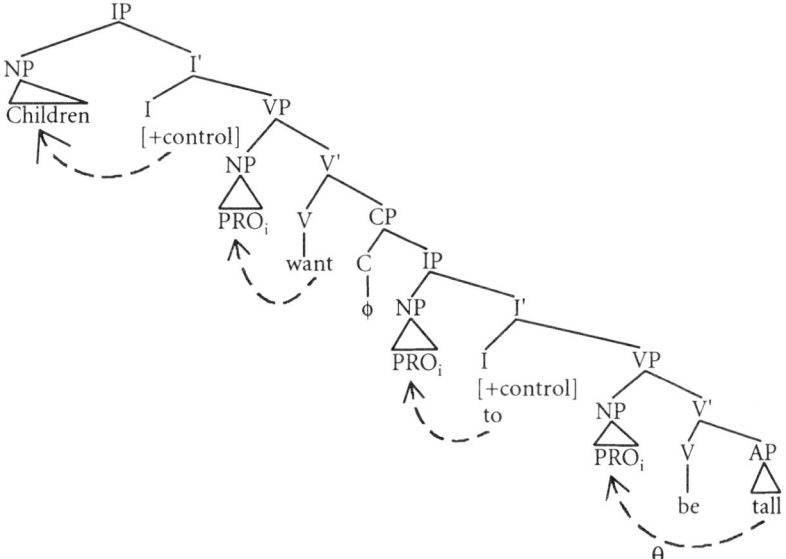

(76) Children want to go for a ride.

```
                IP
              /    \
            NP      VP
            |      /  \
        Children_i I    VP
                [-control]
                    t_i    V'
                          /  \
                         V    CP
                       want  / \
                            C   IP
                            φ  / \
                              t_i  I'
                                  /  \
                                 I    VP
                            [-control]
                                to   t_i  V'
                                         / \
                                        V   AP
                                       go  for a ride
                                         θ
```

Example (75), has the ILP *tall* in the embedded clause. It appears with an Infl in the embedded clause that is [+control] because it "takes" it. This means that the embedded Infl assigns a theta-role to the specifier of the embedded clause; because at most one theta-role can be assigned to a node (and because Diesing assumes that all theta-roles are assigned within the head's maximal projection), *tall* must assign its theta-role to the specifier of VP. By Infl-to-Infl Agreement, the root Infl must be [+control], because the embedded Infl is. From this it follows that the root Infl assigns a theta-role to its specifier, and *want* assigns a theta-role to the specifier of the root VP. In all, four subject theta-roles are assigned. The specifier of the root IP is presumably the only place where abstract Case can be received, so only one overt lexical item is licensed. The other theta-roles thus require three appearances of PRO. Because the overt subject receives its theta-role at the specifier of the root IP, it cannot reconstruct at all. Thus, it cannot possibly move underneath any VP, and it cannot be caught up in unselective, existential closure. The null generic operator will appear and bind the variable in the specifier of the root IP. The sentence is correctly predicted to have only a generic interpretation.

In (76), the head of the embedded predicate is *go*, and it will be assumed to require the embedded Infl to have the feature [−control]. By Infl-to-Infl Agreement, neither Infl in the sentence has a theta-role to assign to its specifier. This means that only two subject theta-roles are assigned—one by *go*, and one by *want*. The overt subject is projected in the specifier of the root VP. It moves to the specifier of IP at surface structure to allow the sentence to survive the Case filter. Since the subject received a theta-role at the specifier of VP, it is permitted to reconstruct to that position by LF. If it does, an existential interpretation will result owing to unselective, existential closure at the root VP node; if it remains at the specifier of IP at LF, however, a generic interpretation results.

2.3 Attitudes

The attitude cases are similar to those with *want* in that the head of the root predicate assigns a theta-role to its subject and the effects are determined by the embedded predicate. These cases are different, however, in that some of them involve a full, finite, clausal complement.

Infl-to-Infl Agreement could account for the attitude data examined above in exactly the same way as we accounted for raising and *want*, if it could be modified so that it can apply to finite Infl. This modification will require every non-root Infl to agree with the Infl in its matrix clause with respect to the [control] feature and its Boolean value. This makes the prediction that a stage-level head like *say, declare, affirm, acknowledge, state, concede, inquire, figure out, decide*, and so on should be grammatical only with a SLP in its complement, but this is clearly false. If Infl-to-Infl Agreement must be abandoned, with it will go any hope of a Diesing-style account for *want* and for propositional attitudes. There would need to be a way to limit the power of Infl-to-Infl Agreement so that it has its effect just in case a head does not require its Infl to have a particular value for the [control] feature. The alternative for a Diesing-style account is to claim that pragmatic, rather than purely syntactic, factors are involved when embedded SLPs yield matrix SLP subject effects. In chapter 7 I will argue that this is a possibility.

2.4 Too *and* Enough

The *too* and *enough* cases differ from the raising, control, and attitude cases in that the trigger of the ILP/SLP effect is located in an adjunct to the head of the predicate, rather than in a complement.

The relevant data involve adjoining an infinitival predicate modifier to an individual-level adjective, with the addition of *too* or *enough* at some suitable node. If a SLP appears in the adjunct, the whole predicate exhibits the subject effects of a SLP (and with *enough*, it might anyhow, but we saw that *too* is transparent). What is significant about these cases is not that the triggering predicate is adjoined rather than in a complement position; Infl-to-Infl Agreement (disregarding its other problems) can be restated in such a way as to apply to adjuncts. The problem is that ordinary ILPs, like *intelligent* and *tall*, must be marked in the lexicon so that they appear with an Infl that is [+control], but when a SLP is adjoined to them, they need to appear with a [−control] Infl. Thus, we would need to posit that every ILP can appear with either kind of Infl, but that certain conditions must license the Infl it appears with.

2.2.5 Specificity Effect

The data from what I have called the specificity effect will be even more problematic for a semantic partition analysis. The data are repeated below:

(77) a. Tycoons own corporations. (generic only)
      b. *Sm tycoons own corporations.

(78) a. Tycoons own that house. (existential possible)
b. Sm tycoons own that house.

In examples like these, the weak construal for an indefinite subject is possible only when a specific description is contained within the predicate. The Mapping Hypothesis would need to require control Infl to appear with SLPs or with ILPs that contain a specific description.

2.6 Conclusion

Infl-to-Infl Agreement might be of use beyond the data considered here for the sequencing of tenses in Romance languages (and to a lesser degree in English). So despite the non-locality of this requirement, it might be independently motivated. However, we found it to be inadequate for the full clause complement cases and for the specificity effect examples. In addition, it has always been worrisome that existential closure was taken to be motivated by a nuclear scope that did not in fact exist; if there is no quantifier in a sentence, there can be no nuclear scope. Although there surely is a mapping between form and meaning in natural language, I take it that it is not as simple as the Mapping Hypothesis suggests. For these reasons, the proposal that will be developed in the following chapter will not include the Mapping Hypothesis.

3. Perceptual Reports and What They Show

Given Carlson's (1977) observation that only SLPs are grammatical in perceptual reports, we might expect that the syntactically complex cases that show SLP subject effects would be acceptable in perceptual reports also. In this section, we find that this is not necessarily the case.

3.1 The data

Below are examples of the raising, control, and full clause complement data that we considered in the discussion of subject effects. Only those predicates that yielded stage-level matrix subject effects are shown. The third example in each set is an attempt to use the predicate in a perceptual report. Clearly, each attempt fails:

(79) a. Workers are likely to be in the field. (existential possible)
b. Sm workers are likely to be in the field.
c. *I saw John likely to go into the field.

(80) a. People want to eat supper. (existential possible)
b. Sm people want to eat supper.
c. ??I saw someone want to eat supper.

(81) a. Surgeons believe that they are ready (for tonight's operation). (existential possible)
b. Sm surgeons believe that they are ready (for tonight's operation).
c. *I saw surgeons believe that they were ready (for tonight's operation).

We have here clear evidence of a divergence between the SLP subject effects and the ability of a predicate to appear in a perceptual report. We will now consider related cases in more detail.

In the discussion of subject effects above, we assigned *seem* and *appear* lexical decompositional interpretations in such a way that a stage-level predicate always results when these heads compose with another predicate. Perceptual reports are somewhat degraded when the predicate is headed by *seem* or *appear*. ILPs and SLPs seem to be about equally grammatical in these environments:

(82) a. I saw Sam seem to eat food.
 b. I saw Sam seem to be intellectual.

Thus, it appears that *seem* is somewhat awkward as an event description, but that it is equally interpretable as such regardless of whether its complement is an ILP or a SLP. The analysis sketched earlier this chapter for the interpretation of *seem* predicts that these should be equally acceptable, and in fact that they should be fully acceptable. I think that they are fully acceptable on a reading in which the individual casting judgment on Sam is an arbitrary person, but they do not allow the reading in which the judge is taken to be the speaker. This fact should not be surprising at all, since the following paraphrase is quite odd:

(83) ??I saw Sam seem to me to eat food.

Thus, *seem* and *appear* are acceptable in the perceptual report, but *likely* is not—as seen in (79c)—even with an embedded SLP, and this poses a challenge.

Next, we consider the control cases. SLPs and ILPs alike are quite odd when *want* is the head of the small clause predicate:

(84) a. ??I saw Marian want to eat supper.
 b. ??I saw Marian want to travel in a spacecraft.

(85) a. ??I saw Marian want to be intelligent.
 b. ??I saw Marian want to be tall.

These are clearly degraded and show no ILP/SLP contrast, even though they did show a contrast with respect to the subject effects.

The propositional attitude predicates are clearly not acceptable in perceptual reports:

(86) a. *I saw surgeons believe that they were intelligent.
 b. *I saw surgeons believe that they were ready (for tonight's operation).

Too and *enough* adjuncts are somewhat acceptable; they clearly are an improvement over the unmodified predicates:

(87) a. ?I saw Leslie skillful enough to please most any audience.
 a'. *I saw Leslie skillful.
 b. ?I saw Sarah clever enough to perform delicate operations.
 b'. *I saw Sarah clever.
 c. ?I saw John too clumsy to walk upright.
 c'. *I saw John clumsy.

I suspect that the modifying clause facilitates evidential coercion, and that this makes it possible for the predicates to be used in the perceptual report.

Finally, let us consider the predicates that gave rise to specificity effects for the subject diagnostics:

(88) a. Tycoons own that house. (existential possible)
b. Sm tycoons own that house.
c. *I saw Robin own that house.

(89) a. Presidents are similar to these senators. (existential possible)
b. Sm presidents are similar to these senators.
c. *I saw Robin similar to these senators.

Clearly, the perceptual reports diverge from the subject effects.

A very clear pattern emerges from the data in this section. With the raising, control, and attitude predicates, placing a SLP in the embedded clause (as opposed to an ILP) resulted in SLP subject effects. We also found that adding a specific argument to an otherwise individual-level predicate facilitated SLP subject effects. That is, bare plurals are given an existential interpretation quite easily, and weak indefinites are acceptable in subject position. However, in each of these cases we found that the corresponding perceptual report turned out to be unacceptable. These sets of data are extremely revealing about the nature of a successful account of the ILP/SLP distinction. Or should we say *distinctions*?

3.2 Two Possibilities, or Three

Two competing analyses seem plausible at this point, and so we will take them up here. Let us assume, for this discussion, Kratzer's idea that SLPs are located in space-time and ILPs are not. Then each of the crucial examples in this chapter involves an attempt to take an unlocated head and add a location to it by some means. In other words, it is an attempt to derive a SLP *compositionally*. Assuming this for the moment, we can ask what is shown by the failure of perceptual reports to pattern with the subject effects. There are three possibilities: (1) the subject effects are completely determined by the presence of a location argument (assuming that the specificity effect can be analyzed in a fashion that is compatible with this), and there is some additional constraint on perceptual reports that has not been respected in the recalcitrant cases; or (2) the perceptual reports reflect the true categorization of the predicate, and pragmatic and contextual factors contribute to the SLP subject effects seen in this chapter; or (3) both these are partly right—there is an additional condition on perceptual reports, and contextual factors can contribute to weak construals of indefinite subjects.

3.2.1 Compositionality

To sort this out, we will bring another diagnostic into the discussion. We concluded earlier that SLPs can delimit cases for quantification and that ILPs cannot. In Kratzer's and Deising's analyses, this distinction is formalized by the presence or absence of the spatiotemporal variable. Seeing whether quantification is allowed by particular predicates should help us decide among the three possible kinds of analyses just mentioned.

First, we consider predicates with raising heads:

(90) a. Whenever volunteers were sought for the campground chores, Robin seemed to be busy.
b. Seeming to be busy, Robin got out of doing a lot of chores.

(90a) clearly is a successful case of quantification, showing that the predicate *seemed to be busy* has a spatiotemporal variable. (90b) very naturally has a non-conditional reading, but it is also fairly easy to get the reading that when Robin seemed to be busy he got out of a lot of chores. We have suggested that *seem* has an interpretation that involves giving evidence on a particular occasion for having the property named by the embedded predicate. Thus, we also expect ILPs to be acceptable on this kind of reading, and they are:

(91) a. Whenever volunteers were sought for the campground chores, Robin seemed to know only Chinese.
b. Seeming to know only Chinese, Robin got out of a lot of chores.

Next are cases with a different raising head:

(92) a. Whenever volunteers were sought for the campground chores, Robin was likely to be busy.
b. ??Likely to be busy, Robin got out of doing a lot of chores.

The first example above is a successful quantification. (92b) sounds odd and so does not tell us anything about whether the predicate has a spatiotemporal argument. It can be improved as follows:

(93) a. Always likely to be busy, Robin got out of a lot of chores.
b. Likely to be busy when volunteers were sought, Robin got out of a lot of chores.

However, these are not quantifications involving the two clauses with the adjunct as the restriction: (93a), for example, does not have a conditional reading but entails that Robin was always likely to be busy and that Robin got out of a lot of chores. Since quantificational readings are not possible in (93), it is clear that the adjunct has no free variable available for a higher quantifier to bind. However, the lack of a free variable is due to the presence of a quantifier within the adjunct itself. (93a) contains *always*, and (93b) has a null generic.

Below, for contrast, are examples with ILPs:

(94) a. Likely to know only Tzotzil, Leslie might have trouble traveling in China. (no conditional)
b. With Leslie likely to know only Tzotzil, she might have trouble traveling in China. (no conditional)

We conclude that SLPs under raising heads do indeed contribute a spatiotemporal variable to the logical representation. Given this conclusion, the fact that raising predicates are sometimes odd in a perceptual report must be due to something else.

We turn now to consideration of control cases. Below, SLPs appear in the adjuncts as complements to *want* or *wanting*:

(95) a. When Sam wants to eat, he steals shrimp cocktails.
 b. Wanting to eat supper, Sam steals shrimp cocktails. (conditional possible)

I find that readings in which the adjunct is taken as the restriction of the modal are clearly possible for these examples. Below we consider cases of embedded ILPs for contrast:

(96) a. ?When Sam wants to be skillful, he spends long hours in the lab.
 b. Wanting to be skillful, Sam spends long hours in the lab.

The question mark for (96a) is intended to indicate the sort of reading one gets when using an ILP in a *when* adjunct; (96b) does not have a conditional reading. These examples indicate that *want to be skillful* does not contribute a spatiotemporal variable to allow quantification. As with raising, we conclude that a SLP embedded under a raising head does contribute a variable to the logical representation, and any oddness associated with using such a predicate in a perceptual report must be due to an additional grammatical requirement on the perceptual report.

Next we look at propositional attitudes:

(97) a. When Elizabeth believes she is ready, we can open the operating room.
 b. With surgeons believing that they are ready, we can open the operating room.

(98) a. ??When Elizabeth believes she is intelligent, we can open the operating room.
 b. ??With surgeons believing that they are intelligent, we can open the operating room.

There is a clear contrast between the embedded SLPs in (97) and the embedded ILPs in (98). (97a) involves an inchoative reading for the predicate, and we can conclude that such a reading is simply easier to obtain when a proposition contains a SLP than when it contains an ILP. (97b), however, is not inchoative, and so it is a very interesting case. It suggests that the matrix VP contributes a variable to the logical representation on its own. But if this were so, we would expect this predicate to be acceptable in a perceptual report, and it is not, so again we will appeal to a constraint on perceptual reports. Repeated below are the relevant examples from (81):

(99) a. Surgeons believe that they are ready (for tonight's operation). (existential possible)
 b. Sm surgeons believe that they are ready (for tonight's operation).
 c. *I saw surgeons believe that they were ready (for tonight's operation).

Notice also that neither (99a) nor (99b) are inchoative. The examples in (97) and (98) raise questions about when inchoative coercion can and cannot occur, but we will not answer these here. And we will find it difficult to treat the predicates in (99) as compositionally derived SLPs, so we will look for an alternative explanation for these cases.

Our efforts to test the compositionality hypothesis has suggested that two factors are involved with the data. Quite clearly, SLPs embedded under raising or control heads contribute a variable for quantification, and certain embedded full clauses seem to as well. All of these were odd in perceptual reports, and this requires an explanation.

3.2.2 Perceivability

If we take the line that some of the examples in the previous section indicate that SLPs can be derived compositionally, we will need an explanation of the fact that they are not acceptable in perceptual reports. Since perceptual reports entail that the eventuality denoted by the small clause is perceived (or not, of course, if the sentence is negative) by the subject, we would actually expect bizarreness to result from placing something imperceivable in the small clause. Recall that there is more to it than this, since we have the contrast below:

(100) a. I saw Lisa tower over her friends. (SLP)
 b. *I saw Lisa taller than her friends. (ILP)

(101) a. I saw Lisa reach a decision. (SLP)
 b. *I saw Lisa know the answer. (ILP)

The perceivability requirement cannot explain why the (b) examples are not acceptable, and for this reason we posited in the first place that ILPs were ungrammatical in perceptual reports. Now we must notice that there are some eventualities that can be described by SLPs but that nevertheless are not perceivable in the manner described by the verb. Fairly obvious examples can be obtained by changing the perception verb:

(102) a. I saw Lisa tower over her friends.
 b. #Robin saw Lisa sing at the other end of the telephone line.
 c. Dave saw Liz slam the door.

(103) a. #I heard Lisa tower over her friends.
 b. Robin heard Lisa sing at the other end of the telephone line.
 c. Dave heard Liz slam the door.

As is customary, the crosshatch indicates that the sentence is semantically bizarre. The small clause in the (a) examples reports an eventuality that can be seen but not heard, and vice versa for (b).[4] The eventuality described in the (c) examples is perceivable in either way. Thus, it follows from the meaning of the perception verb that the eventuality denoted by the small clause complement must be perceivable in the manner indicated by the verb, or else the sentence will be bizarre. Additional support for this comes from the native-speaker intuition that for (101a) to be true, Lisa must make some gesture that indicates she reached a decision. It is not required that the seer know that a decision was reached at that time, although the speaker must know this by speech time. To see this, consider the following:

(104) a. Eleda heard Marena order a hamburger, even though she did it in Hopi (and Eleda doesn't speak Hopi).
 b. I saw Lisa order a hamburger, even though I couldn't tell what she was doing at the time.

Both of these are perfectly acceptable as long as the speaker eventually knows what Lisa was doing by the time the sentence is uttered, and as long as Eleda saw Marena give some evidence for what she was doing. Note that the following are contradictory:

(105) a. →← I saw Lisa order a hamburger, even though I couldn't see her.
 b. →← I saw Lisa order a hamburger, even though I couldn't see her doing anything.

Accepting this, we now must consider whether we can explain any of the recalcitrant perceptual-report data on these grounds. Below are the crucial cases that require explaining:

(106) a. *I saw John likely to go into the field.
 b. ??I saw someone want to eat supper.
 c. *I saw surgeons believe that they were ready (for tonight's operation).
 d. ?I saw Leslie skillful enough to please most any audience.
 e. *I saw Robin own that house.
 f. *I saw Robin similar to these senators.

Let us assume that the small clause predicates in (106) are all compositionally derived SLPs. Can we take the sentences in (106) to be bizarre on the grounds that they cannot be perceived by seeing? This strikes me as plausible for most of the cases. Concerning (a), "likeliness to go into the field" is not something that is ordinarily thought of as perceivable. On the other hand, suppose the speaker knows John very well, and knows that when John scratches his head in a certain manner, he usually heads for the field right away; then suppose the speaker saw John scratch his head in this manner. I take it that (106a) could be used under such circumstances, and perhaps a similar story can be concocted for (106b). And recall that (106a) and (106b) are the examples for which we most need an explanation, since they suggest most strongly that the predicate is a compositionally derived SLP. It may even be possible to say (106c) on an inchoative reading, in a manner similar to (106a) and (106b) (recall that inchoatives are change-of-state SLPs and are distinct from interruption readings, which are ILPs). (106d) is fairly acceptable on an evidential coercion reading. So the strategy we have taken thus far is that the examples in (106a)–(106d) contain derived SLPs but that they are not ungrammatical—they simply express complex eventualities that are so unlikely as to render the sentences fairly useless.

Let us compare (106e) with the example shown below:

(107) I saw that Robin owned that house.

Sentence (107), of course, is factive rather than veridical. Thus, the speaker must have evidence that Robin owns the house, but there is no entailment that the speaker ever actually saw Robin. So (107) can be true, for example, if the speaker saw the deed to the house and saw Robin's name in the appropriate place. Why is it that seeing Robin's name on the deed is not sufficient visual evidence to say (106e)? One reason is that perceptual reports require that the small clause subject be perceived by the root clause subject. But then, why wouldn't it be sufficient for the speaker to see the deed and to see Robin at the same time?

Specificity has little to do with the issue involved in (106e), or (106f), for that matter. We could have made the same claims about the perceivability of (106e) and (106f) if they contained indefinite arguments. And we would say that these indefinite counterparts are ungrammatical in perceptual reports simply because they are ILPs. I think we are better off rejecting the idea that (106e) and (106f) contain SLPs. Indeed, we found no evidence above that they help a predicate to form a quantifier restriction. For (106e) to be usable, it must be possible to see Robin in the flesh as a participant in a *located* eventuality. Ownership simply isn't located, whether we are talking about a particular building or about some building or other. I think that the same considerations apply to similarity. Even though similarity to a particular individual is perceivable, (106f) is unacceptable because similarity isn't a located eventuality.

It is also significant that these examples do not allow Evidential Coercion. This is only partly explained by our characterization of Evidential Coercion. We have said that it requires a stage-level *behavior* to support the inference that the ILP holds of the subject. It seems intuitive, but not fully convincing, to claim that physically holding a deed with one's name on it is not a behavior sufficient to support the inference of ownership, or that standing next to a person one resembles is not a behavior sufficient to support the inference of similarity. These examples strike me as showing where the boundary of Evidential Coercion lies: they are just over it. But explaining exactly why that is the boundary is quite challenging. It is even possible that, coercion being a pragmatic effect, there is no absolute boundary.

We conclude from this discussion that the raising and control cases involve composition, and possibly even the propositional attitude cases do; and we have an explanation for the oddness of these predicates in perceptual reports based on the meanings of the perception verbs themselves. However, we have found that the perceivability requirement cannot explain (106e) and (106f), so we conclude that the specificity effect is not a factor in composing SLPs. Thus, we need some other explanation for the interaction of specificity with the subject effects. This is the subject of the following section.

3.2.3 Specificity Effect

An alternative approach is to assume that existential readings arise by inference. The idea is that if an eventuality is sufficiently situated, then it can be inferred that the participants in it exist. Glasbey (1997) takes this approach and shows some very nice data in which a bare plural sentence seems not to have an existential reading when uttered in isolation, but when given sufficient context, it quite easily allows one:

(108) a. Drinkers were under-age.
    b. I was shocked to discover in the Red Lion last night that drinkers were under-age.

(109) a. Ministers are gay.
    b. In this church, ministers are gay.

Glasbey proposes that these are cases of a pragmatic phenomenon she calls "existential inference." Glasbey implements her proposal in situation semantics, building on Barwise and Cooper (1993). When an eventuality is "situated," the participants in it are entailed to exist. Things can become vague when we try to discern exactly when a given eventuality is adequately situated. In canonical cases, the eventualities are entailed to be situated, and so we have an entailment of existence that follows automatically. In other cases, I take it that the situatedness is a matter of inference, and so the entailment of existence is indirect, following from the inference rather than directly from the truth conditions of the sentence. As is nearly always the case with pragmatics, it would be nice if things could be a little more precise and independently verifiable. However, I believe Glasbey is on the right track for the examples she discusses, which include *Monkeys live in that tree*. With this sentence, the specificity of the tree being referred to is sufficient to situate the proposition and allow the existential inference.

Perhaps this approach could be extended to cover the propositional attitude cases. We will take up this issue in the next chapter. If it can, then Deising's theory could appeal to it.

3.2.4 A Consequence for Copula Effects

Given our conclusions, we no longer are required to believe that every unacceptable perceptual report is odd because it contains an ILP. This might allow us to deflect an issue that Stump (1985) encountered. Stump noticed that some adjectives are acceptable in perceptual reports with or without *be*, that others are acceptable only with *be*, and that still others are acceptable only with *be*, and then there are the ordinary ILPs that are unacceptable with or without *be* (Stump 1985:74):

(110) a. I saw Robin (being) arrested.
I saw Robin (being) hit.
I saw Robin (being) kissed.
b. I saw Robin *(being) a bastard.
I saw Robin *(being) a hero.
I saw Robin *(being) polite.
I saw Robin *(being) paranoid.
c. I saw Robin (*being) drunk.
I saw Robin (*being) alone.
I saw Robin (*being) sick in bed.
I saw Robin (*being) naked.
I saw Robin (*being) in his maroon suit and white shoes.
I saw Robin (*being) on a stage.
d. *I saw Robin (being) intelligent.
*I saw Robin (being) a sailor.
*I saw Robin (being) from Wales.
*I saw Robin (being) fat.

Stump took the perceptual report as an absolute diagnostic for the ILP/SLP distinction. The data above forced the conclusion that, for example, although *drunk* is stage-level, *be drunk* is individual-level. In his analysis, four forms of *be* are necessary—one to map SLPs to SLPs, one to map ILPs to ILPs, one to map SLPs to ILPs, and a final one to map ILPs to SLPs.

Because we are assuming that ungrammaticality in a perceptual report does not necessarily indicate that the embedded predicate is individual-level, we can draw different conclusions from the data in (110). First, we note that the examples in (110b) that have *be* followed by an ILP are cases of Evidential Coercion. Indeed, Stump notes that they have exactly this sort of interpretation. The data in (110d) are less successful attempts at evidential coercion. The ungrammaticality asterisks shown with these examples are consistent with Stump's judgment, but I do not find some of them all that bad. A gradation of acceptability is just what we expect to find from a pragmatic effect like Evidential Coercion.

The examples in (c) are the ones we really need to explain. These are stative stage-level predicates, but they become unacceptable in perceptual reports when they appear with *being*. But *being* carries progressive aspect, which is not normally acceptable with stative predicates. It is acceptable with the examples in (b) because they can be construed as activity descriptions; but it is hard to construe the (c) examples in this way, so they are degraded.

4. Conclusion

In this chapter we have seen evidence that SLPs can be compositionally determined. There are some predicates that appear to be necessarily stage-level due to a lexical requirement. It is clear, however, that having a head, which by itself would constitute an ILP, is not sufficient to guarantee that the whole predicate will exhibit ILP effects. At least under certain circumstances, a SLP in a complement or adjunct position can result in SLP subject effects for the matrix clause.

Carlson (1977) notes that there are lexical differences between heads based not only on the sort of entity that they have as a subject, but also on the sort of entity the head has as its other arguments. Thus, *hit, find*, and *near* are of type $<e^s,<e^s,t>,>$, and *fear* and *hate* are of type $<e^i,<e^o,t>,>$. The investigation in this section has shown variation among heads with clausal complements with respect to whether the clauses contain ILPs or SLPs. An adequate account will need to allow this kind of lexical variation.

In this chapter, we have also found reason to believe both in a specificity effect and in a perceivability constraint. The specificity effect seems to be a pragmatic inference that indefinitely described entities exist in the universe of discourse. The perceivability constraint emerged from the recognition that not every SLP is equally acceptable in a description of a perceived event.

Finally, the data considered in this chapter pose considerable challenges for the Deising/Kratzer Mapping Hypothesis. While there is certainly a mapping from syntax to meaning, the Mapping Hypothesis does not capture all the cases in which a bare plural subject can have an existential interpretation. Despite this, we have repeatedly found it useful to maintain that SLPs have a logical location argument that ILPs lack. This will be the cornerstone of the analysis developed in the next chapter.

7

Of Time and Predicates

1. Predicates

1.1 A Type-Theoretic Distinction

In chapter 5 we saw two reasons to accept part of the Diesing/Kratzer analysis that there is a type-theoretic difference between ILPs and SLPs: SLPs have some sort of argument that ILPs lack. One reason was that SLPs delimit cases for quantification independent of whether their arguments do, and ILPs do not; the other reason was that SLPs are anaphoric and ILPs are not. Of course, this does not necessitate a type-theoretic distinction, but once we need one independently, we can put it to work to take care of the donkey sentences. From this discussion, we concluded that a dynamic account is called for. In the last chapter, we also saw reason to reject the other part of the Diesing/Kratzer analysis—the Mapping Hypothesis. Furthermore, we saw that the ILP/SLP distinction must be visible to the grammar at the clause level. And we saw reason to accept both de Hoop and de Swart's (1989) plurality condition on adverbial quantification, and Kratzer's (1988) prohibition against vacuous quantification. Finally, we concluded that a compositional account of SLPs is required which will allow a spatiotemporally located embedded predicate to determine the status of a matrix predicate. These observations will serve as the basis for our analysis.

Time has figured prominently in characterizations of the ILP/SLP distinction. It is commonly assumed (Milsark 1974, Carlson 1977, Stump 1985, Gawron 1986, Kratzer 1988, Diesing 1992, Chierchia 1995) that ILPs are timeless properties and that SLPs are necessarily anchored in space and time. Kratzer (1988) assumes, without making much of it, that there is a type-theoretic distinction between ILPs and SLPs. SLPs, when saturated, have an extra location argument that ILPs lack. Below are two sentences and the logical interpretations assigned to them by Kratzer's theory:

(1) Robin is asleep.   ∃l asleep'(r,l)   SLP

(2) Robin is a football player.   football-player'(r)   ILP

Since the predicates have different argument structures, they must have different logical types. ILPs are assigned the traditional Montagovian property type <e,t>. But SLPs must combine with a spatiotemporal argument as well as with an entity in order to be saturated. There are two possible types that can be assigned to them: <e,<l,t>> or <l,<e,t>>. I will assume the latter and discuss its alternative in section 3. This type-theoretic distinction is very powerful, and many of the differences between ILPs and SLPs can be explained by this assumption alone. For this analysis, we will disregard the spatio- portion of spatiotemporal, and simply investigate the consequences of positing that SLPs have a temporal argument and that ILPs do not. We also assume that the extra argument of SLPs is not Davidsonian, leaving open the possibility that all predicates have Davidsonian arguments—which Parsons (1990) and de Swart (1991) have found some evidence for believing.

Although I have argued that the ILP/SLP effects are not simply due to a classification of the head of the predicate, predicate heads will be assumed to be underlyingly classified, but it will be made possible for an ILP head to allow SLP effects under the right circumstances.

1.2 Dynamic Interpretations

As we saw in the previous chapter, SLPs display properties of pronouns in that they can be used deictically or anaphorically. And we saw that ILPs do not do this. Suppose that SLPs were definite descriptions of temporal intervals. As such, to assume further that their interpretations include discourse markers associated with temporal locations would be consistent with the assumptions of dynamic semantics. A dynamic adverb of quantification could introduce the discourse referent that is picked up by the SLP in question, or a referent could be supplied by the context or accommodated. This proposal needs to be complicated slightly, because it is counterintuitive to suppose that all SLPs in a discourse pick up exactly the same location discourse referent (cf. *Robin walked in, sat down, and fell asleep*). As Hinrichs (1986) notes, accomplishments and achievements can introduce new reference times in the progression of a discourse, although there is an interaction between Aktionsart and aspect, since the progressive does not allow a new reference time to be introduced. (See Hinrichs 1986 for a discussion of other shifters of reference time.) Atelic sentences, whether they contain ILPs, SLPs, or KLPs, do not shift reference time. What is needed for achievements and accomplishments is something that picks up the current discourse referent and moves one step forward in time (possibly changing the spatial location). Something along these lines is introduced for Discourse Representation Theory in Hinrichs (1986) and Kamp and Ryle (1993). These SLPs combine the characteristics of a definite description in picking up a previously established referent with the ability of an indefinite to introduce a new referent. Thus, telic SLPs are not pure definite descriptions which introduce a new discourse referent without picking up a previously established one; atelic SLPs are, however.

In order to treat SLPs in a manner consistent with the dynamic treatment of anaphora, we will assume the following type assignments:

(3) Stage-level predicates
  dance $<l,<e,cc>>$
  hit $<e,<l,<e,cc>>>$

(4) Individual-level predicates
  be intelligent $<e,cc>$
  own $<e,<e,cc>>$

The type cc is the propositional type for dynamic semantics, mnemonic for "context change" (Chierchia 1992). We will assume that the l arguments are interpreted using discourse referents in the manner that type e arguments are. Thus, they will have the capacity to pick up previously established referents whether they are used deictically or anaphorically. I will assume that tense is what provides the temporal argument for SLPs. Of course, such an assumption requires an explanation of what function tense has with ILPs; we will take up this issue after filling in some of the details of the analysis.

1.3 The Basis of the Clause-Level Distinction

It is easy to see that by positing this sort of type-theoretic distinction between ILPs and SLPs, we can very quickly provide a solution to one of the problems raised in the previous chapter: the fact that the ILP/SLP distinction must be visible at the clause level. If we assign SLPs the type $<l,<e,cc>>$, and provide them with means to compose with their subject arguments, the result will be of type $<l, cc>$, a function from times to context changes. By contrast, ILPs are of the traditional predicate type, $<e,cc>$. Once they compose with their arguments, the result will simply be of type cc. Thus, a subject SLP combination will be of a different type from a subject ILP combination, opening the door for an account of perceptual reports and augmented absolute adjuncts:

(5) see $<<l,cc>,<l,<e,cc>>>$

(6)
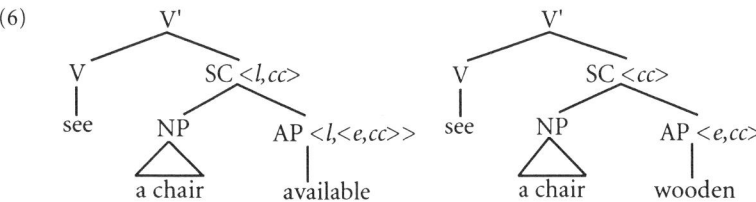

(7) Augmented Absolutes
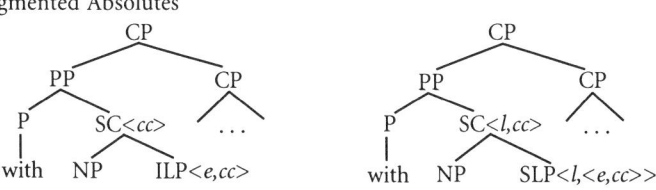

Functional application is the most fundamental way of composing meanings in model-theoretic semantics:

(8) Functional Application
Syntax: If α is of type <a,b> and δ is of type a, then $f_1(α,δ)$ is of type b.
Semantics: If α is of type <s,<a,b>> and δ is of type a, and α and δ translate into α' and δ' respectively, then $f_1(α,δ)$ translates into α'(^δ').

It is not sufficient for us simply to rely on function application for our purposes, because the temporal argument within the small clause needs to be controlled by the matrix clause. I noted above that Kratzer's and Diesing's logical representations would be consistent with SLPs having either type <e,<l,t>> or type <l,<e,t>>. We will now consider each of these possibilities.

1.3.1 <l,<e,cc>>

The inflectional element of a sentence in English has a variety of effects on the interpretation of the sentence. Aspectual information is arrived at compositionally, as Verkuyl (1972) showed, and tense makes a separate contribution to the interpretation of a sentence. However, I will assume for simplicity that there is a single inflectional node in a syntactic tree, and that tense and aspect have already composed into a unified interpretation at this node. In this discussion, I will represent the times of event, reference, and speech as t_E, t_R, and t_S respectively. I will assume that *Judy was asleep* has the interpretation in (9b):

(9) a. Judy was asleep.
   b. $\lambda p \exists t_R[\text{asleep}'(t_E)(j) \& t_R < t_S \& t_E = t_R \& \{t_E/d\} \vee p]$

In the usual dynamic fashion, we can get a truth condition for this formula (with respect to a model) by applying the tautologous proposition as in (10a), which reduces to the saturated formula in (10b):

(10) a. $\lambda p \exists t_R[\text{asleep}'(t_E)(j) \& t_R < t_S \& t_E = t_R \& \{t_E/d\} \vee p]$ (^**true**)
    b. $\exists t_R[\text{asleep}'(t_E)(j) \& t_R < t_S \& t_E = t_R]$

I will assume the following type assignment for variables in this discussion:

Types

Variable	Type		
x, y	e		
P, Q	<s,<e,cc>>		
T, U	<s,<l,<e,cc>>>		
𝒫, 𝒬	<s,<<s,<e,cc>>,cc>>	or	NP
𝒱, 𝒳	<<s,<<s,<e,cc>>,cc>>,cc>	or	<NP,cc>
𝒰, 𝒲	<l,<<s,<<s,<e,cc>>,cc>>,cc>>	or	<l,<NP,cc>>
t, l	l (a sort of type e)		

Let us now see what an analysis would look like if we assume <l,<e,cc>> is the type of SLPs.[1] I assume that times are a sort of entity and so can be values for temporal sorts of discourse markers without adding any machinery to Dynamic Montague

Grammar. I further assume that tense is what introduces a temporal discourse marker (indicated by d^t) that fills the extra argument position of SLPs. Given our current choice of type assignment, tense will combine with the predicate to yield an interpretation of type $<e,cc>$, which can then compose with the interpretation of the predicate's subject. Working from (9b), we can get the interpretation of the simple past tense by abstracting first over the subject and then over the predicate. We also make a distinction between the deictic and the anaphoric use of tense:

(11) a. Simple deictic past$_i$ for SLPs $\Rightarrow$
$\lambda T \lambda x [^{\vee}T(d_i^t)(x); \lambda p \exists t_R [t_R < t_S \; \& \; d_i^t = t_R \; \& \; ^{\vee}p]]$
b. Simple anaphoric past$_i$ for SLPs $\Rightarrow$
$\lambda T \lambda x [^{\vee}T(d_i^t)(x) \; \& \; REL \; (d_i^t, d_j^t); \lambda p \exists t_R [t_R < t_S \; \& \; d_i^t = t_R \; \& \; ^{\vee}p]]$,
where d_i^t is a novel event time and d_j^t is a familiar reference time.

In (11), t_S indicates speech time and is left free since it will be bound by context. The reference time t_R is bound by an existential quantifier. The discourse marker d_i^t represents the event time. As I have argued, the anaphoric use of SLPs combines the qualities of definite and indefinite descriptions, and this is why (11b) includes two discourse markers. *REL* is a relation between these two times that is intended to shift the reference time of the discourse in a manner determined by Hinrich's generalizations (1986:81):

(12) The reference point of a discourse can be shifted by:
(a) the Aktionsart of a main clause; accomplishments and achievements introduce new reference points, while states, activities and events described in the progressive do not.
(b) the use of temporal conjunctions.
(c) the use of flexible anchoring adverbials and dependent adverbials.

Clearly *REL* is a complicated relation and it merits further study, but I will not continue with it here. What is crucial for our analysis is that the interpretation of tense involves discourse markers when SLPs are present. This will allow the reference times in subsequent utterances to refer to them.

The meanings in (11) can compose with a SLP meaning by ordinary function application. The resulting meaning is of type $<e,cc>$, which can be taken as an argument of a subject meaning, again by functional application.

This account poses a challenge for perceptual reports. Since small clauses are tenseless, how are we to compose a meaning from the subject and predicate? It cannot be done by simple function composition because the types are not completely compatible. One possibility is to posit a Montague-style rule to perform the necessary predication:

(13) a. Syntax. If α is of type $<s,<<s,<e,cc>>,cc>>$ and δ is of type $<l,<e,cc>>$, then $f(\alpha,\delta)$ is of type $<l,cc>$.
b. Semantics. If α is of type $<s,<<s,<e,cc>>,cc>>$ and δ is of type $<l,<e,cc>>$, and α and δ translate into α' and δ' respectively, then $f(\alpha,\delta)$ translates into
$\lambda l [\alpha'\{^{\wedge}\delta'(l)\}]$.

No rule beyond ordinary function composition is needed for small clauses containing ILPs. (13) is an ordinary sort of Montagovian rule. The result is of type $<l,t>$.

The temporal argument will need to be filled by the matrix tense. This is consistent with our intuitions about perceptual reports: the perception and the perceived event are taken to be simultaneous.[2] We assume that *see* is of type $<<l,cc>,<l,<NP,cc>>>$, which allows it to combine only with small clause meanings that are described by SLPs. For *Robin saw Judy leave*, we get the following interpretation:

(14) $\lambda p \exists t_R [\text{see}'(r, \lambda l[\text{leave}'(l)(j)], d^t) \,\&\, t_R < t_S \,\&\, d^t = t_R \,\&\, {}^\vee p]$

The time represented by t_E is the time of seeing. We would like this interval to be taken as the argument of *leave*. This can be done either by a meaning postulate, as in (15), or by complicating the rule that composes *see* with its small clause complement, using (17) instead of function composition:

(15) MP: For all α of type $<<l,cc>,<l,<NP,cc>>>$, β of type e, γ of type $<l,cc>$, and δ of type e_l, interpreted as α', β', γ', and δ' respectively,
$[\alpha'(\beta', \gamma', \delta') \Leftrightarrow \alpha_{\#}'(\beta', \gamma'(\delta'), \delta')\,]$.

(Note that e_l is the type for temporal intervals, which I assume to be a sort of entity.) The formula below is the result of applying the meaning postulate to (14):

(16) $\lambda p [\text{see}'(r, \text{leave}'_{\#}(d^t)(j), d^t) \,\&\, \exists t_R [t_R < t_S \,\&\, d^t = t_R \,\&\, {}^\vee p]]$

An equivalent result can be obtained by applying the following rule of composition instead of (13):

(17) a. Syntax. If α is of type $<l,<NP,cc>>$ and δ is of type $<l,cc>$, then $f_2(\alpha, \delta)$ is of type $<l,t>$.

b. Semantics. If α is of type $<l,<NP,cc>>$ and δ is of type $<l,cc>$, and α and δ translate into α' and δ' respectively, then $f_2(\alpha, \delta)$ translates into $\lambda l [\alpha'(\delta'(l))(l)]$.

Either choice is descriptively adequate, and each strikes me as equally ensuring that the event time of the perceived event will match that of the perceiving event. Still, this account offers a compositional way of distinguishing ILPs from SLPs at the small clause level. We will see that this can also be done given the other choice of type assignment.

The proposal sketched here provides the interpretation in (18b) for the discourse in (18a):

(18) a. A woman woke up. She turned on the light. (=33b)
b. $\lambda p \exists x [\text{woman}'(x) \,\&\, \text{woke-up}'(d_1^t)(x) \,\&\, \exists t_R [t_R < t_S \,\&\, d_1^t = t_R \,\&\, \text{turn-on-light}'(d_1^t)(x) \,\&\, \text{REL}(d_1^t),(d_2^t) \,\&\, \exists t_R' [t_R' < t_S \,\&\, d_2^t = t_R' \,\&\, {}^\vee p]$

Discourse markers remain in this expression since I assume the act of deixis supplies the referent. Example (18b), out of context, is analogous to *She left* out of context: one doesn't know the referent of *she*. The theory of Groenendijk and Stokhof (1990) would interpret *She$_i$ left* as $\lambda p [\text{left}'(d_i) \,\&\, {}^\vee p]$. If this sentence were uttered in context, a state-switcher introduced in a previous utterance would replace d_i with a variable or a constant. Or the referent could be supplied by deixis, although Groenendijk and Stokhof do not go into this. The case with (18) is just the same: the referent can be supplied by deixis or by a previous utterance. In the case of adverbial quantification, the quantifier will supply the referent by means of a state-switcher. For example, we can assign *sometimes* the interpretation in (19a), which is equivalent to the interpretation in (19b):

(19) a. sometimes$_i$ $\Rightarrow \lambda P \lambda Q \exists d_i^t [^\vee P(d_i^t); ^\vee Q(d_i^t)]$
b. $\lambda P \lambda Q \exists t \{t/d_3^t\} [^\vee P(d_1^t); ^\vee Q(d_2^t)]$
 & turn-on-light $(d_2^t)(x)$ & REL (d_1^t, d_2^t) & $\exists t_R [t_R < t_S$ & $d_2^t = t_R$ & $^\vee p]]]$

So far I have not said much about tense with ILPs. Certainly ILPs occur in tensed clauses! I have claimed that tense is used to locate the event time of SLPs, but it cannot do the same thing for ILPs since ILPs, by assumption, do not have event time. I propose that tense with ILPs serves to locate the time at which a propositional content of an utterance is to be evaluated. As before, I illustrate this with the simple past:

(20) Simple past$_{ILP}$ $\Rightarrow [\lambda P \lambda x [P\{x\}]]^{t_V}$ & $t_R = t_V$ & $t_R < t_S$

I will explain the motivation for this in section 2.5 after other groundwork is laid for it.

1.3.2 <e,<l,cc>>

The other type possibility for SLPs is <e,<l,cc>>. For this type assignment, composition within a small clause happens differently than with the first proposal:

(21) a. Syntax. If α is of type <s,<<s,<e,cc>>,cc>> and δ is of type <e,<l,cc>>, then $f_3(\alpha, \delta)$ is of type <l,cc>.
b. Semantics. If α is of type <s,<<s,<e,cc>>,cc>> and δ is of type <e,<l,cc>>, and α and δ translate into α' and δ' respectively, then $f_3(\alpha, \delta)$ translates into $\lambda l [\alpha' \{ ^\wedge \lambda y [\delta'(y)(l)]\}]$.

This rule allows the SLP to compose with the nominal expression. This account uses a rule similar to (17) which was used in the previous account to compose the perception verb with its small clause complement. The only difference is that the subject argument of the perception verb is abstracted over to get it in the right order with respect to the temporal argument so that it matches the type of the verb:

(22) a. Syntax. If α is of type <NP,<l,cc>> and d is of type <l,cc>, then $f_2(\alpha, \delta)$ is of type <l,cc>.
b. Semantics. If α is of type <NP,<l,cc>> and δ is of type <l,cc>, and α and δ translate into α' and δ' respectively, then $f_2(\alpha, \delta)$ translates into $\lambda l \lambda x [\alpha' (\delta'(l))(x)(l)]$.

The same basic meanings assigned to the inflectional element in the previous account work for this account as well. Both the small clause composition rule and the VP composition rules are slightly more complex in this account, because this one must provide an entity argument and then abstract over it. For this reason, I adopt the previous account.

1.3.3 Conclusion

On both these accounts, SLPs need special help to compose with their subjects and ILPs do not. Nevertheless, both offer compositional accounts of the fact that the

ILP/SLP distinction can be visible at the small clause level. But if the temporal argument of an SLP is bound within a clause by a quantifier, the type-theoretic distinction is lost at the clause level: a bound SLP-based clause will be of the same type as an ILP-based clause, predicting that bound SLP-based clauses will not be able to compose with perception verbs. This is found to be the case:

(23) a. I saw Kari leave.
      b. *I saw Kari always leave.

We have here strong confirmation that a type-theoretic distinction is what is needed.

So far, we have not explained what role tense plays when it composes with ILPs. Clearly, we cannot say that it does the same thing as what is shown in (11). I will claim that tense with ILPs serves to locate the evaluation time for the propositional content of the sentence in which the ILP appears. We will take this up again later in this chapter.

We can see now that it is crucial to this analysis that the interpretations of SLPs do not emerge from the lexicon with their *l*-arguments already filled; if we were to assume this, we would lose the clause-level distinction. Since we assume that tense is what provides the temporal argument for SLPs, and since small clauses are tenseless, the type-theoretic distinction will be maintained for small clauses but not for full clauses.

1.4 Syntactically complex predicates

In the previous chapter, I argued that raising heads tend to be transparent with respect to the level effects of the predicates contained in their complements. This proposal provides a way of allowing the type of the complement to determine the type of the predicate headed by the raising verb. Raising verbs are systematically assigned two types, accepting a stage-level or individual-level complement, as shown below (following Klein and Sag 1985):

(24) $likely_{ILP}$ a. <<NP,cc>,<NP,cc>>
                  b. $\lambda \mathcal{V} \lambda \mathcal{P}[likely_I^+ (\mathcal{V}(\mathcal{P}))]$

(25) $likely_{SLP}$ a. <<l,<NP,cc>>,<l,<NP,cc>>>
                  b. $\lambda \mathcal{U} \lambda l \lambda \mathcal{P}[likely_S^+ (\mathcal{U}(l)(\mathcal{P}))]$

The types shown in (a) in each case correspond to the relation named by the adjective. In (b), I have shown the translation associated with the adjective after the raising schematic operator posited by Klein and Sag (1985:187) has applied to it.

In the previous chapter I provided a lexical decomposition analysis of the meaning of *seem* and *appear* using Carlson's formalism. Here is a version for the theory I am proposing:

(26) $seem_1$ / $appear_1$ a. <<NP,cc>,<l,<NP,cc>>>
                          b. $\lambda \mathcal{V} \lambda l \lambda \mathcal{P} \exists \mathcal{W}[perceive' (\mathcal{W}(l)(\mathcal{P})) \& G_{y,t}(\mathcal{W}(l')(y')) [\mathcal{V}(y')]]$

(27) $seem_2$ / $appear_2$ a. <<l,<NP,cc>>,<l,<NP,cc>>>
                          b. $\lambda \mathcal{U} \lambda l \lambda P \exists \mathcal{W}[perceive'(\mathcal{W}(l)(P)) \& G_{y,t}(\mathcal{W}(l')(y')) [\mathcal{U}(l')(y')]]$

These verbs, I have argued, always result in a SLP after they compose with their complements. The version in (26) accepts ILP complements, and the version in (27) accepts SLP complements.

Control predicates are of the same semantic type as raising predicates in standard Montagovian treatments (Klein and Sag 1985, Dowty 1985, Jacobson 1990). The differences between them are dealt with in their interpretations. Thus, *want* will have the same pair of type assignments as *likely*, allowing it to be transparent as well:

(28) $want_{ILP}$ a. <<NP,cc>,<NP,cc>>
   b. $\lambda \mathcal{V} \lambda \mathcal{P}[\mathcal{P}\{^\wedge \lambda x[want_I' \ (\mathcal{V}(x^{\cdot}))(x^{\cdot})]\}]$

(29) $want_{SLP}$ a. <<l,<NP,cc>>,<l,<NP,cc>>>
   b. $\lambda \mathcal{U} \lambda l \lambda \mathcal{P}[\mathcal{P}\{^\wedge \lambda x[want_s' \ (\mathcal{U}(l)(x^{\cdot}))(x^{\cdot})]\}]$

The translations in (b) result from applying the Equi schematic operator from Klein and Sag (1985:187).

Finally, we wish to account for some of the predicate adjunction cases we have considered. I concluded somewhat tentatively that *enough* can combine either SLPs or ILPs in the adjoined clause (although the latter tend to be odd, for reasons I did not determine), that either sort of predicate can be modified by *enough*, and that the result of modification is a SLP. Let us assume that *enough* is a relation between the denotation of its complement (the "purpose") and the denotation of the head it modifies. For example, *Rochelle was skillful enough to please the audience* should have the following interpretation (after saturation by the tautologous proposition):

(30) $\exists x,l[$enough' (to-please-the audience'$(l)(x))($skillful'$(r))]$

The following type assignments and translations for *enough* allow it to have a SLP as its first argument and any sort of predicate as its second, and to yield something that is a SLP:

(31) $enough_1$ a. <<l,<NP,cc>>,<<NP,cc>,<l,<NP,cc>>>>
   b. $\lambda \mathcal{U} \lambda \mathcal{V} \lambda l \lambda \mathcal{P}[\mathcal{P}\{^\wedge \lambda x[enough_1' \ (\mathcal{U}(l)(x^{\cdot}))(\mathcal{V}(x^{\cdot}))]\}]$

(32) $enough_2$ a. <<l,<NP,cc>>,<<l,<NP,cc>>,<l,<NP,cc>>>>
   b. $\lambda \mathcal{U} \lambda \mathcal{W} \lambda l \lambda \mathcal{P}[\mathcal{P}\{^\wedge \lambda x[enough_2' \ (\mathcal{U}(l)(x^{\cdot}))(\mathcal{W}(l)(x^{\cdot}))]\}]$

The first type above allows the modifying phrase to adjoin to an ILP, and the second, to a SLP. Two additional translations will be needed if we decide to allow ILPs as the first argument of *enough*. There is certainly more to be said about controlled modifiers and their interaction with the ILP/SLP distinction, but (30) through (32) illustrate the potential that the current analysis offers.

The analysis presented here treats as a complete accident the fact that the predicates headed by *likely* and *want* have the same type as the predicate in the complement. Under some circumstances this should make us unhappy, but it turns out that there are various lexical items that require a complement to be of a certain level and that compose with it to yield a predicate of a different level.

Stump (1985) and Katz (1993) argue that *as* is a lexical item that has these characteristics. In the following sentences, *as* clearly has an ILP as its complement, since the complement is syntactically a NP:

(33) a. Laura saw Jean (as a sailor)/(drinking).
b. Steve hates Ruth (as a lecturer)/(wearing that hat).
c. Jokes about Jim (as a doctor)/(drunk) are funny.
d. There was a chair (as a conversation starter)/(in the room). (Katz's ex. 23)

Each of the environments in which the *as* predicate appears is arguably one that allows only SLPs. All this indicates that, at least some of the time, *as* takes an ILP complement and yields a SLP after composing with it. Katz formalizes his proposal in a manner consistent with Chierchia's (1992) treatment of the ILP/SLP distinction. The following type assignment allows Katz's proposal to be adapted to the current one:

(34) as   <<NP,cc>,<NP,<l,cc>>>

Another case that involves the selection of a predicate of one level to compose a predicate of another level is seen below:

(35) become   <<NP,cc>,<NP,<l,cc>>>

This type assignment allows *become* to take an ILP as its argument and yield a SLP.

If heads could only inherit the types of their complements we might worry more about the stipulative nature of the types assigned for the raising verbs. Since at least two heads can select a predicate of one level and compose with it to yield a predicate of a different level, it seems that the stipulations are justified. (Stump 1985, of course, had two copulas that yield the opposite type of the complement with which they compose.)

1.5 Tensed Clauses and an Alternative Analysis

We now turn our attention to heads that take complements that are full clauses. Since we have assumed that tense saturates a SLP, the type-theoretic distinction will not be visible at the clause level when tense is present in the clause. From our discussion of *believe*, we concluded that tensed embedded clauses can show ILP/SLP effects for the matrix subject, so an independent account is needed for these cases. Before we turn to that part of the proposal, it is worth considering an alternative account.

Suppose, instead of assuming that tense is what provides the l-argument for SLPs, that this argument is provided in discourse. (There would be cases in which a quantifier could provide the argument, Montague style, in which case this wouldn't happen at discourse, but we will focus on simpler cases.) If this were the case, the type-theoretic distinction between ILPs and SLPs would be maintained at the tensed clause level. From the discussion in the previous chapter, we concluded that *say* heads a SLP and can have any level of predicate in its complement. The following type assignment under our strawman assumption allows this:

(36) say   a. <<NP,<l,cc>>,<NP,<l,cc>>>
           b. <<NP,cc>,<NP,<l,cc>>>

Believe, on the other hand, would be transparent to the level of its complement. Assuming that the effects of referential nominals require an independent account, we can propose the following strawman entry for *believe*:

(37) believe   a. <<s,cc>,<NP,cc>>
                b. <<s,<l,cc>>,<NP,<l,cc>>>

This pair of type assignments would allow information to be maintained at the clause level about whether the complement proposition contains a spatiotemporal argument.

One unusual feature of the strawman analysis sketched here has to do with what happens when a propositional attitude verb has a SLP-based clause as its complement. In order to allow the presence of the spatiotemporal argument to be "passed up" to the matrix predicate, the denotation of the complement has to be a function from worlds to sets of spatiotemporal locations. This kind of function is not a proposition, of course; allowing attitudes to compose with this type of logical object means that technically we no longer have a propositional attitude. It is not clear what the attitude is being held of. However, there is probably no logical problem with doing things this way. We do not have a knock-down argument against the strawman—just a gripe about it.

Here is another gripe. Although the subject effects were sensitive to the status of a predicate embedded in a full clause, *see* consistently ignored it. We assumed that *see* selects its small clause complement based on its type; allowing the distinction in the type of the predicate to be preserved at the clause level provided an apparently natural way to account for cases involving simple predicates. *See* was assigned type <<l,cc>,<NP,<l,cc>>>, which required its small clause complements to be a set of spatiotemporal locations. We took pains to allow a raising verb with a SLP complement to denote the same type of object after it composes with its subject, and we did the same thing for other complex predicates. The effect of this, however, is that a predicate containing *likely* and a SLP complement is expected to be grammatical in a small clause complement to *see*. As we have seen, this is an incorrect prediction. However, recall from the discussion of the "perceivability constraint" in the previous chapter that we can rely on the meaning of *see* to take care of most, if not all, of the recalcitrant cases: *see* entails visual perception, and I argued that certain predicates which have a spatiotemporal argument do not describe perceivable eventualities.

To reject the strawman eliminates the type-theoretic distinction at the tensed clause level. It also means that we have two explanations for the unacceptability in a perceptual report of an unlocated head with a SLP embedded in a tensed clause complement: the predicate would not be of the appropriate type to compose with the perception verb, and it would violate the perceivability constraint. Rejecting the strawman also eliminates the question of what sort of thing one has an attitude toward when an attitude head has a SLP clause as its complement: the complement's denotation is a proposition. Neither one of these is a knock-down argument, but I feel my footing is firmer if I reject the strawman—assuming, of course, that an independent explanation is available for the subject effects with full clause complements. The next section develops support for a Glasbey-style analysis of the speci-

1.6 The Consequences of the Specificity Effect

We saw above that specific arguments of what (in Kratzer's terms) are unlocated heads can give rise to SLP subject effects. We took this as one of several pieces of evidence that the correct analysis of the SLP subject effects would not include the Mapping Hypothesis. We can learn more than this from the specificity effect. In our discussion of the prohibition against vacuous quantification, we saw that a satisfactory account will need to achieve the effect of SLPs having an extra variable (assuming a theoretical framework in which quantification is done with variables). Furthermore, our discussion of donkey anaphora supported this idea. We should notice right away that we do not want an account of the specificity effect in which a located nominal contributes a *variable* to the predicate of which it is an argument. This would not make any sense: since the nominal is referential, it cannot be treated as a free variable. This consideration emphasizes an important distinction in the conglomerate of effects that are bound up in the ILP/SLP distinction. The quantification effects—both those subject and those not subject to the Plurality Condition—have been analyzed as showing that SLPs have a *variable* that can be bound by a quantifier. This capability that SLPs have is distinct from the property of locatedness. Glasbey has argued explicitly that the latter is responsible for existential interpretations of bare plural subjects. The prediction, then, is that the specificity effect should allow SLP subject effects, but it should not enhance the ability of an ILP to restrict a quantifier. An ILP with a nonspecific argument should be as unsuccessful at restricting a quantifier as the same ILP with a specific argument. Below we will see that this is exactly what happens.

The prediction is a little difficult to test because the cases in the literature that are supposed to be unacceptable do not seem so bad. For example, Kratzer (1988) cites the following as ungrammatical (Kratzer's ex. 606):

(38) When Pedro has a donkey, he beats it.

Contrary to the prediction of the Mapping Hypothesis, this strikes me as a perfectly acceptable quantification over donkeys. For me, in Kratzer's terms, this sentence involves an "ill-behaved" object; however, I have difficulty finding well-behaved ones. Of course, if we change the indefinite to a definite description, we will lose the ability to quantify over donkeys:

(39) When Pedro has that donkey, he beats it.

Now we try to quantify over times at which Pedro has that donkey, and I find this very easy to do. Below are additional examples comparing an indefinite with a definite argument:

(40) a. When Koko lives in a tree, she is happy.
b. When Koko lives in that tree, she is happy.

(41) a. Living in a tree, Koko is happy.
b. Living in that tree, Koko is happy.

Either the ILPs in the *when* clauses of these sentences are very easily coerced, or it is easy to quantify over some temporal parameter other than the one supplied by SLPs. We will pursue the latter idea in the next section. The key point for testing the specificity effect is to note that, as predicted, substituting a specific argument for a nonspecific one does not make quantification any easier. The examples in (40) and (41) are equally capable of quantifying over some temporal parameter.

What predictions do we make about the specificity effect and perceptual reports? Because the specific/nonspecific distinction is not a type-theoretic one, our analysis of perceptual reports leads us not to expect the specificity effect to be relevant to perceptual reports. And although in the real world we have only direct perception of things that are specific, we have no trouble whatever with using indefinite descriptions in perceptual reports. Thus, we do not expect there to be any specificity effect in perceptual reports, and we predict that any predicate that is unacceptable in perceptual reports without a specific argument will remain unacceptable with a specific argument. This is exactly what we found in (88) and (89) in the previous chapter, repeated below:

(42) a. Tycoons own that house. (existential possible)
b. Sm tycoons own that house.
c. *I saw Robin own that house.

(43) a. Presidents are similar to these senators. (existential possible)
b. Sm presidents are similar to these senators.
c. *I saw Robin similar to these senators.

It could have turned out that situatedness in Glasbey's sense was what was required for perceptual reports as well as for the subject effects. But this turns out not to be the case, as the data show. Glasbey's notion of situatedness, along with our type-theoretic account of the SLP/ILP distinction, allows us to see why the perceptual reports diverge from the subject effects.

Before discussing situatedness as it pertains to propositional attitudes, we will examine a crucial consequence our proposal has for time and propositions.

2. Time

2.1 Timing Is Different

One of the most significant consequences of Kratzer's assumption that only SLPs have a temporal argument has been widely overlooked: time will be part of the propositional content of a sentence containing an SLP, but not of a sentence based on an ILP. Although I assume there is no type-theoretic difference between tensed clauses containing the two sorts of predicates, there is still a semantic difference based on the way time is involved in the two sorts of sentences.

To discuss this, I need to draw some ontological distinctions and define some terms. Considerations of indexicality have led to wide acceptance of the assumption that sentences do not denote propositions, but utterances of sentences do (see, e.g., Levinson 1983:58). Sentences express propositions only after the values of the indexicals have been fixed, and these values are deducible from an utterance. Propositions themselves are commonly held to be temporally rigid (see Frege's 1918 discussion of complete thoughts); that is, they have constant truth value over time with respect to a particular world. Given this view, the evaluation time of a proposition is part of the proposition itself. I need a way to abstract over the evaluation time of propositions so I can talk about the proposition minus its evaluation time. I will call this the "Content of a proposition" (and sometimes I will call it the "Content of an utterance"). The Content, then, includes values for indexicals other then evaluation time. I am not committed to the claim that any linguistic phenomenon corresponds to the Content in the way an utterance corresponds to a proposition and a sentence corresponds to a proposition. It is possible that the act of fixing of values for a particular indexical cannot be separated from the act of fixing values for all indexicals. I am simply going to use term as I have defined it, because it reveals a distinction among SLPs and ILPs. Given this definition, we can say the Content has a truth value with respect to a particular evaluation time. That is, by adding evaluation time to the Content, we get a proposition. And we can say that a proposition is expressed by asserting the Content with respect to an evaluation time. I will also want to talk about sentences that have ILPs and SLPs as their main predicates, and I will want to talk about their utterances, calling the first ILP-based sentences and utterances and the second SLP-based sentences and utterances. And I will sometimes want to talk about the propositions that correspond to these sentences when they are uttered. Thus, I will use the terms "ILP-based proposition" and "SLP-based proposition," but it is entirely possible that a single proposition could be both. That is, I will leave it as an open question whether a single proposition could be described by both an ILP-based sentence and a SLP-based sentence.

I will argue in section 8 that the temporal argument of SLPs corresponds to Reichenbach's event time and not to the evaluation time of a proposition. Giving SLPs a temporal argument has the effect of placing time within the possible Contents for an SLP-based sentences. When the Content is asserted to hold at an evaluation time, the event time is part of the assertion. However, time is not a constituent in the Content corresponding to an ILP-based sentence.

For expository purposes I would like to remove from consideration any sentence that contains an indexical other than the SLP temporal argument. And what I will say here about SLPs assumes that the temporal argument is used indexically rather than being bound by some operator. Cases in which the temporal argument is bound will more closely resemble what I say about ILPs. This will allow us to see a difference between SLP-based and ILP-based sentences. Given that indexicality is intrinsic to the many lexical items that have implicit arguments, the abstraction I have in mind may be nearly impossible in practice, but for this discussion we can imagine it is not. Our analysis allows multiple propositions to correspond to both ILP-based and SLP-based sentences (assuming always that a different evaluation time gives a different proposition), but it allows this in two different ways. SLP-based sentences will correspond to multiple Contents; this is because the only indexical permitted in a Content is the evaluation time. Since the temporal argument of a SLP can be indexical, its value will have to be fixed before a Content is obtained. But each Content corresponding to an SLP-based sentence corresponds to exactly one proposition. Since ILP-based sentences, on the other hand, do not contain any temporal indexicals, they will correspond to exactly one Content. However, since that Content does not have time as a constituent, it will be able to correspond to multiple propositions. This is illustrated below:

(44)

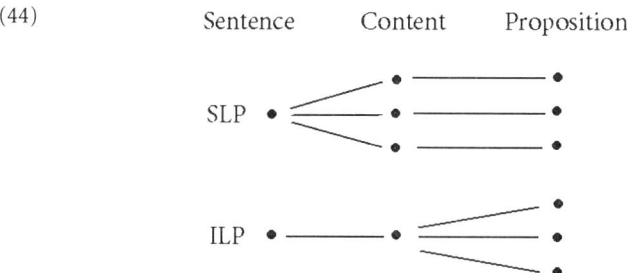

I will leave open the question of whether the fact that other indexicals routinely appear within a sentence is significant. My result can be maintained, at least in a stipulative way, by defining an additional intermediate type between sentences and Contents at which the values of all non-temporal indexicals have been fixed. Then, what I have said above about sentences will correspond instead to this intermediate type.

I will now attempt to show why these results are intuitive. Since time is a constituent in SLP-based propositions, the Content of a SLP-based proposition relative to any given world will necessarily have constant truth value. For example, the Content corresponding to (45a) is either true or false for the real world no matter what the evaluation time is:

(45)   a. Jody was asleep at 10:00 am on July 29, 1994.
         b. Jody is an adult.

However, the value of the Content of an ILP-based proposition like (45b) is something that can vary at different evaluation times in a particular world. Of course, few attested sentences contain temporal information that is as precise as (45a). We are much more likely to say (46) and infer the relevant time from context:

(46)   Jody was asleep.

However, it is clear that (46) has different Contents depending on what is understood to be the event time. (45a) does not have this temporal variability, because the modifiers have pinned down the event time to a punctual interval. This illustrates why I claimed above that SLP-based sentences only have the potential to vary with respect to what proposition they denote.

ILP-based sentences, however, express the same Content no matter when they are uttered. Thus, the Content of (45b) will be false if evaluated at a time when

Jody is a child, and true if evaluated at a time when she is an adult. But the Content has not changed, although technically the proposition has.

In Montague's (1973) intensional logic, propositions are functions from world-time pairs to truth values. This conception of a proposition differs from the one assumed above since it allows values of a proposition to vary over time within a single world. With this kind of view of proposition, what I have said above about Contents can be said directly about propositions. To be completely clear, let us consider (45b) and (46) with respect to a model. Consider a very simple model with three worlds w_1, w_2, w_3, three temporal indices t_1, t_2, t_3, strictly ordered such that $t_1 < t_2 < t_3$, and one individual, Jody. Suppose that Jody is asleep in w_1 at t_1 and t_3, and in w_3 at t_3, that Jody is not asleep in any other world at any other time. Consider now the property, [be asleep at t_3]. The following is a representation of its intension:

(47)
$$\begin{bmatrix} w_1 \to \begin{bmatrix} t_1 \searrow \\ t_2 \to [j \to 1] \\ t_3 \nearrow \end{bmatrix} \\ w_2 \to \begin{bmatrix} t_1 \searrow \\ t_2 \to [j \to 0] \\ t_3 \nearrow \end{bmatrix} \\ w_3 \to \begin{bmatrix} t_1 \searrow \\ t_2 \to [j \to 1] \\ t_3 \nearrow \end{bmatrix} \end{bmatrix}$$

[be asleep at t_3]

The proposition [Jody is asleep at t_3] is true in the model at w_1 and w_3. Because the time at which Jody is asleep is at issue in the proposition, the extension of this proposition at each world is constant from times to characteristic functions of sets of individuals.

Below is the intension of [be asleep at t_1]:

(48)
$$\begin{bmatrix} w_1 \to \begin{bmatrix} t_1 \searrow \\ t_2 \to [j \to 1] \\ t_3 \nearrow \end{bmatrix} \\ w_2 \to \begin{bmatrix} t_1 \searrow \\ t_2 \to [j \to 0] \\ t_3 \nearrow \end{bmatrix} \\ w_3 \to \begin{bmatrix} t_1 \searrow \\ t_2 \to [j \to 0] \\ t_3 \nearrow \end{bmatrix} \end{bmatrix}$$

[be asleep at t_1]

The constancy of these functions (within each world) has nothing to do with the model that was selected for this illustration; it follows directly from the temporal index's being at issue in the proposition. It is not possible to construct a model in which the two propositions whose extensions are characterized in (47) and (48) are not constant over time within each world.

What is crucially different about ILP-based propositions is that they cannot have a temporal index at issue within them. This means that it is logically possible for a model to be constructed in which an individual has some ILP-based property at one temporal index and not at another. Consider the same, simple model that was assumed above, and let Jody be an adult in w_1 at t_3, in w_2 at t_1, t_2, and t_3, and in w_3 at t_2 and t_3. The following function represents the property $[\![be\ an\ adult]\!]$:

(49)
$$\begin{bmatrix} w_1 \to \begin{bmatrix} t_1 \to [j \to 0] \\ t_2 \to [j \to 0] \\ t_3 \to [j \to 1] \end{bmatrix} \\ w_2 \to \begin{bmatrix} t_1 \to [j \to 1] \\ t_2 \to [j \to 1] \\ t_3 \to [j \to 1] \end{bmatrix} \\ w_3 \to \begin{bmatrix} t_1 \to [j \to 0] \\ t_2 \to [j \to 1] \\ t_3 \to [j \to 1] \end{bmatrix} \end{bmatrix}$$

$[\![be\ an\ adult]\!]$

If we evaluate the proposition $[\![Jody\ is\ an\ adult]\!]$ with respect to our model, w_3, say, and time t_1, the proposition is found to be false. In the same world at t_3, however, it is true.

Despite the simplicity of this model, it turned out (with foresight) to be quite well behaved: in no world did it turn out to be the case that Jody was an adult at one index and not an adult at a later index. Nothing about ILPs prevents a model like this from being constructed. In fact, some ILPs would be well-represented in such a model: *Jody is blond* and *Jody is a resident of California* denote propositions that could easily be true for some indices, false for later ones, and true again at still later indices. If we had a model of sufficient complexity to distinguish every (non-tautologous and non-contradictory) proposition from every other, there would surely be some worlds in which (many) ILP-based propositions have truth values that vary over time.

If we wish to maintain that there are no possible worlds in which Jody is an adult at time t_2 and not at some later time, then we have a concern about the theory of possible worlds. Plausibly, we could maintain that part of what it means to achieve adulthood is that is a necessarily permanent state. A meaning postulate could address this concern. The crucial point is, however, that being an ILP alone is not sufficient to impose any such constraint, and something extra would need to be said to impose it. In fantasy and science fiction writing we may encounter fountains of youth, and we are quite able to interpret the sentences in which they appear, so it seems that we really must allow peculiar worlds of the kind being discussed into the set of possible worlds. This might turn out to be the case for every ILP. Discussions of the ILP/SLP distinction often appeal to the temporal persistence of ILPs in the real world. But we are after a theory of grammar, not the world as we perceive it, and we have no difficulty using language to discuss hypothetical scenarios in which some ILP (e.g., *being human*) is not temporally persistent.

We have established a distinction between ILP-based and SLP-based propositions that relies crucially on the requirements that (1) SLP-based propositions must include the time at which the denotation of the predicate is taken to hold (or not hold, if the sentence is negative) of the denotation of the subject, and (2) ILP-based propositions cannot include such information. From these assumptions, it followed that the extension of a SLP-based proposition at each world was necessarily constant over time, but the extension of an ILP-based proposition was not necessarily constant.

If we assume that any world not explicitly prohibited is, by default, permitted, we might conclude that for every ILP-based proposition, there is some world at which its extension is not a constant function over time. But for SLP-based propositions, it is necessarily the case that its extension at every world is a constant function.

It is reasonable to ask whether, for every ILP-based proposition, there is always some world (which could be a science fiction and fantasy world) in which the truth of the proposition varies over time. I will not answer this question here because it would take us too far afield into the vast bizarreness of possible worlds, but I will make a few comments. It should not be unusual to imagine that there are worlds in which Leslie is human and worlds in which she is not: we have no trouble interpreting things like *If Leslie weren't human, she'd be a fish*. The question is, can we imagine a world in which sometimes Leslie is human and sometimes in the same world she is not? The answer is clearly yes. Mythology is full of tales of such changelings. Of course, mathematical properties tend to be represented by individual-level predicates, so we would have to consider allowing them to vary over time as well. We do routinely assume the existence of very bizarre worlds when we create counterfactual utterances. Hofstadter (1985:36) attributes the following clever counterfactual question to Scott Kim:

(50) What would this sentence look like if π were 3?

The suggestion, of course, is that the curvy letters would be somehow contorted. Now we could imagine the value of π varying over time and saying:

(51) When π has its usual value, the sentence looks normal, but when π equals 3, I can't quite make out the words.

We can even imagine the fundamental principles of logic as variable:

(52) Whenever modus ponens gives unreliable results, you might as well stay in bed since there is no point in constructing arguments.

An even more extreme case is:

(53) When I am not self-identical I just don't know what to do.

It is tempting to answer in the affirmative to the query about whether there is always some world in which the truth value for an ILP-based proposition is variable. However, nothing in my analysis rests on this point and deep philosophical issues are at stake, so I will stop short of this claim.

What is a clear consequence of the temporal distinction between ILPs and SLPs is that the Contents of SLP-based propositions cannot have variable truth values within a world, but the Contents of ILP-based propositions can. SLP-based sentences, on the other hand, correspond to multiple Contents, but ILP-based sentences correspond to a single Content. If the temporal argument is bound by a quantifier of some sort, the proposition denoted by the sentence will be constant across time (within a particular world, of course).

2.2 What Time Is It?

Claiming that SLPs have a temporal argument and that ILPs do not has consequences for theories of tense and aspect. I will not attempt to provide a complete analysis of this here, but certain questions need to be answered.

Reichenbach (1947) claimed that the interpretation of sentences involves three kinds of temporal information: speech time, reference time, and event time. Speech time is the time at which a sentence is uttered. Event time is the interval during which the eventuality described occurs, and reference time is the time to which the sentence refers. Tense, in its non-deictic use, typically establishes a relation between speech time and reference time, but the relation does not pick out a specific reference time. Adverbials, if present, may fix the reference time more precisely. They can do other things as well (see Hinrichs 1986). Aspect typically establishes a relation between reference time and event time.

Since we (with Kratzer) have argued that SLPs have a temporal argument that ILPs do not have, we should ask what exactly that temporal argument is in Reichenbach's terms. Hinrichs (1986), building on Partee (1973), observed that the deictic use of tense locates the event time of a sentence. Since, as we claimed in the previous chapter, ILPs do not have a deictic use, I take this as an indication that ILPs do not have event time and that SLPs do. Thus, I claim that the temporal part of Kratzer's spatiotemporal argument is Reichenbach's event time.

Given this conclusion, we expect no event time interactions for ILPs; that is, we expect no aspectual material with uncoerced ILPs that requires event time for its analysis. Aspect is a very complex area, and I will leave this prediction partly hanging, but I will consider the most obvious consequences. Our proposal is consistent with the conjecture that the progressive appears only with SLPs (Dowty 1985):

(54) Socks are lying under the bed.

(55) *New Orleans is lying at the mouth of the Mississippi River.

However, our assumption raises the question of what the aspectual information is operating on in sentences like the following:

(56) John had known French for six years by the time I met him.

In this sentence, the reference time is fixed to the time when the speaker met John; six years before the reference time is something that seems to be event time. It is important to note, however, that this apparent event time is not the period of time over which the ILP held of the subject: since (56) will usually implicate that John still knows French, the run time of that eventuality is ongoing. Rather, the apparent event time is the initial point at which the ILP began to hold of John: that is, we are getting an inchoative reading for *know French*. And inchoatives, being changes of state and therefore non-stative, cannot be individual-level because all ILPs describe stative eventualities. The following section continues the discussion of temporal differences between ILPs and SLPs.

2.3 Other Times

2.3.1 LeGuin Time

Hitzeman (1993) argues for a fourth time in addition to Reichenbach's speech, reference, and event times. She points out that a temporal adverbial can be used to describe "a property of something other than the eventuality overtly expressed by the sentence" (1993:31) in which it appears. An unusual reading of the following sentence illustrates this:

(57)   Lincoln was a communist for an hour.

The sentence is ambiguous. The easiest reading to notice is the one by which Lincoln was a communist for one hour and then stopped being one. The other reading is what interests Hitzeman. She calls it the "LeGuin reading." A character in Ursula LeGuin's novel *The Lathe of Heaven* (1971) has the peculiar property that whatever he dreams is true turns out actually to be true when he awakes. Hitzeman invites us to suppose that he dreams that Lincoln was a communist for Lincoln's entire life. The character wakes up and, behold, it is true that Lincoln was a communist. Suppose the character falls asleep an hour later and dreams that Lincoln was never a communist. Hitzeman points out that under such circumstances (57) and (58a) are true, with the paraphrase given in (58b):

(58)   a. It was true for an hour that Lincoln was a communist.
        b. Lincoln was a communist for his whole life for an hour.

(Note that it is also true—for a while—that Lincoln never was a communist! Hitzeman does not discuss this.) Of course, with LeGuin time there is no contradiction involved, because which world is the real one keeps changing. Hitzeman's point is that the temporal adverbial is pinning down the duration of the temporal interval over which the proposition modified by the adverbial was true. The time of evaluation does not correspond to event time, reference time, or speech time; therefore, she adds a fourth time to Reichenbach's three. Furthermore, she points out that this fourth time, which she calls L, interacts with reference time (R) and speech time (S) in a way that closely resembles the way event time (E) interacts with them. In the example below, Hitzeman notes that $E < R < S$ (that is, the event described is entailed to have taken place before the reference time which was prior to speech time) and $L < R < S$ as well:

(59)   For an hour, Hinkley had shot Bush.

We turn now to the question of what the *L* is. In possible world semantics, a proposition is identified with the set of worlds in which it is true. Thus, we might ask whether L is simply the evaluation time of a proposition. Evaluation time is represented in classical treatments of semantics as the *t* shown below:

(60) $[p]^{M,w,t,g}$

This whole expression represents the truth value of *p* in a model *M*, with respect to world *w*, at the evaluation time *t*, for the assignment function *g*. Crucially, a particular world is part of this evaluation, and this fact shows that LeGuin time is not the same as the evaluation time. Evaluation is done with respect to a particular world. In LeGuin's novel, the effect of the character's dreaming is to identify different possible worlds as the real world. Which world is the real one keeps changing, and the adverbials indicate the duration of the interval over which a particular world happens to be identified as the real one. Thus, the evaluation time is distinct from LeGuin time.

Hitzeman discusses LeGuin readings only in their interaction with durational adverbials; however, punctual adverbials are compatible with LeGuin readings as well. The following sentence is ambiguous depending on whether the adverbial is taken to modify evaluation time or LeGuin time:

(61) At 2:32 last Saturday, Lincoln was a communist.

This sentence clearly has a LeGuin reading paraphrasable as "The world that was the real world at 2:32 last Saturday was one in which Lincoln was a communist." The evaluation time reading can be paraphrased as "The proposition that Lincoln was a communist was true at 2:32 last Saturday." To eliminate the possibility of attributing a LeGuin reading to this paraphrase, we might append the comment, "and in fact that proposition is true at any evaluation time."

An explanation of the use of aspect in ILP sentences is crucial for us. The following is an example:

(62) Lenin had been a communist for fifteen years by the time of the Russian revolution.

The interpretation we get is that there is a temporal interval spanning fifteen years prior to the Russian revolution, during which the proposition expressed by *Lenin is a communist* is evaluated as true. Thus, we see that the time of evaluation of a proposition can interact with reference time and speech time in just the way that LeGuin time does. We conclude that evaluation time is a fifth use of time in natural language alongside speech, reference, event, and LeGuin time. The LeGuin readings are probably the least commonly used of these, since we rarely need to talk about whole worlds changing their identities. Evaluation time, however, is widely referred to in ILP-based sentences. I take it that this is the time that is modified in the following examples:

(63) a. In 1967, Greg believed Humphrey would become president.
      b. Carter was president from 1977 to 1981.

2.3.2 Evaluation Time

Hitzeman points out that stage-level predicates do not always allow a LeGuin reading. The following example contrasts with (57) in this respect (Hitzeman's ex. 4.116c):[3]

(64) #Lincoln built the Panama Canal for an hour.

No LeGuin reading is possible for this sentence, although we can easily see what it would mean: that, for an hour, the real world was one in which Lincoln was the one who built the Panama Canal. The following, however, allows this reading, as Hitzeman points out (Hitzeman's ex. 4.117):

(65) Lincoln had built the Panama Canal for an hour.

Hitzeman also notes the following contrast (Hitzeman's exx. 4.124 and 4.126):

(66) a. #For an hour Lincoln was seated (during the Gettysburg Address).
b. For an hour Lincoln had been seated (during the Gettysburg Address).

However, as Greg Carlson pointed out to me, it seems much easier to understand (66a) as having a LeGuin reading with the situating modifier *during the Gettysburg Address* than without it:

(67) a. #For an hour Lincoln was seated.
b. For an hour Lincoln was seated during the Gettysburg Address.

Hitzeman also noted that SLPs understood generically allow LeGuin readings:

(68) For an hour, this machine crushed oranges.

This sentence is ambiguous, of course, between a LeGuin reading based on the machine's having the property of being an orange crusher, and a reading in which the adverbial modifies event time. Following Farkas and Sugioka (1983) and many others since, we assume this sentence has a null generic adverbial in its logical representation. Overt generic operators also allow LeGuin readings:

(69) For an hour, John always smoked when he was nervous.[4]

Now we can see a contrast in the possibility of a LeGuin reading between the following:

(70) a. #John was on the porch for twenty minutes.
b. John was on the porch at 2:00 P.M. for twenty minutes.

We need to explain why ILPs naturally allow LeGuin readings while SLPs do so only if the sentence in which one appears has additional aspectual information or additional temporal modification.

The data in this section provide a strong confirmation of our assumption that SLPs have a temporal argument and ILPs do not. The availability of a LeGuin reading depends on the ability of a sentence to identify a set of worlds to serve as alternatives to the world that was the real one before LeGuin's character's dream. For a sentence to allow such a reading, it must be able to pick out a unique proposition. For the utterance of a SLP-based sentence to identify a unique proposition, the temporal argument of the SLP must be bound somehow. This can happen in several ways: it can be bound by a quantifier, or by aspectual operators, or it can be used deictically. We have seen that SLP-based sentences allow LeGuin readings when the temporal argument is bound by aspectual operators or by adverbial quantifiers. Seen this way, the question we need to answer is why LeGuin readings are difficult to have when the argument is used deictically. Answering this question will explain why (64), (67a), and (70a) do not have LeGuin readings.

For a sentence containing a deictic expression to be felicitous, it must be possible for the hearer to identify the referent of the deictic. This seems to be the reason for the difficulty with the LeGuin readings in (64), (67a), and (70a). Suppose LeGuin's character had a dream in which Lincoln was seated, and then the character wakes up. Which world is it that he wakes up in? Will Lincoln still be seated when the character wakes up? There could be many different times at which Lincoln was seated, but the LeGuin character must have dreamt of a particular one. Possibly the character dreamed that Lincoln was seated at the time of the dream. In that case, Lincoln might or might not still be seated when the character awakes; all that is required is that Lincoln must have been sitting when it was dreamed that he was sitting. The event time is dependent on the dreaming time. We find no such dependency with ILP-based propositions. I take this fact as strong confirmation for the temporal-argument distinction between ILPs and SLPs.

We should note another case in which a LeGuin reading is not possible. Another way to bind the temporal argument of the SLP is with an existential operator. But LeGuin readings are difficult to obtain for SLP-based propositions in which the temporal operator is bound by an existential. I take it that this reading is disfavored for the same reason that it is disfavored in the following:

(71)   Lincoln was seated.

The most natural interpretation of this sentence uses the temporal argument deictically—that is, it refers to a particular time when Lincoln was seated. It is fairly difficult to express concisely the reading in which the temporal argument is bound by an existential quantifier. The following are possibilities:

(72)   a. Lincoln has been seated before.
       b. Lincoln has been seated from time to time.

These seem to be usable only in a context in which the question of whether Lincoln ever sat down is already at issue. Otherwise, the proposition expressed by these sentences is not very informative and so it is not very useful pragmatically. Any realistic world in which Lincoln exists is likely to be one in which he was seated at some time or other. A LeGuin reading for (67a) would have us, for twenty minutes, identify the real world with a world in which Lincoln sat at some time or other. Such sentences do very little to identify the alternative world. But I take it that the reason (67a) does not seem to have an existential-LeGuin reading follows from the fact that the existential reading is so strongly disfavored in (71).

But then, why does adding *at 2:00* or *during the Gettysburg address* help in (67b) and (70b)? If we remove the durational adverbial that we used to trigger the LeGuin readings, we see that the temporal argument is interpreted existentially in these sentences:

(73)   a. Lincoln was seated during the Gettysburg Address.
       b. John was on the porch at 2:00 pm.

Since an existential interpretation is readily available for the basic sentence without the LeGuin time modifier, we expect the reading to continue to be possible when the extra modifier is added.

Finally, we note that once-only SLPs can be used existentially with little difficulty:

(74) a. Lyle blew up the pier.
 b. Leslie destroyed the Washington Monument.

Certainly they are most natural on their deictic interpretation, but an interpretation in which the existential binds the temporal argument is also acceptable. Since the SLP is once-only, the sentence is informative even with an existential interpretation. They are also acceptable with LeGuin readings:

(75) a. Lyle blew up the pier for an hour.
 b. Leslie destroyed the Washington Monument for an hour.

2.3.3 Conclusion

I have claimed that the temporal argument of SLPs is event time and that ILPs lack this. This leads us to ask what temporal modifiers do in ILP-based sentences. The answer given here is that they modify evaluation time, a time distinct from Reichenbach's three and distinct from Hitzeman's LeGuin time. I also argued that there is a contrast between the availability of LeGuin readings for SLPs and ILPs, and I claim the explanation verifies the potential use of SLP anaphora as deictic.

2.4 Situated Propositions

It is time to make good on the promissory note to attempt an explanation of the peculiar cases in which SLPs within full clause complements yield SLP subject effects in the matrix clause. I will accept Glasbey's (1997) suggestion that these cases involve situating the matrix eventuality. In addition, I would like to argue that some propositions are situated and others are not, and further, that beliefs about situated propositions are themselves situated in a way that beliefs about unsituated propositions are not.

What I mean by this distinction is akin to the classical distinction between singular and general propositions. Singular propositions are about particular individuals (e.g., the propositions that the Earth is round, and that Nixon was president), while general propositions are only about properties and not about particular individuals (e.g., the propositions that the shortest spy is human, and that all snow is white) (Crimmins 1997: 298). But there are many varieties of individual. In fact, a particular spatiotemporal location is a sort of individual. Hence, a logical formula containing a referential spatiotemporal argument will correspond to a singular proposition. That is, any SLP-based sentence in which the temporal argument is interpreted deictically (rather than bound to something internal to the sentence) will have a singular proposition as its interpretation. Thus, *A horse kicked over some boxes* is interpreted as a singular proposition because it refers to a particular spatiotemporal location, even though the sentence does not directly reference the participants in the eventuality. The class of singular propositions will also include ILP-based propositions that involve reference to particular individuals. *Clinton is tall* is one example, since it refers to Clinton; *Monkeys live in that tree* will be another, since interpreting it involves reference to a particular tree. On the other hand, *The President is tall* and *Monkeys live in trees* are not singular propositions, since there is no reference to any particular individual.

This way of sorting propositions gives us something very close to the set of sentences which, when embedded as a propositional attitude complement, trigger SLP effects on the matrix subject. I have argued that an embedded SLP-based sentence will yield these effects. However, ILP-based sentences that involve referential nominals do not trigger these effects. Thus, the class of particular propositions is too inclusive for the purpose of identifying the full clause complements that allow matrix SLP subject effects. The class of particular propositions does seem to describe adequately the environments which, somewhere or other, yield SLP subject effects.

An alternative that is more successful with the sentences involving full clause complements is simply to define the class of situated propositions as required for our purposes. I will define a situated proposition as any proposition that involves a deictic use of a temporal argument. (As usual, we set aside the spatial portion of the issue. Ultimately, it may be productive to distinguish temporal arguments from spatial ones; then we would probably admit into the class of situated propositions those that involve a deictic use of a spatial argument.) Then I claim that an attitude with respect to a situated proposition is itself situated. From this, I rely on Glasbey's notion of existential inference to predict the SLP subject effects.

2.5 Tense and ILPs

Since my proposal for the ILP/SLP contrast assumes that tense provides the event time discourse referent which fills the temporal argument of SLPs, we must try to understand what tense does in ILP-based sentences.

I conclude from the discussion of Reichenbach's theory, LeGuin time, and evaluation time, along with the considerations raised in Partee (1984, 1989), Hinrichs (1986), and others, that tense introduces a temporal discourse referent which can have deictic or anaphoric usage. However, different things happen with ILPs than with SLPs. Since only the latter have event time, and only the latter have a temporal argument of any kind, only with the latter can tense be used to designate event time. Hence, with ILPs, the temporal discourse referent must have a different function. As suggested above, I propose that it designates the evaluation time for the proposition. Clearly evaluation time can be indicated by deixis. This is what I claim happens with most ILP-based propositions (e.g., *Sam was intelligent*). We have also encountered cases in which it seems that anaphoric uses of evaluation time are possible. But progress with these cases will require finer-grained distinctions in interpretation than have been made in the literature thus far.

I propose that tense with ILPs works as follows:

(76)   Simple past$_{ILP}$ $\Rightarrow$ $[\lambda P \lambda x [P\{x\}]]$ ^{tv} & $t_R = t_V$ & $t_R < t_S$

Evaluation time is represented by t_V, thus associating the proposition to speech time.

3. Conclusion

The ILP/SLP distinction is a conglomerate of dichotomies that overlap almost completely. Several of these dichotomies are subject to pragmatic influence. Environments subject to the plurality condition trigger evidential coercion. We have seen that evidential coercion converts ILPs into SLPs. Perceptual reports can trigger inchoative coercion. This kind of coercion converts statives into non-statives, thus converting ILPs into SLPs, but affecting the interpretations of stative SLPs as well. Context plays a large role in the success of coercion. We have also seen that an inference of interruption is subject to contextual factors, although this does not affect the ILP/SLP status of the predicate. And the specificity effect influences the interpretations of bare plurals, possibly leading to an existential inference.

With all these pragmatic influences, it is not surprising that some researchers have questioned whether there is anything left of the ILP/SLP distinction that is purely grammatical. I have claimed that there is a substantial core left over after the pragmatic effects have been accounted for. Several non-pragmatic factors are significant to the ILP/SLP distinction. I have adopted Carlson's idea that there is a type-theoretic distinction between ILPs and SLPs, but I have adopted Kratzer's ontology in assigning SLPs an implicit temporal argument. Tense, when filling this argument, can be anaphoric, and this provides an account of the donkey anaphora cases, including the ability of a SLP to restrict a quantifier or modal operator. The type-theoretic distinction also provides one way of identifying the level of a predicate at the small or infinitival clause level. But if the temporal argument is bound within a clause by a quantifier, the type-theoretic distinction is lost and the SLP is unable to appear as the predicate of a perceptual report. Thus, the type-theoretic distinction is exploited in several ways by the grammar, and these different uses explain the non-uniformity seen in the individual-level and stage-level effects.

Notes

Notes to Chapter 2

1. McCawley (1988:86) claims that more than 100 verbs can appear with the expletive *there* as subject. Other verbs have not played any role in investigations of the ILP/SLP distinction.

2. *There* can also appear as the subject of non-existential sentences. On the so-called "presentational" reading (e.g., *There was Sam*), (d) becomes more acceptable. See Milsark (1974), Rando and Napoli (1978), and Lumsden (1988) for further discussion.

3. See also Kortmann (1991) for a corpus-based study of free and absolute adjuncts. Kortmann distinguishes a number of relations that can hold between the adjunct and the main clause, and he argues that pragmatic factors are crucial in determining which relation is relevant to a particular utterance.

4. Kortmann (1991:200) writes that, in a cursory survey, British speakers found conditional interpretations possible with unaugmented absolutes, but American speakers tended to agree with Stump's intuitions.

5. Bolinger (1973:61) writes, "The starred examples would be understood but would be accepted, if at all, only as freshly coined and rather strained figures of speech."

Notes to Chapter 3

1. Carlson notes the existence of "a rather enigmatic class of bare plural NPs which do not seem to denote kinds as we have imagined them" (1977:194). These NPs are always modified by a relative clause or a PP. Carlson cites the following examples (his ex. 107):

(i)   a. parts of that machine
      b. people in the next room
      c. books that John lost yesterday
      d. bears that are eating (now)

Carlson lists a number of reasons why these cannot be considered kind-denoting: KLPs cannot be predicated of them; they allow opaque/transparent ambiguities in contexts that allow them with *a*-indefinites; they cannot be associated with adverbs of quantification or modals; and they are ungrammatical as subjects to ILPs. Carlson points out that not all bare plurals that are modified in this way have these effects (his exx. 110 and 111):

(ii) a. ??Parts to this machine are quite common.
b. Keys to this door are quite common.

(iii) a. ??Dogs that are sitting here are rare.
b. Dogs that sit here are rare.

Carlson suggests that one of the key factors in interpreting bare plurals as non-kinds is taking the NP to refer to a finite set. He discusses this line further, but he concludes that "there is possibly no necessary and sufficient set of GRAMMATICAL criteria that will serve to separate those bare plurals that denote kinds from those that denote only a set of objects. Rather what we are dealing with here i[s] a conceptual scheme, one where we take a CN that denotes a set of individuals, and in some cases we associate a kind with it, and in some cases we cannot" (1977:197).

2. Carlson uses the double prime in his initial exposition to indicate a set of stages. I have followed him in doing this for the initial exposition.

3. The idea that an ILP is the basis of the characteristic reading is discarded in Carlson's chapter 5 in favor of an analysis of *Zippy ran* as a generalization over stages. This will be discussed shortly.

4. *iotf* abbreviates *is of the form*.

5. T21 requires the argument of G to be intensional since, as Carlson argues (1977:166 ff.), generic readings are intensional with respect to objects of the verb and VP modifiers. Thus:

(i) Procedure P picks out the coldest state. (from Bennett 1974)

(ii) Bill eats peas with a knife.

"On the event reading, when there is an existential claim made about some stage of the subject, no intensional context is introduced, and hence the extensionality of certain verbs in the event sense, but there is apparent intensionality on the generic reading" (Carlson 1977:169).

6. The conditions on reconstruction must be slightly different for Kratzer than for Diesing. Diesing assumes that the subject of an ILP cannot move to the specifier of VP because, when the predicate is individual-level, the specifiers of both IP and VP receive independent theta-roles; if the NP in the specifier of IP moved to the specifier of VP, a chain with two thematic roles would be formed, and this would violate the constraints on chain well-formedness imposed by the Theta Criterion (Chomsky 1981:335). Kratzer cannot use this constraint because she assumes that no theta-role is assigned to the specifier of VP for ILPs. Kratzer must allow reconstruction of a constituent only to a position that holds a trace of the constituent. (An alternative formulation that is equivalent for the simple cases under consideration is that a constituent can reconstruct only to the point at which it was projected or at which it received a theta-role.)

7. The external role is italicized. To account for the ordering of the agent and the theme roles of *hit*, Kratzer suggests that internal agent arguments might occupy the specifier position, and internal theme arguments might occupy the object position (1995:135–136).

8. Of course, it is possible that the NP originates as a sister of *known*, but this issue is not relevant to our concerns.

9. Diesing acknowledges that there is potentially a problem with PRO being governed in (37). She points out that some recent work has called into question the assumption that

PRO must be ungoverned. As an alternative, she suggests that perhaps PRO could move into Pesetsky's μP and avoid getting Case.

10. Diesing assumes that reconstruction is an undoing of NP movement (following May 1977, 1985), suggesting that a nominal is permitted to reconstruct to the point at which it was projected (where it received a theta-role). An alternative way of stating this restriction would be to allow reconstruction to any node as long as the argument chain in which the nominal appears is associated with exactly one theta-role. This makes no difference for the current discussion, but it will become significant in efforts to extend Diesing's analysis to cover a broader range of data.

11. Another alternative would be for the complement to select its head. This would be quite unorthodox in a theory which assumes that only complements can be selected, but something like this might be possible with head movement and feature checking. If the complement selects the head, then the head of an ordinary ILP would select a control Infl (which may be finite or non-finite depending on the clause in which it appears). The head of unaccusative ILPs and SLPs would select a raising Infl. There seems to be no reason why SLPs and unaccusative ILPs cannot appear with a control Infl as long as they can also appear with a raising Infl, so the only crucial matter is that ordinary ILPs must appear with control Infl.

12. The discussion in this section is largely unchanged from Fernald (1994). Tsai (1994) made the same observations independently. Tsai (1994:147) proposes the following:

(i) Extended Mapping Hypothesis
   a. Material from a syntactic predicate is mapped into the nuclear scope.
   b. Material from the XP immediately dominating a syntactic predicate (excluding the predicate) is mapped into a restrictive clause.

13. cb in this expression is a constant of type $<s,<<s,t>,t>>$, denoting the conversational background in any context of use. D, Stump writes, "(a constant of type $<<s,<<s,t>,t>>, <<s,t>,<s,<<<s,t>,t>,t>>>>$) is to denote that function D' such that for any function g of type $<s,<<s,t>,t>>$, any proposition p, and any index $<w,i>$, $D'(g)(p)(<w,i>)$ is the set of all consistent subsets of the union of $g(<w,i>)$ with the unit set of p which contain p" (1985:52).

14. There is more to it than this, however. Stump argues that, in general, *because* cannot be the appropriate interpretation, and that pragmatic effects are involved (1985:60 ff.). This is discussed at length in his final chapter (325 ff.).

15. P^t is a variable of type $<s,<i',t'>$. L is a free variable of type $<<s,t>,<<s,t>,t>>$ ranging over the various, pragmatically determined, logical relations which hold between a free adjunct and the root clause (Stump 1985:60). K is a constant of intensional logic having the same denotation as the following expression:

$$\lambda L \lambda p \lambda q [L(p)(q) \; \& \; \forall r \forall s [L(r)(s) \rightarrow [{}^\vee r \; \& \; {}^\vee s]]] \quad (1985:61)$$

If L is used to establish the relation between an adjunct and the main clause, there will be no entailment that the adjunct eventuality holds in the real world; this is used with weak adjuncts. When $K(L)$ establishes the relation, the eventuality in the adjunct is entailed to hold; this yields strong readings. M_n is a free variable of type $<i,<i,t>>$, taking as its value a binary relation between time intervals. Its value is inferred by language users (1985:170).

Notes to Chapter 5

1. See Dimitriadis (1993) for a discussion related to these issues.

2. In $<<s,t>,t>,t>$, s stands for 'state' rather than standing for 'world-time pair' as in Montague (1973).

Notes to Chapter 6

1. This is simplified for the sake of clarity: the full form would have a stage of the speaker as the perceiver, and the stage would need to be related to the individual speaker by R.

2. Note that APs with *too* or *enough* modifiers appear postnominally very easily:

(i)   a. Surgeons clever enough to perform the operation waited outside.
         b. Students too short to be varsity basketball players were disappointed.

It is very difficult with the existential construction to force these APs into a coda to test their status, so I will not consider them here, and I will make the argument only on the basis of indefinites and bare plurals.

3. Only non-finite Infls are required to agree, since the constraint would fail at once on empirical grounds if it applied to all embedded Infls. *Say* and *declare*, for example, always head SLPs, but their complement clauses are free to be headed by either a SLP or an ILP.

4. By labeling (102b) bizarre, I do not mean to suggest that you (gentle reader) are not imaginative enough to concoct a reasonable reading for the sentence, but that it is bizarre on the obvious reading for (103b) in which Lisa is somewhere out of sight, singing on the phone to Robin.

Notes to Chapter 7

1. This is the assumed type for intransitive SLPs. Transitive SLPs would be $<e,<l,<e,cc>>>$.

2. I assume that this is so for English. Of course, the study of astronomy is full of cases in which an event, like a star going supernova, is perceived millions of years after it actually happened. If we can describe such an observation with a perceptual report (*The astronomer saw the star go supernova*), that would have difficult consequences for our analysis. If we must bind the temporal argument in the small clause with an existential quantifier at the small clause node, we would lose the clause-level, type-theoretic distinction between ILPs and SLPs.

3. Throughout this section # indicates that a LeGuin reading is not possible. It does not mean that no reading is possible.

4. LeGuin readings are harder to get if the quantifier's restriction is not supplied by the sentence and has to be inferred from context:

(i)   (#) For an hour, John always smoked.
(ii)   a. (#) For an hour, this machine always crushed oranges.
         b. For an hour, this machine always crushed oranges when it was operational.

References

Akmajian, Adrian. 1977. "The Complement Structure of Perception Verbs in an Autonomous Syntax Framework." In Peter W. Culicover, Thomas Wasow, and Adrian Akmajian, eds., *Formal Syntax*, pp. 427–460. New York: Academic Press.

Bach, Emmon, Eloise Jelinek, Angelika Kratzer, and Barbara H. Partee, eds. 1995. *Quantification in Natural Languages*. Dordrecht: Kluwer.

Barss, Andrew. 1995. "Extraction and Contraction." *Linguistic Inquiry* 26:681–694.

Barwise, Jon. 1981. "Scenes and Other Situations." *Journal of Philosophy* 78:369–397.

Barwise, Jon, and Robin Cooper. 1981. "Generalized Quantifiers and Natural Language." *Linguistics and Philosophy* 4:159–219.

Barwise, John, and Robin Cooper. 1993. "Extended Kamp Notation: A Graphical Notation for Situation Theory." In P. Aczel et al., eds., *Situation Theory and Its Applications*, vol. 3, 29–53. Stanford, Calif.: CSLI Publications.

Barwise, Jon, and John Perry. 1983. *Situations and Attitudes*. Cambridge, Mass.: MIT Press.

Bäuerle, Rainer. 1979. *Temporal Deixis, Temporal Frage*. Tübingen: Gunter Narr Verlag.

van Bentham, Johan. 1996. *Exploring Logical Dynamics*. Stanford, Calif.: CSLI Publications.

Bennett, Michael. 1974. Some Extensioins of a Montague Fragment. Dissertation, UCLA.

Bolinger, Dwight. 1967. "Adjectives in English." *Lingua* 18:1–34.

Bolinger, Dwight. 1973. "Essence and Accident: English Analogs of Hispanic *Ser-Estar*. In B. Kachru et al., eds., *Issues in Linguistics: Papers in Honor of Henry and Renée Kahane*, pp. 58–69. Chicago: University of Chicago Press.

Carlson, Gregory N. 1977. *Reference to Kinds in English*. Dissertation, University of Massachusetts, Amherst. Published, New York: Garland, 1980.

Carlson, Gregory N. 1979. "Generics and Atemporal *When*." *Linguistics and Philosophy* 3:49–98.

Carlson, Gregory N. 1982. "Generic Terms and Generic Sentences." *Journal of Philosophical Logic* 11:145–181.

Carlson, Gregory N., and Francis Jeffry Pelletier, eds. 1995. *The Generic Book*. Chicago: University of Chicago Press.

Chierchia, Gennaro. 1992. "Anaphora and Dynamic Binding." *Linguistics and Philosophy* 15:111–184.

Chierchia, Gennaro. 1995a. *Dynamics of Meaning*. Chicago: University of Chicago Press.
Chierchia, Gennaro. 1995b. "Individual-Level Predicates as Inherent Generics." In Carlson and Pelletier 1995, 176–223.
Chomsky, Noam. 1981. *Lectures on Government and Binding*. Dordrecht: Foris.
Chomsky, Noam. 1986. *Barriers*. Cambridge, Mass.: MIT Press.
Condoravdi, Cleo. 1992. "Individual-Level Predicates in Conditional Clauses." Paper presented at the Annual Meeting of the Linguistic Society of America, Philadelphia.
Condoravdi, Cleo. 1994. *Descriptions in Context*. Dissertation, Yale University.
Cooper, Robin. 1986. "Tense and discourse location in situation semantics." *Linguistics and Philosophy* 9:17–36.
Crimmins, M. 1997. "Singular/General Proposition." In Peter V. Lamarque, *Concise Encyclopedia of Philosophy of Language*, pp. 297–298. Oxford: Pergamon.
Davidson, Donald. 1966. "The Logical Form of Action Sentences." In Nicholas Rescher, ed., *The Logic of Decision and Action*, pp. 81–95. Pittsburgh: University of Pittsburgh Press.
Dekker, Paul. 1993. *Transsentential Meditations*. Dissertation, University of Amsterdam.
Diesing, Molly. 1988. "Bare Plural Subjects and the Stage/Individual Contrast." In M. Krifka, ed., *Genericity in Natural Language*, pp. 107–154. University of Tübingen.
Diesing, Molly. 1992. *Indefinites*. Cambridge, Mass.: MIT Press.
Dimitriadis, Alexis. 1993. "Events and Quantification." In *MIT Working Papers in Linguistics* 20:51–66.
Doherty, Cathal. 1996. "Clausal Structure and the Modern Irish Copula." *Natural Language and Linguistic Theory* 14:1–46.
Dowty, David R. 1979. *Word Meaning and Montague Grammar*. New York: Kluwer.
Dowty, David R. 1985. "On Recent Analyses of the Semantics of Control." *Linguistics and Philosophy* 8:291–331.
Farkas, Donka F., and Yoko Sugioka. 1983. "Restrictive If/When-clauses." *Linguistics and Philosophy* 6:225–258.
Fernald, Theodore B. 1994. *On the Nonuniformity of the Individual- and Stage-Level Effects*. Dissertation, University of California, Santa Cruz.
Fernald, Theodore B. 2000. "Generalizations in Navajo." In Theodore Fernald and Paul Platero, eds., *Athabaskan: Language & Linguistics*. Oxford and New York: Oxford University Press.
Fernald, Theodore B. 1999. "An Anaphoric Account of Stage-Level Predicates." In *North East Linguistic Society* 29.
Frege, Gottlob. 1918. "Der Gedanke." Translated as "Thought." In Michael Beaney, ed., *The Frege Reader*, 325–345. Oxford: Blackwell, 1997.
Gawron, Jean Mark. 1986. "Types, Contents, and Semantic Categories." *Linguistics and Philosophy* 9:427–476.
Gazdar, Gerald, Ewan Klein, Geoffrey Pullum, and Ivan Sag. 1985. *Generalized Phrase Structure Grammar*. Cambridge, Mass.: Harvard University Press.
Geach, Peter. 1962. *Reference and Generality*. Ithaca, N.Y.: Cornell University Press.
Gee, James Paul. 1977. "Comments on the Paper by Akmajian." In Peter W. Culicover et al., eds., *Formal Syntax*, pp. 461–481. New York: Academic Press.
Glasbey, Sheila. 1997. "I-Level Predicates That Allow Existential Readings for Bare Plurals." In Aaron Lawson, ed., *Proceedings from Semantics and Linguistic Theory VII*. Ithaca, N.Y.: Cornell University Press. 169–179.
Green, Georgia. 1973. "A Syntactic Syncretism in English and French." In Braj Kachru, ed., *Issues in Linguistics*. Urbana: University of Illinois Press.

Groenendijk, Jeroen, and Martin Stokhof. 1990. "Dynamic Montague Grammar." In L. Kalman and L. Polos, eds., *Papers from the Second Symposium on Logic and Language.* Budapest: Akadémiai Kaidó.

Groenendijk, Jeroen, and Martin Stokhof. 1991. "Dynamic Predicate Logic." *Linguistics and Philosophy* 14:39–100.

Halliday, M. A. K. 1967. "Notes on Transitivity and Theme in English, Part 1." *Journal of Linguistics* 3:37–81.

Heim, Irene. 1982. *The Semantics of Definite and Indefinite Noun Phrases.* Dissertation, University of Massachusetts, Amherst.

Higginbotham, James. 1983. "The Logic of Perceptual Reports: An Extensional Alternative to Situation Semantics." *Journal of Philosophy* 80:100–127.

Hinrichs, Erhard. 1981. *A Compositional Semantics for Aktionsarten and NP-reference.* Dissertation, Ohio State University.

Hinrichs, Erhard. 1986. "Temporal Anaphora in Discourses of English." *Linguistics and Philosophy* 9:63–82.

Hitzeman, Janet. 1993. *Temporal Adverbials and the Syntax-Semantics Interface.* Dissertation, University of Rochester.

Hofstadter, Douglas R. 1985. *Metamagical Themas: Questing for the Essence of Mind and Pattern.* New York: Basic Books.

de Hoop, Helen. 1992. *Case Configuration and Noun Phrase Interpretation.* Dissertation, Rijksuniversiteit Groningen.

de Hoop, Helen. 1995. "On the Characterization of the Weak-Strong Distinction." In Bach et al. 1995, 421–450.

de Hoop, Helen, and Henriette de Swart. 1989. "Over indefinite objecten en de relatie tussen syntaxis en semantiek." *Glot* 12:19–35.

de Hoop, Helen, and Henriette de Swart. 1990. "Indefinite Objects." In Reineke Bok-Bennema and Peter Coopmans, eds., *Linguistics in the Netherlands* 91–100. Dordrecht: Foris.

Jackendoff, Ray. 1990. *Semantic Structures.* Cambridge, Mass.: MIT Press.

Jacobson, Pauline. 1990. "Raising as Function Composition." *Linguistics and Philosophy* 13:423–475.

Jäger, Gerhard. 1997. "The Stage/Individual Contrast Revisited." In Brian Agabayani and Sze-Wing Tang, eds., *Proceedings of the Fifteenth West Coast Conference on Formal Linguistics,* 225–239. Stanford, Calif.: CSLI Publications.

Johnston, Michael. 1994. *The Semantics of Adverbial Adjuncts.* Dissertation, University of California, Santa Cruz.

Kamp, Hans. 1981. "A Theory of Truth and Semantic Interpretation." In Jeroen Groenendijk et al., eds., *Truth Interpretation and Information*, pp. 277–322. Dordrecht: Foris.

Kamp, Hans, and Uwe Ryle. 1993. *From Discourse to Logic.* Dordrecht: Kluwer.

Karttunen, Lauri. 1976. "Discourse Referents." In James McCawley, ed., *Syntax and Semantics 7*, pp. 363–385. New York: Academic Press.

Katz, Graham. 1993. "The Interpretation of *As*-headed Adjuncts." In Erin Duncan et al., eds., *Proceedings of the 12th West Coast Conference on Formal Linguistics*, pp. 547–560. Stanford, Calif.: CSLI Publications.

Kayne, Richard. 1984. *Connectedness and Binary Branching.* Dordrecht: Foris.

Kenny, Anthony J. P. 1963. *Actions, Emotion, and Will.* New York: Humanities Press.

Klein, Ewan, and Ivan Sag. 1985. "Type-Driven Translation." *Linguistics and Philosophy* 8:163–202.

Kortmann, Bernd. 1991. *Free Adjuncts and Absolutes in English: Problems of Control and Interpretation.* New York: Routledge.

Kratzer, Angelika. 1977. "What 'Must' and 'Can' Must and Can Mean." *Linguistics and Philosophy* 1:337–355.
Kratzer, Angelika. 1979. "Conditional Necessity and Possibility." In R. Bauerle et al., eds., *Semantics from Different Points of View*. Berlin: Springer-Verlag.
Kratzer, Angelika. 1988. "Stage-level and Individual-level Predicates." In M. Krifka, ed., *Genericity in Natural Language*, 247–284. Tübingen: University of Tübingen. Reprinted in Carlson and Pelletier 1996, 125–175.
Krifka, Manfred, Francis Jeffry Pelletier, Gregory N. Carlson, Alice ter Meulen, Gennaro Chierchia, and Godehard Link. 1995. "Genericity: An Introduction." In Carlson and Pelletier 1996, 1–124.
Kuroda, S.-Y. 1972. "The Categorical and the Thetic Judgment." *Foundations of Language* 9:153–185.
Kuroda, S.-Y. 1992. *Japanese Syntax and Semantics*. Dordrecht: Kluwer.
Ladusaw, William A. 1979. *Polarity Sensitivity as Inherent Scope Relations*. Dissertation, University of Texas at Austin. Published, New York: Garland, 1980.
Ladusaw, William A. 1994. "Thetic and Categorical, Stage and Individual, Weak and Strong." In Mandy Harvey and Lynn Santelmann, eds., *Proceedings from Semantics and Linguistic Theory IV*. Ithaca, N.Y.: Cornell University Press. 220–229.
Lakoff, George. 1965. *On the Nature of Syntactic Irregularity*. Dissertation, Indiana University. Published as *Irregularity in Syntax*. New York: Holt, Reinhart and Winston, 1970.
Levin, Beth and Malka Rappaport. 1986. "The Formation of Adjectival Passives." *Linguistic Inquiry* 17:623–661.
Levinson, Stephen C. 1983. *Pragmatics*. Cambridge: Cambridge University Press.
Lewis, David. 1975. "Adverbs of Quantification." In E. L. Keenan et al., eds., *Formal Semantics of Natural Language*, pp. 3–15. Cambridge: Cambridge University Press.
Lumsden, Michael. 1988. *Existential Sentences: Their Structure and Meaning*. London: Croom Helm.
May, Robert. 1977. *The Grammar of Quantification*. Dissertation, MIT.
May, Robert. 1985. *Logical Form: Its Structure and Derivation*. Cambridge, Mass.: MIT Press.
McCawley, James D. 1988. *The Syntactic Phenomena of English*. Chicago: University of Chicago Press.
McNally, Louise. 1992. *An Interpretation for the English Existential Construction*. Dissertation, University of California, Santa Cruz.
McNally, Louise. 1993. "Adjunct Predicates and the Individual/Stage Distinction." In Erin Duncan et al., eds., *Proceedings of the 12th West Coast Conference on Formal Linguistics*, 561–576. Stanford, Calif.: CSLI Publications.
McNally, Louise. 1995. "Stativity and Theticity." In S. Rothstein, ed., *Events and Grammar*. Dordrecht: Kluwer. 293–307.
McNally, Louise. 1998. "Existential Sentences without Existential Quantification." *Linguistics and Philosophy* 21:353–392.
Milsark, Gary L. 1974. *Existential Sentences in English*. Dissertation, MIT.
Milsark, Gary L. 1977. "Toward an Explanation of Certain Peculiarities of the Existential Construction in English." *Linguistic Analysis* 3:1–29.
Moens, Marc, and Mark Steedman. 1988. "Temporal Ontology and Temporal Reference." *Computational Linguistics* 14:15–28.
Montague, Richard. 1973. "The Proper Treatment of Quantification in Ordinary English." In J. Hintikka et al., eds., *Approaches to Natural Language*, pp. 221–242. Dordrecht: Reidel.

Parsons, Terence. 1985. "Underlying Events in the Logical Analysis of English." In E. LePore and B. McLaughlin, eds., *Actions and Events: Perspectives on the Philosophy of Donald Davidson*. Oxford: Blackwell.

Parsons, Terence. 1990. *Events in the Semantics of English: A Study in Subatomic Semantics*. Cambridge. Mass.: MIT Press.

Partee, Barbara H. 1973. "Some Structural Analogies between Tenses and Pronouns in English." *Journal of Philosophy* 70:601–609.

Partee, Barbara H. 1977. "John is Easy to Please." In Antonio Zampolli, ed., *Linguistic Structures Processing*, pp. 281–312. Amsterdam: North-Holland.

Partee, Barbara H. 1984. "Compositionality." In Fred Landman and Frank Veltman, eds., *Varieties of Formal Semantics*, 281–311. Dordrecht: Foris.

Partee, Barbara H. 1989. "Binding Implicit Variables in Quantified Contexts." *Chicago Linguistic Society* 25:342–365.

Percus, Orin. 1996. "Consequences of a Predication-Based Analysis of Semantic Partition." In José Camacho et al., eds., *Proceedings of the Fourteenth West Coast Conference on Formal Linguistics*. Stanford, Calif.: CSLI Publications.

Pesetsky, David. 1982. *Paths and Categories*. Dissertation, MIT.

Pesetsky, David. 1994. *Zero Syntax: Experiencers and Cascades*. Cambridge, Mass.: MIT Press.

Pollard, Carl, & Ivan A. Sag. 1994. *Head-Driven Phrase Structure Grammar*. Chicago: University of Chicago Press.

Postal, Paul. 1969. "On So-called Pronouns in English." In David Riebel and Sanford Shane, eds., *Modern Studies in English*, pp. 201–224. Englewood Cliffs, N.J.: Prentice-Hall.

Rando, E., and Donna Jo Napoli. 1978. "Definites in *There*-Sentences." *Language* 54:300–313.

Rapoport, Tova. 1991. "Adjunct-Predicate Licensing and D-structure."1 In S. Rothstein, ed., *Syntax and Semantics 25: Perspectives on Phrase Structure*, pp. 159–187. New York: Academic Press.

Raposo, Eduardo, and Juan Uriagereka. 1995. "Two Types of Small Clauses (towards a Syntax of Theme/Rheme Relations)." In Anna Cardinaletti and Maria Teresa Guasti, eds., *Syntax and Semantics 28: Small Clauses*, 179–206. New York: Academic Press.

Reichenbach, Hans. 1947. *Elements of Symbolic Logic*. New York: Free Press.

Reuland, Eric, and Alice ter Meulen. 1987. *A Representation of (In)definiteness*. Cambridge, Mass.: MIT Press.

Rizzi, Luigi. 1990. *Relativized Minimality*. Cambridge, Mass.: MIT Press.

Safir, Ken. 1992. "On the Directness of Perception: Naked Infinitives and Clausal Structure." Ms., Department of Linguistics, Rutgers University.

Saito, Mamoru. 1989. "Scrambling as Semantically Vacuous A´-Movement." In M. Baltin and A. Kroch, eds., *Alternative Conceptions of Phrase Structure*, 182–200. Chicago: University of Chicago Press.

Sasse, Hans-Jürgen. 1987. "The Thetic/Categorical Distinction Revisited." *Linguistics* 25:511–580.

Schubert, Lenhart K., and Francis Jeffry Pelletier. 1989. "Generically Speaking: Or, Using Discourse Representation Theory to Interpret Generics." In Gennaro Chierchia et al., eds., *Properties, Types and Meaning*, vol. 2, *Semantic Issues*, 193–268. Dordrecht: Kluwer.

Smith, Carlota S. 1991. *The Parameter of Aspect*. Dordrecht: Kluwer.

Smith, Carlota S. 1995. "The Range of Aspectual Situation Types: Derived Categories and a Bounding Paradox." In P. Bertinetto et al., eds., *Temporal Reference: Aspect and Actionality*, 105–124. Turin: Rosenberg and Sellier.

Stalnaker, Robert C. 1978. "Assertion." In P. Cole, ed., *Syntax and Semantics 9: Pragmatics*, 315–322. New York: Academic Press.

von Stechow, Arnim. 1982. "Three Local Deictics." In R. Jarvella and W. Klein, eds., *Speech, Place, and Action: Studies in Deixis and Related Topics*, 73–99. New York: John Wiley and Sons.

von Stechow, Arnim, and Wolfgang Sternefeld. 1988. *Bausteine syntaktischen Wissens: Ein Lehrbuch der generativen Grammatik*. Opladen: Westdeutscher Verlag.

Stowell, Timothy A. 1981. *Origins of Phrase Structure*. Dissertation, MIT.

Stowell, Timothy A. 1989. "Subjects, Specifiers, and X-Bar Theory." In M. Baltin and A. Kroch, eds., *Alternative Conceptions of Phrase Structure*. Chicago: University of Chicago Press.

Strawson, Peter. 1952. *Introduction to Logical Theory*. London: Methuen.

Stump, Gregory T. 1985. *The Semantic Variability of Absolute Constructions*. Dordrecht: Reidel.

Svenonius, Peter. 1994. *Dependent Nexus*. Dissertation, University of California, Santa Cruz.

de Swart, Henriette E. 1991. *Adverbs of Quantification: A Generalized Quantifier Approach*. Dissertation, Rijksuniversiteit Groningen.

de Swart, Henriette E. 1998. "Aspect Shift and Coercion." *Natural Language and Linguistic Theory* 16:347–385.

ter Meulen, Alice G. B. 1995. *Representing Time in Natural Language*. Cambridge, Mass.: MIT Press.

Tsai, W.-T. D. 1994. *On Economizing the Theory of A-Bar Dependencies*. Dissertation, MIT.

Vendler, Zeno. 1967. *Linguistics in Philosophy*. Ithaca, N.Y.: Cornell University Press.

Vendler, Zeno. 1972. *Res Cogitans*. Ithaca, N.Y.: Cornell University Press.

Verkuyl, Henk J. 1972. *On the Compositional Nature of the Aspects*. Dordrecht: Reidel.

Verkuyl, Henk J. 1993. *A Theory of Aspectuality*. Cambridge: Cambridge University Press.

Webelhuth, Gert. 1985. "German is Configurational." *Linguistic Review* 1:81–114.

Webelhuth, Gert. 1989. *Syntactic Saturation Phenomena and the Modern Germanic Languages*. Dissertation, University of Massachusetts, Amherst.

Willie, MaryAnn. 1999. "Individual and Stage Level Predication and the Navajo Classificatory Verbs." Paper presented at the West Coast Conference on Formal Linguistics XVIII, Tucson, Arizona.

Williams, Edwin. 1980. "Predication." *Linguistic Inquiry* 11:203–238.

Williams, Edwin. 1981. "Argument Structure and Morphology." *Linguistic Review* 1:81–114.

Williams, Edwin. 1983. "Against Small Clauses." *Linguistic Inquiry* 14.287–308.

Index

absolute adjuncts, 21–23, 56–58, 77–78, 119
adverbs of quantification, 21, 50, 56, 59–62, 66, 73, 79–81
Aktionsart, 6–9
  See also stativity
anaphora, 81–86, 118
anaphoric nature of SLPs, 85–86
argument structure, 43–49, 89
aspect, 8, 26, 43, 65, 72, 118, 120, 135
  See also progressive aspect
atelic eventualities. *See* telic/atelic eventualities

bare plurals, 14–17, 36, 40, 50–51, 54–56
Barss, A., 29
Bolinger, D., 24–29

Carlson, G., 3–5, 8–10, 13, 16–18, 23, 36–41, 43, 50, 53–56, 64, 67, 70–71, 74–77, 88–92, 107, 117, 124, 138, 142–144
case assignment, 45–46, 50–51
categorical/thetic judgments, 64
change of state, 31, 69, 93–94, 113, 135
Chierchia, G., 4–5, 24, 49, 61–62, 64, 82–83, 117, 119, 126

clausal complements, 24–27, 54–56, 87–97, 111, 124–127
  See also small clauses
clause-level distinction between ILPs and SLPs, 74–76, 119–124, 126–127
closure of nuclear scope, 41–42, 47, 49–53, 99–100
coercion, 10, 23, 31, 57, 63–73, 90–91, 111, 113–114
complement selection, 24–27
complete thoughts, 129
compositionality of SLPs, 75–76, 109, 111, 113–114
conditional interpretations, 21–22, 57–58, 80
conjunction of predicates, 28
content of a proposition, 130–132
context, 23, 45, 57, 83, 87, 109
context-change potential, 118–119
control, 21, 30, 51–56, 92–95, 103–106, 108, 111, 114, 125
copulas, 52–53, 56–57, 115–116

Davidsonian arguments. *See* event arguments
diagnostics. *See* ILP/SLP distinction, diagnostics for
definite nominals, 94, 98
deixis, 85, 98, 118, 122, 139–140

153

depictives. *See* modifiers, depictive
Diesing, M., 3, 10–11, 41–42, 45–46, 49–56, 67, 72, 74–78, 89, 93, 98–100, 104–106, 117, 120, 144–145
discourse anaphora, 82–83
discourse referent, 83–86, 118–119, 122
donkey anaphora, 81–86
dynamic semantics, 82–86, 118–123

episodic eventualities, 24, 65
evaluation time, 73, 78, 124, 130, 137–141
event arguments, 43, 53, 61, 118
event time, 120–121, 130, 135, 137
evidential coercion, 64, 66–73, 90, 114, 116
existential closure, 41–42, 47, 49, 51
existential construction, 12–15, 29–33, 52, 64, 66, 68, 82
existential inference, 114–115, 140–141
existential interpretations, 15–17, 39–40, 45, 47, 50–51, 54, 56, 89
existential quantifier, dynamic, 83

frequency adverbial. *See* adverbs of quantification
functional application, 120

general propositions. *See* propositions, general/singular
generalized quantifiers, 15
generic interpretations, 16, 18–19, 21–23, 40–41, 48, 50–51, 54, 56, 61
Glasbey, S., 98, 114–115, 127–129, 140–141

habitual interpretations, 8, 40, 61, 70
Hinrichs, E., 85, 118, 135, 141
Hitzeman, J., 136–138, 140
de Hoop, H., 10, 19–20, 59–62, 74, 79–80, 117

ILP. *See* ILP/SLP distinction
ILP-based proposition, 130–135
ILP-based sentence, 130–131
ILP/SLP distinction
  analysis of (summary), 10–11, 117, 142
  characterizations of, 3–6, 63
  diagnostics for, 9, 34
    See also bare plurals
    See also existential construction
    See also indefinite subjects
  See also perceptual reports
  See also subject effects
  See also type-theoretic distinction between ILPs and SLPs
  lexical classification, 9, 116, 118
  time and space as a basis for, 43, 63–65, 135–139
implicature, 15, 31, 80, 90, 92
inchoative. *See* change of state
inchoative coercion, 69, 111, 113
indefinite nominals, 15–20, 41–42, 48–50
indefinite subjects, 15–17, 42, 45–46, 73, 89, 148
indexical, 130–131
individual-level predicate. *See* ILP/SLP distinction
INFL, 50–53, 56, 76, 100, 102
INFL-to-INFL agreement, 100, 102, 106–107
intensifier *all*, 28
interruption, 70–73, 81, 113

Jäger, G., 49

kind-level predicates (KLP), 6, 38, 40
kinds, 36, 40
Kratzer, A., 3, 5, 9–11, 18–20, 23, 26, 34, 42–49, 52–54, 57–59, 61–62, 64, 67, 70–72, 74–75, 77–80, 85, 88–89, 98–99, 109, 117, 120, 128–129, 135, 142, 144
Krifka, M., 3, 6, 16, 65, 70, 77

LeGuin time, 136–141
lexical rule, 47–48
located eventualities, 24, 43, 71, 77, 88, 114, 117, 128
  See also situatedness
locative modifiers. *See* modifiers, locative

mapping hypothesis, 42, 49, 52, 55, 87, 99, 107, 117, 128
McNally, L., 12, 24, 30–32, 44, 64, 71–72
Milsark, G., 3, 5, 12–16, 48, 117
modals, 21–23, 26, 57–58, 80
modifiers
  depictive, 29–33, 71–73
  locative, 7, 23–24, 43, 47
  reduced relative clause, 30, 33

temporal, 23–24, 43–44, 47, 57, 99, 136–140
  See also absolute adjuncts
  See also when adjuncts

nominal predicates, 4, 13, 68
nonuniformity, 10, 49, 87, 107–109, 127

once-only predicates, 19, 59–61, 79–81

Partee, B., 68, 85, 135, 141
passives, 47–49
perceivability, 112–114, 127
perceptual reports, 17–18, 29–30, 64, 68, 73–77, 87, 91, 107–109, 112–114, 119, 122–123, 127
plurality condition on generic quantification, 60–62, 73, 79–81, 117, 128
possible worlds, 133–136
pragmatics, 64–65, 114, 116
  See also coercion
predicate
  individual-level. *See* ILP/SLP distinction
  stage-level. *See* ILP/SLP distinction
  stative predicates. *See* stativity
  See also kind-level predicates
  See also modifiers, depictive
  See also nominal predicates
  See also once-only predicates
presupposition, 19, 59–60
progressive aspect, 7–8, 34, 68–69, 72–73, 116, 118, 135
prohibition against vacuous quantification, 19, 59, 61, 79–81, 117
propositional attitudes, 96–97, 106, 111, 126–127
propositional content, 130–132
propositions
  general/singular, 140–141
  situated, 140–141
  temporal rigidity of, 129
  and time, 129–137

quantification, 18–19, 21–22, 42, 49, 55, 59–61, 78–81, 111
  See also adverbs of quantification
  See also existential interpretations
  See also generalized quantifiers
  See also generic interpretations
  See also ILP-based proposition
  See also SLP-based proposition

raising, 51–54, 88–92, 100–103, 110, 114, 124
Rapoport, T., 30, 71
Raposo, E., 76–77
reduced relative clauses. *See* modifiers, reduced relative clause
reference time, 120–121, 135, 137
Reichenbach, H., 130, 135–136, 140–141
relative clauses. *See* modifiers, reduced relative clause

saturation, 21
scrambling, 48–49, 128
sieves, 15
singular propositions. *See* propositions, general/singular
situated propositions. *See* propositions, situated
situatedness, 114–115, 129, 140–141
SLP. *See* ILP/SLP distinction
SLP-based proposition, 130–135
SLP-based sentence, 130–131
sm, 14
small clauses, 17–18, 27, 54, 74–78, 121, 123–124, 127
sorted ontology, 36–38, 56–58
spatiotemporal argument, 43–49, 62, 65, 67, 71, 77, 86, 118, 127
  See also temporal argument
specificity effect, 98–99, 106–109, 114–115, 128–129
specifying *in*, 28
speech time, 120–121, 135, 137
stage, definition of, 36
stage-level predicate. *See* ILP/SLP distinction
stativity, 18, 24, 31, 65, 69, 77, 116, 135
strong/weak interpretations of absolutes, 21, 57–58
strong/weak nominals, 14–16
structural ambiguity, 29–33
Stump, G., 5, 9–10, 21–22, 52, 54–59, 68, 77, 115–117, 126, 145
subject effects, 9, 34, 128
  and control, 92–95
  and deviation from perceptual reports, 87, 107–109, 127

subject effects (*continued*)
   and full clause complements, 95–97, 127
   and raising, 88–92
   See also bare plurals
   See also existential construction
   See also indefinite subjects
de Swart, H., 10, 19–20, 49, 59–62, 65, 73–74, 79–80, 117–118

telic/atelic eventualities, 43, 69, 89, 118
tense, 120, 122, 135, 141
   See also evaluation time
   See also event time
   See also reference time
   See also speech time
temporal argument, 118, 122, 130, 138
temporal modifiers. *See* modifiers, temporal
temporal persistence of predicates, 80
temporal persistence of propositions. *See* propositions, temporal rigidity of
there insertion. *See* existential construction
theta-roles, 44–53, 88, 105
thetic/categorical judgments, 64
type-theoretic distinction between ILPs and SLPs, 36–38, 117–119
   See also sorted ontology

unaccusative ILPs, 46–49, 53–54, 76
unselective closure of nuclear scope, 42, 45, 49, 51
Uriagereka, J., 76–77

vacuous quantification. *See* prohibition against vacuous quantification

weak interpretations of absolutes. *See* strong/weak interpretations of absolutes
weak nominals. *See* strong/weak nominals
when adjuncts, 18–20, 56–59, 79–81, 111